GUIDE TO NATURAL FOOD RESTAURANTS

IN THE U.S. AND CANADA

1990-91 Edition

From the Editors of VEGETARIAN TIMES
Foreword by JOHN ROBBINS

Compiled by CAROL WILEY

THE BOOK PUBLISHING COMPANY
SUMMERTOWN, TENNESSEE

Because dining establishments may change location or hours and days of operation, it is strongly suggested that readers call before visiting any restaurant they are not familiar with.

Cover design by Estelle Carol

Cover photo by Alison Miksch

Library of Congress Cataloging-in-Publication Data

Guide to natural food restaurants in the U.S. and Canada / from the editors of Vegetarian times; foreword by John Robbins.
   p. cm.
   ISBN 0-913990-66-3
   1. Vegetarian restaurants–United States–Directories. 2. Natural food restaurants–United States–Directories. 3. Vegetarian restaurants–Canada–Directories. 4. Natural food restaurants–Canada–Directories. I. Vegetarian times. II. Title.
TX907.2.G84 1989
647.9573–dc20   89-15090
                                                                  CIP

Copyright © 1989 by *Vegetarian Times*

Printed in the USA

10 9 8 7 6 5 4 3 2 1

All rights reserved. No portion of this book may be reproduced by any means whatsoever except for brief quotations in reviews, without written permission from the publisher or *Vegetarian Times*.

The Book Publishing Company
Summertown, TN 38483

CONTENTS

Guide to Natural Food Restaurants in the U.S.

Alabama	2	Missouri	102
Alaska	2	Montana	105
Arizona	4	Nebraska	105
Arkansas	5	Nevada	106
California	6	New Hampshire	106
Colorado	46	New Jersey	107
Connecticut	51	New Mexico	110
Delaware	54	New York	112
District of Columbia	54	North Carolina	124
Florida	58	Ohio	127
Georgia	66	Oklahoma	130
Hawaii	70	Oregon	131
Idaho	73	Pennsylvania	132
Illinois	74	South Carolina	138
Indiana	79	South Dakota	140
Iowa	80	Tennessee	140
Kansas	82	Texas	144
Kentucky	83	Utah	149
Louisiana	83	Vermont	151
Maine	85	Virginia	151
Maryland	86	Washington	154
Massachusetts	90	West Virginia	163
Michigan	95	Wisconsin	164
Minnesota	99	Wyoming	166
		Puerto Rico	167

Guide to Natural Food Restaurants in Canada

British Columbia	170	Ontario	171
Nova Scotia	171	Quebec	178

Appendix: Mexico • 181

FOREWORD

As the numbers of people who are choosing a vegetarian lifestyle continue to mount, and the need for meatless cuisine rises accordingly, more and more vegetarian restaurants are opening their doors. I like going to vegetarian restaurants, and now there are more to enjoy: there are more than 1,000 in this guide, and the number is growing all the time.

Why the growing demand for vegetarian dining? People are looking to vegetarian food for all sorts of reasons. For some, the reason is health. They know that heart disease, strokes, cancers, diabetes and other degenerative diseases are directly and mathematically correlated to diets high in animal fat. Or they might be alarmed by the presence of artificial hormones, pesticides and antibiotics in modern-day meats. Perhaps they just feel better on a lighter diet.

There also are many people today who are choosing vegetarian fare for ethical reasons. Throughout history, there have been special people who have chosen not to consume meat because they did not want to cause killing. As George Bernard Shaw put it in one of his not-overly-subtle moments: "A man of my spiritual intensity does not eat corpses." The ranks of revered people who have been vegetarians for humanitarian reasons include Tolstoy, Gandhi, Thoreau, da Vinci and Pythagoras. Today there is a new ethical dilemma: Animals are raised in factory farms, where methods are so cruel and violently frustrating to the animals' natural habits that many caring people who can easily accept the killing of an animal for food are making the switch. It's not the deaths of the animals that's so much the issue for these people, but the obscene and utter deprivation in which the animals are forced to live.

And then there are those who seek vegetarian cuisine because they can't condone what's being done to the environment by the meat industry. Perhaps they know that every fast-food hamburger represents 55 square feet of tropical rainforest that was destroyed for cattle-grazing. Or that every individual who switches from a meat-centered diet to a purely vegetarian one saves an acre of trees a year. Or that it takes 2,500 gallons of water to produce a single pound of beef, compared to only 25 gallons for a pound of wheat. This means that you can save more water by becoming a vegetarian than 10 ecologically-conscious citizens ever could by home water conservation methods. The environmental devastation directly attributable to contemporary meat production is so extreme that many environmental scientists are saying today that the single most important step an individual who cares about our planet and its future can take is to become a vegetarian.

Whatever your reasons for wanting to dine in the friendly atmosphere of a vegetarian restaurant, you are in good and growing company. Vegetarians used to be viewed as perhaps a trifle odd, but that attitude is found only among the most unenlightened today. Instead, the choice to move toward vegetarianism is being seen as a decision that brings renewed health, vitality, self-respect and well-being. And a statement that you, at least, are making the healing choice, for youself, for the animals and for the planet.

John Robbins

INTRODUCTION

Earlier this year, I spent a week at a vegetarian health retreat in northern California. When it was time to return home, my vegetarian friends pressed a brown bag into my hands. "We made lunch for you," they said. "You're going to need this." I thanked them and headed for the San Francisco airport and my flight home to Chicago. I planned to buy lunch at the airport and save the brown bag for the plane—one never knows what a vegetarian meal in the air is going to be like—but as I nosed around the restaurants in the airport terminal, I was glad I had that brown bag. In a world of burgers, hot dogs and soft drinks, my portable lunch was a lifesaver.

Although this guide would have been of little use in the airport terminal, you get the picture: Travelers have more than a difficult time finding good vegetarian restaurants. Despite these more nutritionally enlightened times, finding a good vegetarian meal in a restaurant can be a real challenge, particularly if you're in unfamiliar territory. This guide, an indispensable traveling companion, is here to make the search easier.

But don't leave it in the suitcase between trips. It's your local dining guide as well. Planning a night out is simple when you can turn to a listing of all of the vegetarian or natural-food restaurants in the area.

The guide is the most comprehensive, up-to-date listing of vegetarian restaurants ever published. The first guide, published by *Vegetarian Times* in 1978, listed 350 restaurants; this guide—*VT*'s fourth—lists more than 1,000 vegetarian and natural-food restaurants in the United States, Canada, Mexico and Puerto Rico, and the listings are more descriptive than ever.

Defining a vegetarian restaurant is not always easy. A vegetarian restaurant can be something as simple as a back-of-the-store lunch counter (as with Chip 'N Dale's in Oak Park, Ill.), or something as elegant as San Francisco's Greens, where reservations are required. It could even be a hospital dining room, such as St. Helena Health Center in St. Helena, Calif. Don't be put off by the setting: Several hospital dining rooms are in the guide, and they offer healthful vegetarian fare to the public.

In addition to the differences in ambiance, the restaurants differ in what might be called their "degree of vegetarianism." Some restaurants call themselves vegetarian, but have fish on the menu; many vegetarian restaurants would never serve fish dishes. Likewise with alcohol. You'll never find it on the menu at a Country Life restaurant, but you'll find a great selection of beers at Bloodroot in Bridgeport, Conn. You also will find that many of the restaurants listed in this guide are not vegetarian restaurants at all, but we have included them if they'll accommodate vegetarians, particularly in areas where vegetarian restaurants are scarce.

Most of the information in the guide is self-explanatory. The book is organized alphabetically by state and province. Within each state, restaurants are listed alphabetically by city and then by restaurant name. If you're not familiar with the area, we've provided lists of neighboring communities in major metropolitan areas that offer additional dining choices.

A dot before the restaurant's name indicates the restaurant serves only vegetarian food. No fish, poultry or meat is served, although dairy products and eggs may be. Entries without the dot serve fish, poultry or other meat, along with a selection of vegetarian dishes.

Whenever possible, we've listed special dishes, described the atmosphere, listed special directions and let you know what's unique about the restaurant—be it live entertainment or outdoor dining. Symbols at the end of each listing indicate what kinds of food and drink are served, how casual or formal the place is, if credit cards are accepted, and whether children are welcome or easily accommodated. In addition, a general price range is noted.

This guide should get you through all of the major cities, but what if you find yourself in South Dakota, for example, where we list only one natural-food restaurant in the entire state? Breakfast usually isn't a problem for vegetarians. Even in the most mainstream of restaurants you can find juices and one or two hot, whole-grain cereals on the menu. (My children and I always travel with soymilk and a loaf of whole-grain bread to round out what we find on the usual breakfast menus.)

Even for lunch and dinner, you have several options. Italian restaurants offer pizza and spaghetti, of course, but variations on the theme are endless: manicotti, pasta primavera, fettucini Alfredo, mostaccioli, lasagna. Almost all Indian restaurants have a complete vegetarian section on the menu. Indian dishes may contain dairy products, but you'll probably never find an egg in Indian cuisine. Middle Eastern restaurants offer a wealth of vegetarian dishes: hummus, falafel, baba ganouj, tabouli, pita bread. Kosher delis offer blintzes, potato pancakes, borscht, kugels, salads and bagels. And Chinese restaurants, of course, have always had menu staples. Most are happy to substitute meat with tofu. Be careful of meat stocks in soups and sauces, however, and in some stir-fries. You also could try a steakhouse; many of them have great salad bars, complete with potatoes and pasta. One well-known, fast-food hamburger chain offers a "superbar," where you can find vegetarian salads and pasta.

Armed with that knowledge—and with this guide—traveling should be easier. *Bon appetit*, and may your brown bags be few.

Carol Wiley
Vegetarian Times

GUIDE TO NATURAL FOOD RESTAURANTS

IN THE U.S.

ALABAMA

BIRMINGHAM

- **Golden Temple Cafe**
  1901 11th Ave. S., Birmingham, AL 35205 (205) 933-6333

  Juice bar in a natural food store. Vegetable stew over rice or pasta, some Mexican food. Salads and sandwiches, too. Cafe closed Sunday. SB,I,M,N,CC,CH,$

HOOVER

- **Golden Temple Cafe**
  3309 Lorna Rd., Hoover, AL 35216 (205) 823-7002

  See entry above.

HUNTSVILLE

Pearly Gates Natural Foods
2308 Memorial Pkwy. S.W.
Huntsville, AL 35801 (205) 534-6233

They have their own organic garden here, and grow many of the natural and primarily organic foods offered on the menu. Homemade, organic breads and pastries contain no sugar or preservatives. Open for 15 years. Reservations recommended for large parties. Also a grocery, deli, bakery, and frozen dinner and catering service. Closed Sunday. FS,V,M,N,J,CC,$$

ALASKA

ANCHORAGE

Marx Brothers Cafe
627 W. Third Ave., Anchorage, AK 99501 (907) 277-6279

Open 10 years, the cafe is in an old home (built in 1916) and maintains the beautiful ambience of the era, including stained glass and works of original Alaskan art. Mainly American food, with a definite French twist. (Recently rated a mention in *Bon Appetit*.) They'll cook you a good veggie meal upon request. Try freshly made pasta or simple sautéed veggies, or go for Van's Caesar salad, the house special. How about Melitzano Salata (roasted eggplant paté)? Open 6 p.m. to 9:30 p.m. Monday through Saturday; closed Sunday. FS,V,A,N,CC,CH,$$$

ALASKA

Zeppo's
328 G St., Anchorage, AK 99501   (907) 272-3663

Wine bar and grill. A representative mixture of American and international cuisine. Enjoy many veg specials in a modern cuisine: roasted eggplant paté, Thai spring rolls or Thai sauté, spinach salad, wild mushroom gratin and sautéed veggies. Top it off with either espresso or a smoothie. Closed Sunday. Call for winter/summer hours. FS,I,V,A,N,CC,CH,$$-$$$

FAIRBANKS

A Moveable Feast
338 Old Steese Hwy., Fairbanks, AK 99701   (907) 456-4701

At least two vegetarian specials for lunch and dinner every day, and breakfast menu is chock full of vegetarian selections, including homemade cinnamon rolls and freshly baked croissants. Pasta's a specialty; they make their own here. Lunch is soup, salad, sandwich or pasta. Dinner is pasta, stir-fry, quiche, fondue or a Greek salad. "Disgustingly delicious desserts are another specialty," the owner said. Closed Sunday. I,A,CC,CH,$$

Cafe de Paris
801 Pioneer Rd., Fairbanks, AK 99701   (907) 456-1669

A converted 65-year-old house with three dining rooms, a fireplace and a cozy atmosphere. Offerings include one or two vegetarian specials every day, six salads, quiches and soups. Open for lunch only. Closed Sundays. Personal checks accepted. FS,I,N,CC,CH,$$

El Sombrero
1420 Cushman St., Fairbanks, AK 99701   (907) 456-5269

Mexican and American. Vegetarian dishes include veggie burritos, the Veggie Lo-Cal Lunch, pizza and other pasta dishes. Other Mexican entrées are available without meat. FS,I,A,J,CC,CH,$$$

Gambardella's Pasta Bella
706 2nd Ave., Fairbanks, AK 99701   (907) 456-3417

Italian. Everything here is fresh and high-quality. Meatless specialties include eggplant parmigiana, fettucini alfredo and fettucini romano. The sauces are fresh-made. Try the fettucini pesto and the fettucini marinara. Open for lunch and dinner. Closed Sundays. FS,V,N,$$$

KEY TO DINING GUIDE
• Vegetarian food only

FS Full service	**V** Vegan options	**CC** Major credit cards accepted
CAF Cafeteria/buffet	**M** Macrobiotic options	**CH** Children welcome
SB Salad bar	**A** Alcoholic drinks	**$** Average dinner under $5
I Informal	**N** Nonalcoholic beer/wine	**$$** Average dinner $5 to $10
F Formal	**J** Freshly squeezed juices	**$$$** Average dinner over $10

ALASKA / ARIZONA

Los Amigos
636 28th Ave., Fairbanks, AK 99701   (907) 452-3684
The mainly Mexican menu includes vegetarian specialties like rice and beans served with a tostada and enchilada or cheese rellenos with rice. Closed Sundays. FS,I,A,N,J,CC,CH,$$

JUNEAU

Fiddlehead
429 W. Willoughby
Juneau, AK 99801   (907) 586-9431 or 586-3150
Gourmet and eclectic cuisine. Named for the ferns that grow in abundance on the mountainsides of southeast Alaska. The Fiddlehead specializes in vegetarian dishes. Try the bean burger, pasta in peanut sauce, eggplant sandwich or tofu croissant, or what they call the "Pauper's Prerogative": veggie soup du jour, salad and bread. The French onion soup is made with a miso base. Three meals a day, seven days a week, plus an excellent Sunday brunch. Children's menu available. A true Juneau tradition for family dining. FS,V,A,N,J,CC,CH,$$

Udder Culture
245 Maine Way, Juneau, AK 99801   (907) 463-3559
A combo yogurt and deli shop in a country decor. Fast—and delicious—food. All the yogurt is honey-sweetened from Alta Dena dairies, and you can also order a variety of hearty vegetarian sandwiches, both hot and cold, on the good Jewish rye bread that deli sandwiches deserve. Try the veggie-based soups, too. Juices aren't homemade, but they're all natural. Open daily. V,CH,$-$$

Udder Culture
2092 Jordan Ave., Juneau, AK 99801   (907) 789-1991
See entry above.

PETERSBURG

Helse Restaurant
Singley Alley, Petersburg, AK 99833   (907) 772-3444
Whole foods are the trademark here for lunch: natural sandwiches, soups and delicious bread. Daily specials. Closed Sunday. FS,I,CH,$

ARIZONA

PRESCOTT

- **Super Carrot Natural Foods**
  236 S. Montezuma, Prescott, AZ 86303   (602) 776-0365
  A natural food restaurant tucked inside a natural food retail store. Specialties include lasagna, stuffed cabbage, falafel. Fresh carrot juice. Two blocks south of town square. Closed Sunday. FS,V,N,J,$

SCOTTSDALE

  Marche Gourmet
  4121 Marshall Way, Scottsdale, AZ 85251   (602) 994-4568
  Many vegetarian options here; there's even an entirely veg section of the menu with items like vegetable melt, tofu provençale, miso soup, and vegetarian chili. Authentic vegetarian Moroccan-style couscous is also available, and the management says they "will gladly try to accommodate any special dietary requests." Try the blue-corn pancakes or Irish oatmeal for breakfast, too. Closed Monday. FS,I,V,M,A,N,J,CC,CH,$$$

TEMPE

- **Gentle Strength Co-op & Restaurant**
  234 W. University Dr., Tempe, AZ 85281   (602) 968-4831
  Deli in a whole-foods co-op. Outdoor cafe when it's cool enough. Nut burgers and tofu burgers, vegan tamales, vegan soups, veggie lasagna, sandwiches and pasta. Homemade baked goods. Open daily. Brunch only on Saturday and Sunday. Nonalcoholic beverages available in store. Even when deli's closed, sandwiches are available. I,M,J,CC,CH,$

ARKANSAS

LITTLE ROCK

Beans & Grains & Things
300 S. Rodney Parham
Little Rock, AR 72201   (501) 221-2331 or 227-9700
Natural food store with deli for take-outs. They're planning to add a couple of tables. Closed Sunday. I,V,$

KEY TO DINING GUIDE
• Vegetarian food only

FS Full service	**V** Vegan options	**CC** Major credit cards accepted
CAF Cafeteria/buffet	**M** Macrobiotic options	**CH** Children welcome
SB Salad bar	**A** Alcoholic drinks	**$** Average dinner under $5
I Informal	**N** Nonalcoholic beer/wine	**$$** Average dinner $5 to $10
F Formal	**J** Freshly squeezed juices	**$$$** Average dinner over $10

CALIFORNIA

- **Wheatberry**
  5602 Asher Ave., Little Rock, AR 72204   **(501) 562-4307**
  A nonprofit educational program offering whole, natural, international vegan meals and cooking lessons. Complete meal for $3.50. Reservations required for groups of more than five. Closed weekends, but will serve meals if advance notice is given. FS,I,V,CH,$

CALIFORNIA

ANAHEIM

The Greenery Natural Kitchen
323 S. Magnolia, Anaheim, CA 92804   **(714) 761-8103**
A delightfully wide-ranging menu devoted to health and good taste. "If anything is sacred," the menu notes, quoting Walt Whitman, "the human body is sacred." With that, they give you unique, delicious soups, juices and smoothies, many sandwiches (including one called Cottage Tofu), and several specialties, including quesadillas, burritos, veggie lasagna and a daily quiche. Special desserts daily. Juice bar service available. Carryout available. Sister restaurant in Fullerton. Closed Sunday. FS,F,V,N,J,CH,$

ARCATA

- **The Tofu Shop**
  768 18th St., Arcata, CA 95521   **(707) 822-7409**
  A deli specializing in homemade fresh tofu. Find a full line of tofu cold cuts, burgers, salads and desserts. Open since 1980. Closed on holidays. V,M,J,$

- **The Wildflower Cafe & Bakery**
  1604 G St., Arcata, CA 95521   **(707) 822-0360**
  Homemade pastries, breads, salsa, sauces and salad dressings. Locally grown organic produce used whenever possible. International entrées a specialty. Great breakfast menu. Open for three meals a day Monday through Saturday. Open Sunday 10 a.m. to 2 p.m. FS,M,CH,$$

AUBURN

- **The Kitchen**
  4020 Grass Valley Hwy., Auburn, CA 95603   **(916) 885-9535**
  International vegetarian cuisine at a restaurant with a sense of humor and a sense of community: A local herbalist sells products here. Local artists display their works. Brunch is scrambled tofu, omelets, crêpes, pancakes, burgers, sandwiches and burritos. Dinner specials include eggplant scallopini, vegetable curry, Persian tempeh, black-bean enchiladas,

CALIFORNIA

stroganoff and shepherd's pie. Only the best and freshest ingredients are used. Catering available. Closed Monday and Tuesday. Located at the corner of Dry Creek Rd. and Highway 49. FS,I,V,M,A,N,J,CC,CH,$$

BERKELEY

- **The Blue Nile**
  2525 Telegraph Ave., Berkeley, CA 94704   (415) 540-6777

  Ethiopian. Standard Ethiopian fare, but the specialty vegetarian combinations are very good. Lunch and dinner Monday through Saturday; dinner only on Sunday. Casual dress. FS,N,A,CC,$$

  Brick Hut
  3222 Adeline, Berkeley, CA 94703   (415) 658-5555

  Natural foods. Breakfast and lunch. Specialties: tofu sauté, vegetarian chili. Open daily. FS,I,CH,$

  Good Earth
  2175 Allston Way, Berkeley, CA 94705   (415) 841-2555

  Natural, fresh, international foods include Mexican, Chinese and Continental specialties. Organic grains used in bakery items. No fried foods. Lunch buffet. Open daily. Brunch on Sunday. Locations throughout California. FS,V,M,N,A,J,CC,CH,$$

  Long Life
  2129 University, Berkeley, CA 94704   (415) 845-6072

  Chinese. Authentic Chinese cuisine, all vegetarian except for a couple of seafood dishes. Complement it with jasmine tea. Open daily. Brunch on weekends. FS,A,CC,$

  Pasand Madras
  2286 Shattuck Ave., Berkeley, CA 94704   (415) 549-2559

  Southern Indian-style cuisine. Nightly entertainment. Open daily. FS,A,CC,CH, $$

  Petrouchka
  2930 College Ave., Berkeley, CA 94705   (415) 848-7860

  What a treat! Russian cuisine with several vegetarian options. FS,A,J,$$

KEY TO DINING GUIDE
• Vegetarian food only

FS Full service	**V** Vegan options	**CC** Major credit cards accepted
CAF Cafeteria/buffet	**M** Macrobiotic options	**CH** Children welcome
SB Salad bar	**A** Alcoholic drinks	**$** Average dinner under $5
I Informal	**N** Nonalcoholic beer/wine	**$$** Average dinner $5 to $10
F Formal	**J** Freshly squeezed juices	**$$$** Average dinner over $10

CALIFORNIA

- **Vegi Food**
  2083 Vine St., Berkeley, CA 94709   (415) 548-5244

  Natural foods. A great place to eat, said a reader who contacted us about Vegi. Closed Monday. FS,V,$

BEVERLY HILLS

Bombay Palace
8690 Wilshire Blvd.
Beverly Hills, CA 90211   (213) 659-9944

Indian. Tandoor dishes. Lunch buffet. Open daily. FS,CAF,F,V,A,CC,CH,$$$

Breadwinner
200 S. Beverly Dr.
Beverly Hills, CA 90212   (213) 550-0590

Natural foods. Fresh fruit, salads, natural food specialties. CAF,A,J,$

CAMPBELL

Bread of Life
1609 S. Bascom Ave., Campbell, CA 95008   (408) 371-5000

Deli in an "alternative food store." Salad bar with more than 50 items, homemade soup and sandwiches, plus more than 35 prepared salads, running the gamut from brown rice to tempeh to eggless egg salad. Cookies and pastries made with whole-grain flour and fruit juice or other natural sweeteners. Take-out available. Open daily. SB,V,CC,CH,$$

CANOGA PARK

- **Follow Your Heart**
  21825 Sherman Way
  Canoga Park, CA 91303   (818) 348-3240

  Since 1970. A menu for true natural foodists. Start with homemade cornbread (and raw butter) if you'd like, then move on to salads—lots of salads: raw veggies, Italian, falafel, tofu, even high-protein salad. For your entrée, try spaghetti, or enchiladas with rennetless cheese, or check out the sandwiches, both hot and cold. (Mmm-m-m-m... vegetarian barbecue, made with soy protein!) Good beverage selection too: juices, shakes, teas, raw milk. And dessert! Whole wheat cinnamon rolls, among other items. All without eggs. Open daily. FS,I,V,N,CC,CH,$$

- **Krishna Cafe**
  7147 Winnetka Ave.
  Canoga Park, CA 91306   (818) 594-5803

Southern Indian. Everything cooked fresh. The daily lunch and dinner specials appear generous, and there's a wide selection of appetizers, side orders and entrées. Closed Monday. I,N,CH,$$

CASTRO VALLEY

Health Unlimited
3446 Village Dr., Castro Valley, CA 94546   (415) 581-0220

It's no longer a soup-and-sandwich place, but stop in for a smoothie, a frozen yogurt or a glass of carrot juice. Sister location in San Leandro. V,J,$

CENTURY CITY

• Raja
**Century City Market Place
10250 Santa Monica Blvd.
Century City, CA 90067   (213) 282-CURRY**

See Los Angeles listing.

CHICO

• Chico Natural Foods Cafe
818 Main St., Chico, CA 95928   (916) 891-1737

A full-service indoor cafe with full-spectrum lighting and a full menu, attached to a fully vegetarian health foods store, but it's open for lunch only. Almost everything is macrobiotic, from the vegan soups to the unleavened poncé bread for the sandwiches. Non alcoholic beers and wines are available in the store, and sandwiches are always available when the store's open. Closed weekends. FS,I,V,M,J,CH,$

COSTA MESA

• Mother's Market and Kitchen
225 E. 17th St., Costa Mesa, CA 92626   (714) 631-4741

Natural foods. Full lacto-ovo menu and vegetarian deli! Breakfasts, soups, salads, sandwiches, entrées, Mexican fare, desserts. Weekly macrobiotic specials. Carryout available. Open daily. FS,V,M,J,CC,CH,$

KEY TO DINING GUIDE
• Vegetarian food only

FS Full service	**V** Vegan options	**CC** Major credit cards accepted
CAF Cafeteria/buffet	**M** Macrobiotic options	**CH** Children welcome
SB Salad bar	**A** Alcoholic drinks	**$** Average dinner under $5
I Informal	**N** Nonalcoholic beer/wine	**$$** Average dinner $5 to $10
F Formal	**J** Freshly squeezed juices	**$$$** Average dinner over $10

CALIFORNIA

COTATI

Markey's Cafe and Coffee House
8240 Old Redwood Hwy.
Cotati, CA 94928   (707) 795-7868
See Petaluma listing.

CUPERTINO

Hobee's
The Oaks Shopping Center
21267 Stevens Creek Blvd.
Cupertino, CA 95014   (408) 255-6010
See Palo Alto listing. Closed Monday. FS,SB,I,V,A,CC,CH,$$

- **Sun 'N' Soil**
20700 Stevens Creek Blvd.
Cupertino CA 95014   (408) 257-8887
Natural foods. Nature Burger, quiche and soups are available. Closed Sunday. FS,V,J,CC,$

DAVENPORT

New Davenport Cash Store
On Coast Highway 1, Davenport, CA 95017   (408) 426-4122
Natural foods. Also a bed-and-breakfast inn. Visit the popular gift shop, and watch the whales as you dine. Veggie burgers, salads, veggie beans, tofu dishes, veggie lasagna and buckwheat pancakes. Open daily. FS,A,CC,$$

DAVIS

The Blue Mango
330 G St., Davis, CA 95616   (916) 756-2616
International vegetarian. Cooperatively managed. Organic produce. Nightly specials. With a name like this, The Blue Mango can't help being creative. Entertainment Friday, Saturday and Sunday. Closed Monday. FS,N,J,$

DUNCANS MILLS

The Blue Heron
1 Steelhead Blvd., Duncans Mills, CA 95430   (707) 865-2269
International cuisine featuring pasta and Mexican specialties. They've won awards for their veggie appetizers. At least one vegetarian special nightly. Open weekends, but call for hours. FS,A,$$-$$$

CALIFORNIA

EL CAJON

- **L'Chaim Cafe**
  134 W. Douglas St., El Cajon, CA 92020   (619) 442-1331

  Natural vegetarian foods, with a down-home style. Pritikin-approved. Closed Sunday. Take the Magnolia Street south exit off Interstate 8 east of San Diego. Turn right into an alley a half block past the fourth traffic light. L'Chaim is located half a block further on the left. Parking at rear of cafe. FS,I,V,M,N,CH,$$

EL TORO

P.J.'s Casa Fiesta
23696 El Toro Rd., El Toro, CA 92630   (714) 581-2529

Mexican. No lard in anything here. Veggie dishes include quesadillas, beans, enchiladas. They'll accommodate your diet. Counter service only. It's the first of a franchised operation, so there'll be more in the area soon. Open daily. I,V,A,N,CC,CH,$

EMERYVILLE

Hobee's
Powell Street Plaza, 5765 Christie Ave.
Emeryville, CA 94608   (415) 652-5944

See Palo Alto listing.

ENCINITAS

Roxy Restaurant and Ice Cream
517 First St., Encinitas, CA 92024   (619) 436-5001

Natural and fun foods. Falafel burger, vegetarian burrito, hummus. It's an ice cream parlor, too. Open daily. FS,I,A,N,J,CC,CH,$$

- **Shepherd**
  1126 First St., Encinitas, CA 92024   (619) 753-1124

  International. Natural foods. Open since 1972, but under new management in the past year. Nightly specials, monthly dessert specials, children's menu. Enjoy Russian stroganoff or Oriental sweet-and-sour under the stars, and be serenaded by live music every night. FS,SB,I,V,A,N,J,CC,CH,$$

KEY TO DINING GUIDE
• Vegetarian food only

FS Full service	**V** Vegan options	**CC** Major credit cards accepted
CAF Cafeteria/buffet	**M** Macrobiotic options	**CH** Children welcome
SB Salad bar	**A** Alcoholic drinks	**$** Average dinner under $5
I Informal	**N** Nonalcoholic beer/wine	**$$** Average dinner $5 to $10
F Formal	**J** Freshly squeezed juices	**$$$** Average dinner over $10

CALIFORNIA

ENCINO

Good Earth
17212 Ventura Blvd., Encino, CA 91316   (818) 986-9990
See Berkeley listing.

EUREKA

Tomaso's Tomato Pies
216 E St., Eureka, CA 95501   (707) 445-0100
Italian specialties include spinach pie, spinzone and calzone. Dairyless pizza is available, as well as occasional dairyless soups. Happy to cater to customers' dietary restrictions. Reservations recommended for large parties or during peak times (noon, and 6 p.m. to 7 p.m.). FS,A,J,CC,$$

FAIR OAKS

Blue Iris Cafe
10118 Fair Oaks Blvd., Fair Oaks, CA 95628   (916) 961-7675
A gourmet restaurant known for its calamari, but wait...there's a macrobiotic and vegetarian menu, too: stir-fries, sautés, noodle and rice dishes, and a popular Veggie Box Lunch featuring tempura. Open Tuesday through Friday for lunch and dinner; open weekends for dinner. Closed Mondays. FS,M,A,N,CC,$$$

- **Sunflower Drive Inn**
10344 Fair Oaks Blvd., Fair Oaks, CA 95628   (916) 967-4331
Juice bar. Nut burgers, falafels, smoothies. Open daily. CH,$

FREMONT

Hobee's
39222 Fremont Blvd., Fremont, CA 94538   (415) 796-4779
See Palo Alto listing.

FULLERTON

The Greenery
119 E. Commonwealth Ave.
Fullerton, CA 92632   (714) 870-0981
Soups and salads. Carryout available. Counter service available. Open daily. Personal checks accepted. FS,I,A,J,CH,$

CALIFORNIA

GARBERVILLE

Wood Rose Cafe
911 Redwood Dr., Garberville, CA 95440   (707) 923-3191

Natural foods. Homemade soups, tofu dishes, organic produce. Patio dining in the summer. No smoking indoors. Easy access from Highway 101. Open daily for lunch. FS,A,CH,$$

GARDEN GROVE

Souplantation
5939 Chapman Ave.
Garden Grove, CA 92645   (714) 895-1314

See San Diego listing. This is one of two locations in suburban Los Angeles. A,J,$$

GLENDALE

- **Glendale Adventist Medical Center**
1509 Wilson Terrace, Glendale, CA 91207   (818) 409-8090

Natural food cafeteria. Open daily. CAF,SB,I,CH,$

Good Earth
50 W. Broadway, Glendale, CA 91204   (818) 502-1970

See Berkeley listing.

GOLETA

Good Earth
5955 Calle Real, Goleta, CA 93117   (805) 683-6101

See Berkeley listing.

HACIENDA HEIGHTS

- **Macrobiotic Living Center**
14426 Cabinda Dr.
Hacienda Heights, CA 91745   (818) 330-1246

Take-out orders only, so call in your order before you go. Closed weekends. The macrobiotic store is closed Saturday. M,N,$$

KEY TO DINING GUIDE
• Vegetarian food only

FS Full service	**V** Vegan options	**CC** Major credit cards accepted
CAF Cafeteria/buffet	**M** Macrobiotic options	**CH** Children welcome
SB Salad bar	**A** Alcoholic drinks	**$** Average dinner under $5
I Informal	**N** Nonalcoholic beer/wine	**$$** Average dinner $5 to $10
F Formal	**J** Freshly squeezed juices	**$$$** Average dinner over $10

CALIFORNIA

HERMOSA BEACH

- **The Spot**
  110 Second St., Hermosa Beach, CA 90254   (213) 376-2355
  Natural foods. Just half a block from the beach. Everything is homemade: fresh bread, soups, lasagna, Mexican foods, terrific salads. Only wholegrain and honey-sweetened desserts: cobblers, cookies, tofu cream pies and more. The owners recently published their own vegetarian cookbook, *Recipes from the Heart*. Established in 1977. FS,V,A,J,CC,$$

HOLLYWOOD

- **I Love Juicy**
  7174 Melrose Ave., Hollywood, CA 90025   (213) 935-7247
  Natural foods. Should be open at this new address by the time we go to press. (Formerly located down the street.) Open 24 hours a day. Completely vegan. One of the premier vegetarian restaurants in California, if not the country. A "must go to" if you're in the area. Where else can you find mochi or manna bread, or even organic oatmeal for breakfast? Several fresh soups and veggie appetizers daily, many salads, lots of sandwiches and too many entrées to count. No salt or preservatives in any of the products, and even distilled water is used in their soups. Everything made fresh from the finest, purest ingredients available. The regulars include John Astin, Olivia Newton-John and Peter Falk. Herb Alpert gets carryout here almost every day. Healthpital, the adjacent store, is a natural and herbal boutique. Catering service, too. Another I Love Juicy is set to open in Westwood in July 1989. CAF,V,M,J,CH, $-$$

- **Orean The Health Express**
  1320 Vine, Hollywood, CA 90028   (213) 462-9945
  Fast and natural vegan take-out. Pancakes and "soysage" for breakfast, Monday through Friday. Tofu and tempeh burgers, chili and Mexican food, salads, dairyless cheese, "super-shakes" and homemade pastries. No refined sugar used. Counter service. Open daily. SB,V,M,CH,$

- **Paru's**
  5140 Sunset Blvd., Hollywood, CA 90027   (213) 661-7600
  Southern Indian vegetarian cuisine. No eggs. Closed Tuesday. FS,I,A,CC,CH,$$

- **La Toque**
  8171 Sunset Blvd.
  West Hollywood, CA 90028   (916) 444-0966
  French gourmet. Any diet can be accommodated because nothing is created until it's ordered. FS,V,A,J,CC,$$$

CALIFORNIA

Natural Fudge Cafe
5224 Fountain Ave.
North Hollywood, CA 91606   **(213) 669-8003**

Natural foods. Daily blackboard specials; daily fresh pastries and pies are sugarless. Champagne brunch on Sunday. Entertainment nightly, featuring musicians, comedians, improvisation groups. Children always welcome, but the entertainment may not always be appropriate for kids. Closed major holidays. FS,I,V,M,A,J,CC,$$

• Leonor's
11403 Victory Blvd.
North Hollywood, CA 91606   **(818) 980-9011**

Mexican. Whole-wheat pizza. Soy sausage, "meatballs" and "chicken." Closed Sunday. FS,I,A,N,CH,$$

Trumps
8764 Melrose Ave.
West Hollywood, CA 90069   **(213) 855-1480**

Nouvelle cuisine. Certainly not primarily veg, but if you want to indulge in gourmet treats, stop by for grilled vegetables or salad. FS,A,J,CC,$$$

HUNTINGTON BEACH

• Mother's Market and Kitchen
19770 Beach Blvd.
Huntington Beach, CA 92648   **(714) 963-6667**

Natural foods. Open daily. Entertainment 10 a.m. to 2 p.m. Sunday. FS,V,J,CC,$

LAGUNA BEACH

• The Stand
238 Thalia, Laguna Beach, CA 92651   **(714) 494-8101**

Salads, soups, sandwiches, Mexican, smoothies, avocado sandwiches, hummus, desserts and more. All vegan, and all without sugar or salt. Closed only on Christmas. V,J,CH,$

KEY TO DINING GUIDE
• Vegetarian food only

FS Full service	**V** Vegan options	**CC** Major credit cards accepted
CAF Cafeteria/buffet	**M** Macrobiotic options	**CH** Children welcome
SB Salad bar	**A** Alcoholic drinks	**$** Average dinner under $5
I Informal	**N** Nonalcoholic beer/wine	**$$** Average dinner $5 to $10
F Formal	**J** Freshly squeezed juices	**$$$** Average dinner over $10

CALIFORNIA

LAKEPORT

Nature's Bounty
301 N. Main St., Lakeport, CA 95453 (707) 263-4575

Juice bar. A lunch place. Superb salads. Closed weekends. FS,N,J,CH,$$

LA MESA

Souplantation
9158 Fletcher Pkwy., La Mesa, CA 92041 (619) 462-4232

See San Diego listing. A,J,$$

LEUCADIA

• Vegetarian Express
1470 N. Highway 101, Leucadia, CA 92021 (619) 942-2320

Fast food. All-you-can-eat buffet, with salad, two dairyless soups and other homemade gourmet entrées. Lunches: salad bar, soups, homemade bread, rice and a tostada bar. Homemade desserts. Entertainment twice a week. Closed Monday. CAF,SB,I,N,J,CH,$$

LOMA LINDA

• Loma Linda University Medical Center
Anderson and Barton Rds.
Loma Linda, CA 92354 (714) 824-4365

Open daily for all meals. No alcohol and no smoking on premises. Take-out available. Open 22 hours a day. CAF,CH,$

• The Soup Stone
11306 Mountain View
Loma Linda, CA 92354 (714) 796-1162

(Formerly Bradford's.) Strictly veg. A 40-item salad bar, soup bar, potato bar, bread and dessert bar graces this combination restaurant, bakery and catering service, and you can find veggie burgers, pasta dishes and six soups on the menu daily. Children pay 50 cents for every year of their age. Eat indoors or out, and if you need to, request the private banquet room. Closed Friday and Saturday. Sunday brunch starts at 10 a.m. CAF,SB,N,CC,CH,$$

LOS ALAMITOS

Good Earth
4232 Katella Ave., Los Alamitos, CA 90721 (213) 598-0503

See Berkeley listing.

CALIFORNIA

LOS ANGELES

A Votre Sante
13016 San Vicente Blvd.
Los Angeles, CA 90049   **(213) 451-1813**

Natural foods. Vegetarian enchiladas, tamales, black beans with brown rice. FS,V,M,J,CC,$$

The Artful Balance
525½ N. Fairfax Ave.
Los Angeles, CA 90036   **(213) 852-9091**

Natural foods. Reservations recommended. Call ahead for hours: they change. FS,V,M,CC,CH,$$$

- ## Beverly Hills Juice Club
  8382 Beverly Blvd., Los Angeles, CA 90048   (213) 655-8300

  Juice bar. Fast food. All foods are raw and vegan, but you might not believe it. Fresh veggies, fruits, nuts, herbs and spices from around the world are inventively blended to create an amazing array of exotic dishes. And because nothing is cooked, all of the vitamins and minerals are retained. Look at the possibilities: Vegetable Curry, Tree Fish (made from a vegetarian tree food grown in the tropics), barbecued mushrooms, chili, and corn beet paté. Even vegetarian caviar (a nori roll with a delicious combination of seeds, veggies and other sea vegetables). The Hollywood hip hang out here. Fabulous carrot juice, by the way. Closed Sunday. V,J,CH

Break-Away Garden
11970 Venice Blvd., Los Angeles, CA 90066   (213) 559-1922

(Formerly the Green Bean.) Natural foods featuring "California cuisine". Soba stir-fry, for example. Open daily. V,M,A,J,CC,$$

- ## Country Life
  888 S. Figueroa, Los Angeles, CA 90017   (213) 489-4118

  Natural foods. Enormous international buffet. Located downstairs, next to a Nautilus health spa. Buffet is all-you-can-eat variety. Completely vegan. Homemade soups, breads, spreads and desserts. Carry-out available. Usually closed weekends, but owners were considering serving on Sunday; phone first. CAF,SB,V,J,CC,CH,$$

KEY TO DINING GUIDE
• Vegetarian food only

FS Full service	**V** Vegan options	**CC** Major credit cards accepted
CAF Cafeteria/buffet	**M** Macrobiotic options	**CH** Children welcome
SB Salad bar	**A** Alcoholic drinks	**$** Average dinner under $5
I Informal	**N** Nonalcoholic beer/wine	**$$** Average dinner $5 to $10
F Formal	**J** Freshly squeezed juices	**$$$** Average dinner over $10

CALIFORNIA

Erewhon Foods Healthycatessen
8001 Beverly Blvd.
Los Angeles, CA 90048 (213) 655-5441
Natural foods. CAF,A,,J,$$

• Fragrant Vegetable
11859 Wilshire Blvd.
Los Angeles, CA 90025 (213) 312-1442
Chinese Buddhist dining. Some dishes include eggs. Elegant variety of selections. FS,I,A,N,CC,$$$

Gitanjala of India
414 N. La Cienega Blvd.
Los Angeles, CA 90048 (213) 657-2117
Indian. Hand-rolled bread, yogurt dressing. Interesting range of veggie entrées exquisitely seasoned with herbs and spices to your taste—mild, medium or hot. Authentic six-bowl thali. Open daily. FS,A,N,CC,CH,$$

In the Los Angeles area . . .

For the traveler who is not familiar with the Los Angeles area, we suggest looking under the following listings for additional dining choices.

Anaheim
Beverly Hills
Canoga Park
Costa Mesa (1 hour drive)
Encino
Glendale
Hermosa Beach (45 minutes)
Hollywood
Huntington Beach (45 minutes)
Loma Linda (1 hour)
Manhattan Beach (40 minutes)
Marina del Rey
Monterey Park
Murrieta (1 hour)

Northridge
Norwalk (30 minutes)
Pasadena (30 minutes)
San Gabriel (30 minutes)
Santa Monica
Sherman Oaks
Sierra Madre
Topanga Canyon
Torrance
Venice (45 minutes)
Westwood (45 minutes)
Westwood Village (40 minutes)

CALIFORNIA

- **Golden Temple**
  7910 W. Third St., Los Angeles, CA 90048   **(213) 655-1891**
  Natural foods. International "home cookin'," including homemade fresh desserts and bread. No eggs used. Dairy and nondairy dishes available; will cater to special diets. Closed Sunday. FS,SB,I,V,N,J,CC,CH,$$

  Good Earth
  1002 Westwood Blvd.
  Los Angeles, CA 90024   **(213) 208-8215**
  See Berkeley listing.

  Good Earth
  11819 Wilshire Blvd., Los Angeles, CA 90025   **(213) 479-0177**
  See Berkeley listing.

- **Govinda's**
  9624 Venice Blvd., Los Angeles, CA 90232   **(213) 836-1269**
  Indian, Mexican and purely natural. Sandwiches, enchiladas, lasagna, tostadas, quesadillas, nut loaves, veggie burgers and grilled tofu. No eggs. Bakery and juice bar. Closed Sunday. Personal checks accepted. FS,I,V,CH,$$

  The House of Stewart
  3151 Wilshire Blvd., Los Angeles, CA 90010   **(213) 384-4155**
  Full service or fast—it's your choice. The menu's pretty broad, with some purely vegetarian items mixed in. Everything's homemade. Most of the soups are veggie-based, and there are several veggie sandwiches; and the veggies are organic. The desserts sound delightful. Closed Sunday. V,M,J,CC,CH,$

- **Inaka**
  131 S. La Brea Ave., Los Angeles, CA 90036   **(213) 936-9353**
  All-vegan, Japanese foods. Most foods are organic, and none contain preservatives, artificial flavors or colors. Carryout available. BYOB. Closed Monday. FS,V,M,CH,$$

KEY TO DINING GUIDE
- Vegetarian food only

FS Full service	**V** Vegan options	**CC** Major credit cards accepted
CAF Cafeteria/buffet	**M** Macrobiotic options	**CH** Children welcome
SB Salad bar	**A** Alcoholic drinks	**$** Average dinner under $5
I Informal	**N** Nonalcoholic beer/wine	**$$** Average dinner $5 to $10
F Formal	**J** Freshly squeezed juices	**$$$** Average dinner over $10

CALIFORNIA

Keste Demena
5779 W. Venice Blvd.
Los Angeles, CA 90019 (213) 933-6522

Ethiopian. Some veggie dishes, including mustard greens, lentils and a mixed veggie dish. Closed Wednesday. FS,I,N,CC,CH,$-$$

• The Kingsley Garden
4070 W. Third St., Los Angeles, CA 90020 (213) 389-5527

Here's an exciting concept: the only restaurant in the country offering a complete, all-natural and vegan menu of Mexican, Italian, Indian, Oriental and other international specialties, as well as traditional dishes. All-natural, sugarless desserts include shakes, sundaes, cakes and pies. And it's 90 percent organic. Eat on the patio in nice weather. Open daily. FS,SB,V,M,N,J,CC,CH,$$$

Mother Earth
11277 National Blvd.
Los Angeles, CA 90064 (213) 477-0555

Many vegan dishes. Closed at lunchtime Saturday through Monday and at dinnertime Monday. FS,CAF,I,V,M,N,CH,$$

• Naturally Fast
11661 Santa Monica Blvd.
Los Angeles, CA 90025 (213) 444-7886

Natural foods. The setting is clean and bright; the cuisine is healthfully varied. Choose from Pritikin-style, vegan, macrobiotic or regular vegetarian offerings. No dish contains eggs. House specials include vegetarian lasagna, a variety of veggie burgers and soups. Low-oil and no-sodium dishes are also a specialty. Counter service available. Closed on major holidays. CAF,V,M,CH,$$

Nowhere Cafe
8009 Beverly Blvd., Los Angeles, CA 90048 (213) 655-8895

Natural foods. California elegance. Vegetarian dishes include Moo Shi Vegetables, Blue Enchilada and Meatless Loaf. Open daily. Open Sunday for dinner only. FS,V,M,N,J,CC,$$-$$$

Old World Restaurant
8782 Sunset Blvd., Los Angeles, CA 90069 (213) 652-2520

Natural foods since 1965. Eight vegetarian entrées, plus breakfasts and salads. For dessert, there's the Ultimate Belgian Waffle. Open daily. FS,V,A,CC,CH,$$$

• Organic-Ville
Alexander and Sixth Street
Los Angeles, CA 90020 (213) 386-1440

Natural foods. Wide variety of entrées, soups, sandwiches, salads. No eggs. Daily specials include steamed veggies, curries, stroganoffs, and Thai dishes. Entrées: Vegetarian scallops (braised gluten), nut loaf, burgers and tamales. All sandwiches—avocado, burgers, tofu salad—can be served on bible bread if requested. Also salads, sides and fresh vegetable and fruit juices. Organic fruits and veggies whenever possible. Open daily. FS,V,J,CC,CH,$$

- **Osteria Romana Orsini**
  9575 W. Pico Blvd., Los Angeles, CA 90035   (213) 277-6050

  California cuisine. Many vegetarian items on the lunch buffet. No eggs. Closed Sunday. FS,SB,A,N,CC,CH $$$

- **Racers Cafe**
  359 N. La Cienega Blvd.
  Los Angeles, CA 90048   (213) 652-8896

  International vegetarian. Along with 16 kinds of raw foods, Racers also has a large selection of cooked vegetarian entrées, including tofu lasagna (all foods with cheese have either tofu or dairy cheese), stir-fried vegetable plates, and meatless tacos and other Mexican dishes. Take-out and delivery, too. Closed Sunday. FS,V,N,J,CC,$$

- **Raja**
  8875 W. Pico Blvd., Los Angeles, CA 90035   (213) 550-9176

  Indian. Eat from the buffet at lunch or from the table at dinner. Spinach and cheese, curries, and eggplant, potato and cauliflower dishes are the specialties. Open daily. A Century City location, also. FS,CAF,I,A,CC,CH,$$

Sisters
3884 Crenshaw Blvd.,
Los Angeles, CA 90008   (213) 294-3018

Juice bar. Some veg offerings, including falafel, lentil burgers, quiche and sandwiches on whole-grain breads. Open daily. CAF,I,V,$

The Source
8301 Sunset Blvd., Los Angeles, CA 90069   (213) 656-6388

Natural foods. Open daily. FS,I,V,A,CC,CH,$$

KEY TO DINING GUIDE
• Vegetarian food only

FS Full service	**V** Vegan options	**CC** Major credit cards accepted
CAF Cafeteria/buffet	**M** Macrobiotic options	**CH** Children welcome
SB Salad bar	**A** Alcoholic drinks	**$** Average dinner under $5
I Informal	**N** Nonalcoholic beer/wine	**$$** Average dinner $5 to $10
F Formal	**J** Freshly squeezed juices	**$$$** Average dinner over $10

CALIFORNIA

- **White Memorial Medical Center**
  1720 Brooklyn Ave., Los Angeles, CA 90025   (213) 268-5000
  Natural foods. Cafeteria in Seventh-day Adventist hospital features a variety of vegetarian dishes. Open daily. No breakfast or lunch served on weekends. FS,J,$$

MANHATTAN BEACH

St. Estephe
2640 N. Sepulveda Blvd.
Manhattan Beach, CA 90266   (213) 545-1334

California cuisine. Modern Southwestern cuisine with a French twist. Try the avocado cake entrée or the chili rellenos. Closed Sunday and Monday. FS,A,CC,$$$

MARINA DEL REY

Good Earth
4730 Lincoln Blvd.
Marina del Rey, CA 90291   (213) 822-9033
See Berkeley listing.

MENLO PARK

Flea Street Cafe
3607 Alameda, Menlo Park, CA 94025   (415) 854-1226

Natural foods. Innovative menu featuring organic produce from local growers, fresh goat cheeses and eggs from free-range chickens. Menu includes pastas and many vegetarian items. Menu items offer fresh seasonal food "which honors the earth from which it is grown and the hardworking farmers who produce it."Lunch Tuesday through Friday. Dinner Tuesday through Saturday. Sunday is brunch only. FS,I,A,J,CC,CH,$$

Late for the Train
150 Middlefield Rd., Menlo Park, CA 94025   (415) 321-6124

Natural foods. Mostly vegetarian items including omelets, salads, sandwiches, soups. Also stews and pasta. Sunday brunch. Closed Monday. FS,I,V,J,CC,CH,$$

MIDDLETOWN

Stonefront Restaurant
18424 Harbin Springs Rd.
Middletown, CA 95461   (707) 987-9012

CALIFORNIA

Some macrobiotic dishes and some veggie dishes without eggs available. Open daily. I,M,CH,$$

MONTEBELLO

Raja
3414 W. Beverly Blvd.
Montebello, CA 90640   (213) 725-8905
See Los Angeles listing.

MONTEREY PARK

Fragrant Vegetable
108 N. Garfield, Monterey Park, CA 91754   (818) 280-4215
Chinese Buddhist dining. See Los Angeles listing.

MOUNTAIN VIEW

• The Blue Sky Cafe
336 Bryant St., Mountain View, CA 94041   (415) 961-2082
Natural foods. Many fruits and vegetables freshly picked from the backyard garden. Patio dining in nice weather. All food made on premises with a "caring and loving consciousness." Closed Monday. FS,V,A,CC,CH,$$

Hobee's
2312 Central Expressway
Mountain View, CA 94040   (415) 968-6050
See Palo Alto listing. FS,V,A,N,J,CC,$$

MURRIETA

Murrieta Hot Springs Resort and Health Spa
39405 Murrieta Hot Springs Rd.
Murrieta, CA 92362   (714) 677-7451
Called "a mecca for the healing arts," this family-oriented resort features three natural mineral springs, Olympic-sized pool, tennis courts, mineral baths, tule-root mud baths, body wraps, saunas and a lacto-vegetarian

---

KEY TO DINING GUIDE
• Vegetarian food only

FS Full service	**V** Vegan options	**CC** Major credit cards accepted
CAF Cafeteria/buffet	**M** Macrobiotic options	**CH** Children welcome
SB Salad bar	**A** Alcoholic drinks	**$** Average dinner under $5
I Informal	**N** Nonalcoholic beer/wine	**$$** Average dinner $5 to $10
F Formal	**J** Freshly squeezed juices	**$$$** Average dinner over $10

CALIFORNIA

menu that is out of this world. Stay overnight if you can (pure luxury), or just stop by for a meal. (One hour by car from Los Angeles.) Make sure you come hungry—you'll want to sample everything. Open daily. FS,CAF,SB,A,N,J,CC,CH,$$-$$$

NATIONAL CITY

- **Paradise Valley Hospital**
  2400 E. Fourth St., National City, CA 92050   (619) 470-6311
  Natural foods. Lunch and dinner specials, $2. Open daily. CAF,SB,J,CH,$

NEEDLES

Irene's Drive Inn
703 Broadway, Needles, CA 92363   (619) 326-2342
Juice bar. Drive-in food for vegetarians: cheeseburgers, tacos and burritos. Closed Saturday. FS,J,CH,$

NEVADA CITY

Earth Song Market and Cafe
727 Zion St., Nevada City, CA 95959   (916) 265-9392
Natural foods. All-natural ingredients including organic grains, beans and produce used whenever possible. Daily specials. FS,V,M,J,CC,$$

NEWPORT BEACH

Good Earth
Fashion Island, 210 Newport Center Dr. E.
Newport Beach, CA 92660   (714) 640-2411
See Berkeley listing.

NORTH PARK

- **Govinda's**
  3102 University Ave., North Park, CA 92109   (619) 284-4826
  Indian natural foods. Open daily. Buffet style, all you can eat. Soups, salads. CAF,SB,V,M,N,CC,CH,$-$$

NORTHRIDGE

Good Earth
19510 Nordhoff St., Northridge, CA 91324   (818) 993-7306
See Berkeley listing.

CALIFORNIA

NORWALK

- **Our Daily Bread Bakery**
  12201 Front St., Norwalk, CA 90650   **(213) 863-6897**

  Whole-foods bakery, general store and vegetarian take-out restaurant with dairy-, sugar- and oil-free entrées, soups and salads. Closed weekends. $

OAKLAND

Alpha Health Foods
468 20th St., Oakland, CA 94612   **(415) 465-7410**

Juice bar. Soups and sandwiches. J,$

Granny Feels Great
5020 Woodminster Lane
Oakland, CA 94602   **(415) 530-6723**

Juice bar. Sandwiches, salads, soups, box lunches, homemade cookies. Reservations recommended for large parties. Closed Sunday. Located in the Oakland Hills, above the Mormon Temple, east of Highway 13. I,V,A,N,CH,$

- **Macrobiotic Grocery**
  1050 40th St., Oakland, CA 94608   **(415) 653-6510**

  Natural food restaurant and store. Reservations recommended for dinner. Take-out available. Open daily. Brunch on Sunday. FS,M

Royal India Cuisine
1400 Franklin St., Oakland, CA 94612   **(415) 268-9000**

Indian. A nutritionally well-balanced, all-you-can-eat 20-course buffet is available on Saturday nights, and it is sure to have something for everyone (like the belly dancer, for example). Similar lunch buffets during the week. Only the freshest ingredients are used—even the spices are fresh-ground. Homemade cheese and yogurt. Open daily. FS,CAF,V,N,J,CC,CH,$$$

OCEANSIDE

- **Pacific Yeast Free Bakery & Macrobiotic Center**
  429 S. Hill St.
  Oceanside, CA 92054   **(619) 757-6020 or 967-0710**

KEY TO DINING GUIDE
• Vegetarian food only

FS Full service	**V** Vegan options	**CC** Major credit cards accepted
CAF Cafeteria/buffet	**M** Macrobiotic options	**CH** Children welcome
SB Salad bar	**A** Alcoholic drinks	**$** Average dinner under $5
I Informal	**N** Nonalcoholic beer/wine	**$$** Average dinner $5 to $10
F Formal	**J** Freshly squeezed juices	**$$$** Average dinner over $10

CALIFORNIA

Organic grains, vegetables, nuts and fruit. All breads free of sugar, honey, eggs, dairy, oil, yeast, baking powder and baking soda. Open daily for breakfast and lunch. Dinner by reservation only. I,M,V,$$

OROVILLE

- **Vega Study Center**
  1511 Robinson St., Oroville, CA 95965   **(916) 533-7702**
  It's what the name says: A center for the study of vegetarianism and macrobiotics. Open to the public by reservation only. One menu item daily, unless fish is served; then there's a vegan alternative (a rare occurrence). Meals are served at 11:30 a.m. and 5:30 p.m. Call by 9 a.m. for reservations for lunch and by 2 p.m. for dinner. I,V,M,CC,$$

PACIFIC GROVE

Tillie Gort's
111 Central Ave., Pacific Grove, CA 93950   **(408) 373-0335**
Natural foods. Nonmeat loaf, pasta, sandwiches and quiche. (Real men *do* eat quiche!) Now open for breakfast. Homemade desserts. Open daily. FS,V,A,CC,CH,$$

PALO ALTO

Country Sun
440 California Ave., Palo Alto, CA 94306   **(415) 328-4120**
Select from a variety of fresh vegetarian soups, salads and entrées. Fresh juice and espresso bar. Open daily. V,M,CH,$

Good Earth
185 University Ave., Palo Alto, CA 94301   **(415) 321-9449**
See Berkeley listing. Natural food restaurant and bakery. Open daily. Closed Christmas. FS,V,A,J,CC,CH,$$

Hobee's
4224 El Camino Real, near Charleston/Arastradero
Palo Alto, CA 94306   **(415) 856-6124**
All-fresh salad bar. Meatless soups and chili. Gourmet tofu burgers, omelets and sandwiches. Energy blends. Open daily, including breakfast. Other Hobee's in Palo Alto, Tahoe City, Mountain View, San Jose, Cupertino, Santa Cruz, San Bruno, San Luis Obispo, Fremont and Emeryville. Mountain View and San Jose restaurants are not open for dinner. FS,SB,I,V,CC,CH,$$

CALIFORNIA

Hobee's
67 Town and Country Village
El Camino Real and Embarcadero
Palo Alto, CA 94301   (415) 327-4111

See above entry. FS,SB,V,A,N,J,CC,$$

PALOMAR

- ### Mother's Kitchen
  Junction S6 & S7
  Palomar Mountain, CA 92060   (619) 742-3496

  Natural foods. Located atop Palomar Mountain amid beautiful wooded area. "Stargazer sandwiches" and make-your-own omelets. FS,A,J,CC,$$

PARADISE

- ### Feather River Hospital Cafeteria
  5974 Pentz Rd., Paradise, CA 95969   (916) 877-9361

  Natural foods. Spanish, Chinese and American cuisine. Open to the public. CAF,N,J,CH,$

PASADENA

Good Earth
257 N. Rosemead Blvd., Pasadena, CA 91107   (818) 351-5488

See Berkeley listing. Closed Sunday.

Uncle Nick's Falafel
1579 E. Colorado Blvd., Pasadena, CA 91106   (818) 795-5073

Middle Eastern. This Middle Eastern version of a fast-food restaurant is open every day except Sunday. $

Grass Roots
1119 Fair Oaks Ave.
South Pasadena, CA 91030   (818) 799-0156

A natural food store and a restaurant. Very casual and homey (with a sawdust-sprinkled maroon cement floor.) Homemade soups, muffins (eight varieties), banana nut bread, frozen yogurt and shakes. No dinners, but come in for sandwiches until about 5:30. Fresh, open space. Counter service. Closed Sunday. I,V,M,J,CC,CH,$$

KEY TO DINING GUIDE
- Vegetarian food only

FS Full service	**V** Vegan options	**CC** Major credit cards accepted
CAF Cafeteria/buffet	**M** Macrobiotic options	**CH** Children welcome
SB Salad bar	**A** Alcoholic drinks	**$** Average dinner under $5
I Informal	**N** Nonalcoholic beer/wine	**$$** Average dinner $5 to $10
F Formal	**J** Freshly squeezed juices	**$$$** Average dinner over $10

CALIFORNIA

PETALUMA

Markey's Cafe
316 Western Ave., Petaluma, CA 94952   **(707) 763-2429**

Natural foods. Combination natural food deli and coffeehouse, serving three meals daily. Casual atmosphere and menu. Light classics from the piano, and folk music on weekends. Open daily. FS,V,A,N,J,$

SACRAMENTO

The Good Earth
2024 Arden Way, Sacramento, CA 95825   **(916) 920-5544**

Natural and wholesome. Incredibly large menu ranging from soups, salads, entrées, sandwiches, and even a weekend champagne brunch (lots of eggs). Their favorites? The vegetable-and-bean Planet Burger, the Magic Eggplant casserole with Spanish Basque sauce and the Good Earth tostada on a whole-wheat chapati with adzuki and pinto beans. Veg dinner menu features walnut and mushroom casserole, Cajun veggie tempeh, and veggie sweet-and-sour. You can even get sautéed tofu for a side order. Good desserts, too. FS,A,J,CC,$

• India Restaurant
729 J St., Sacramento, CA 95814   **(916) 448-9046**

A small Indian cafe with some outdoor seating. Entrées include sag paneer (spinach with cheese) and several vegetarian appetizers. Open Monday through Saturday for lunch and dinner, and Sunday for dinner only. FS,N,CC,CH,$$

Juliana's Kitchen
1800 L St., Sacramento, CA 95814   **(916) 444-0966**

Natural foods. A lunch place, but what a lunch! Middle Eastern specialties: homemade falafel, tabouli salad, tahini salad, baba ganouj, and fried zucchini and cauliflower sandwiches. Two locations in Sacramento. Closed Sunday. FS,I,V,A,J,CH,$

Juliana's Kitchen
1401 G St., Sacramento, CA 95814   **(916) 444-0966**

See entry above.

• Marline's Vegetable Patch
1119 8th St., Sacramento, CA 95814   **(916) 448-3327**

Lunch only, but what a lunch! Everything's vegan: burritos, tostadas, nachos, burgers, sandwiches salads. Smoothies and fresh juices, too. One VT reader says she goes out of her way to eat lunch here a couple of times a week. Closed weekends. FS,SB,I,CAF,V,N,J,CH,$

CALIFORNIA

- **Mums**
  2968 Freeport Blvd., Sacramento, CA 95818   (916) 444-3015

  Gourmet. Dinner items include tofilo, spanakopita and tempeh flauta. The specialties incorporate imaginative spices and an array of herbs. Reservations recommended for four or more persons. Brunch on Saturday and Sunday. Live entertainment on holidays. Closed Monday. FS,V,M,A,N,J,CC,CH,$$

- **Taj Mahal**
  2355 Arden Way, Sacramento, CA 95825   (916) 924-8378

  Indian restaurant, with the usual complement of vegetarian dishes: cauliflower and potatoes or peas, eggplant, curries. Open daily. FS,CAF,V,A,N,CC,CH,$$

ST. HELENA

- **St. Helena Health Center Dining Room**
  650 Sanitarium Rd., St. Helena, CA 94576   (707) 963-6214

  Natural foods. Completely vegetarian resort and health spa. The dining room serves an all-you-can-eat buffet, including salad bar and desserts, three times a day: from 7:45 a.m. to 8:30 a.m., 12:30 p.m. to 1:30 p.m., and 5:30 p.m. to 6:30 p.m. Reservations are required. Take Highway 29 to Deer Park Road and turn left on Sanitarium Road. Go about one mile to the health center. See spa listings for more information. CAF,SB,I,V,CH,$$

SAN BRUNO

Hobee's
12 Bayhill Shopping Center
San Bruno, CA 94066   (415) 588-9662

See Palo Alto listing. Open daily. FS,SB,CC,CH,$$

SAN DIEGO

- **Cornucopia**
  112 W. Washington St., San Diego, CA 92107 (619) 299-4174

  Greek and Middle Eastern. Home-style cooking without preservatives or

---

KEY TO DINING GUIDE
• Vegetarian food only

FS Full service	**V** Vegan options	**CC** Major credit cards accepted
CAF Cafeteria/buffet	**M** Macrobiotic options	**CH** Children welcome
SB Salad bar	**A** Alcoholic drinks	**$** Average dinner under $5
I Informal	**N** Nonalcoholic beer/wine	**$$** Average dinner $5 to $10
F Formal	**J** Freshly squeezed juices	**$$$** Average dinner over $10

CALIFORNIA

pesticides. Tabouli, hummus, guacamole and homemade cream of mushroom soup. Wheatless pancakes; homemade desserts with whole-wheat flour. Personal checks accepted. Open daily. Open Sunday for lunch only. FS,F,CH,$$

- **Govinda's**
  3102 University Ave., San Diego, CA 92104   (619) 284-4826
  Natural foods. No eggs used in the cooking. Open daily. CAF,SB,V,M,N,CC,CH,$-$$

In the San Diego area . . .

For the traveler who is not familiar with the San Diego area, we suggest looking under the following listings for additional restaurant choices.

El Cajon
Encinitas
La Mesa
Leucadia
National City

Needles
North Park
Palomar Mountain
Paradise

- **Grain Country**
  3448 30th St., San Diego, CA 92104   (619) 298-1052
  Natural foods. Macrobiotic. Natural food store, too. Open daily for lunch and on Friday and Saturday nights for dinner. Sunday brunch. CAF,I,M,CC,CH,$$

- **Kung Food**
  2949 Fifth Ave., San Diego, CA 92103   (619) 298-7330
  Natural foods. Large, creative selection of natural foods. Home-style and gourmet entrées and desserts. Low-fat, low-salt and Pritikin specialties. Open daily for breakfast, brunch and dinner. FS,V,A,N,J,CC,$$

- **O. B. People's Food Store**
  4765 Voltaire St., San Diego, CA 92107   (619) 224-1387
  A take-out deli specializing in vegan and raw foods. Closed on major holidays. Personal checks accepted. I,V,N,J,CH,$

- **Souplantation**
  6171 Mission Gorge Rd.
  San Diego, CA 92120   (619) 280-7087

CALIFORNIA

Juice bar. More than 60 items on the all-you-can-eat, self-serve salad bar, including soup, fresh fruit and muffins. Open daily. Locations throughout southern California. SB,CAF,I,A,N,CH,$$

Souplantation
3960 W. Point Loma Blvd.
San Diego, CA 92110   **(619) 222-7404**

See above entry. A,J,$$

Soups Unlimited
660 University Ave., San Diego, CA 92103   **(619) 296-4030**

Juice bar. Closed on major holidays. CAF,SB,I,V,A,J,CH,$

SAN FRANCISCO

A.J.'s Falafel King
420 Geary St., San Francisco, CA 94102   **(415) 776-2683**

Falafel, asharma and frozen yogurt are the specialties here. Open daily. FS,I,V,M,N,CH,$$

All You Knead
1466 Haight St., San Francisco, CA 94117   **(415) 552-4550**

Natural foods. Pasta and pizza. FS,A,J,$$

- **Amazing Grace**
216 Church St., San Francisco, CA 94114   **(415) 626-6411**

Juice bar. Two-soup, two-entrée specials daily. Open for lunch and dinner. Closed Sunday. CAF,SB,CH,$$

- **Ananda-Fuara**
3050 Taraval, San Francisco, CA 94114   **(415) 564-6766**

Natural foods for the whole family in this peaceful restaurant run by students of Sri Chinmoy. Try it for delicious, wholesome, hearty breakfasts, or for barbecued tofu burgers later in the day. Seniors receive a 10 percent discount. Carryout available. Closed Sunday. FS,V,M,J,$

Bombay Palace
2801 Leavenworth, Beach St., (in the Cannery)
San Francisco, CA 94113   **(415) 776-3666**

KEY TO DINING GUIDE
• Vegetarian food only

FS Full service	**V** Vegan options	**CC** Major credit cards accepted
CAF Cafeteria/buffet	**M** Macrobiotic options	**CH** Children welcome
SB Salad bar	**A** Alcoholic drinks	**$** Average dinner under $5
I Informal	**N** Nonalcoholic beer/wine	**$$** Average dinner $5 to $10
F Formal	**J** Freshly squeezed juices	**$$$** Average dinner over $10

CALIFORNIA

Indian. Homemade cottage-cheese dishes, beans, lentils, curry. Closed Christmas and Labor Day. Locations also in Great Britain, Canada and Hong Kong. FS,F,V,A,N,CC,CH,$$$

Cafe International
508 Haight St., San Francisco, CA 94117 (415) 552-7390

De Paula's
2114 Fillmore St., San Francisco, CA 94115 (415) 346-9888

Brazilian restaurant and pizzeria. A couple of veg entrées—eggplant parmigiana and sautéed vegetables with cream on rice—besides their vegetarian pizza, which is available with a large number of veggie toppings. Open for dinner seven days a week, lunch Monday through Friday. Reservations for parties of more than four. Take-out available. FS,V,N,CC,CH,$$

El Moro Tacqueria
1799 Fulton, San Francisco, CA 94117 (415) 921-1183

- **The Ganges**
775 Frederick, San Francisco, CA 94117 (415) 661-7290

Indian. Authentic Gujarat (western Indian) cuisine; menu changes daily. In a residential area, but it's reportedly worth the hunt. Live music Thursday through Saturday. FS,A,$$-$$$

- **Greens**
Fort Mason, Building B
San Francisco, CA 94123 (415) 771-6222

Featured in *VT* as one of the country's best vegetarian restaurants. Call ahead for reservations. The raised dining room overlooks the marina of San Francisco Bay. Some of the food is grown at the nearby Tassajara Zen Monastery farm. Most popular items: Vegetable and Tofu Brochette, pizza, pasta and rich desserts. Lunch and dinner Tuesday through Saturday. Brunch on Sunday. Closed Monday. FS,A,CC,CH,$$$

The Haven
One Post St., San Francisco, CA 94104 (415) 397-1299

Juice bar. Closed weekends. CAF,N,$

Indian Garden Restaurant
120 Hazelwood, San Francisco, CA 94080 (415) 952-8482

(Formerly Nirvana Restaurant.) Several veg dishes on the traditional Indian menu, including homemade cheese with peas in sauce, lentils with sweet butter and spices, and spinach with cheese curry. Many veggie appetizers, too. Closed Monday. Reservations encouraged. FS,I,A,N, CC,CH,$$

CALIFORNIA

> **In the San Francisco area . . .**
>
> For the traveler who is not familiar with the Bay Area, we suggest looking under the following listings for additional dining choices.
>
> Berkeley
> Castro Valley
> Cupertino (1 hour)
> Menlo Park (45 minutes)
> Mountain View
>
> Oakland
> Palo Alto
> San Bruno
> San Leandro
> San Rafael (45 minutes)

The Jasmin Cafe
1251 Third Ave., San Francisco, CA 94122   (415) 566-3776

International/Middle Eastern. Fine art and fine food. Enjoy exhibits of the Bay Area's finest artists with your breakfast, lunch or dinner. Breakfast entrées include steamed eggs—not poached—with curry sauce, pesto sauce, or the house sauce made with sautéed tomatoes, garlic, bell peppers, mushrooms and onions. Also six-grain cereal, waffles and bagels. For lunch and dinner, there's standard Middle Eastern fare, plus Armenian pizza, stuffed cabbage and lasagna. Greek salads, couscous and many soups. Everything available to go. At Hugo Street between Irving and Lincoln. Closed weekends. FS,A,N,$

La Fuente
2 Embarcadero Center
San Francisco, CA 94111   (415) 982-3363

Lo Naturo Italiano
600 Fifth Ave. (at Balboa)
San Francisco, CA 94118   (415) 752-1044

Natural Italian (if you couldn't tell). Wide variety of special pizzas, whole-wheat crust, Chicago-style stuffed pizza (soy cheese available), vegetable specials, zucchini specials, whole-grain pastas. A *VT* reader called to tell us that "the food is always good, the service is impeccable, and the chef is always creative." Take-out available. Closed Monday. FS, A,CH,$$

KEY TO DINING GUIDE
• Vegetarian food only

FS Full service	**V** Vegan options	**CC** Major credit cards accepted
CAF Cafeteria/buffet	**M** Macrobiotic options	**CH** Children welcome
SB Salad bar	**A** Alcoholic drinks	**$** Average dinner under $5
I Informal	**N** Nonalcoholic beer/wine	**$$** Average dinner $5 to $10
F Formal	**J** Freshly squeezed juices	**$$$** Average dinner over $10

CALIFORNIA

- **Lotus Garden**
  532 Grant Ave., San Francisco, CA 94108   **(415) 397-0707**
  Chinese. Daily specials. Soy products replace traditional Chinese meat items. Closed Monday. FS,I,V,N,CC,$$

- **Lucky Creation**
  854 Washington St.
  San Francisco, CA 94108   **(415) 989-0818**
  Chinese vegetarian food, and it's all natural. Sixty-five menu items to choose from. If you love Chinese food, this is definitely the place to go. Closed Wednesday. FS,V,CH,$$

  Pasand Madras
  1875 Union St., San Francisco, CA 94123   **(415) 922-4498**
  Indian. Southern Indian style. Nightly entertainment. FS,A,CC,$

  Real Good Karma
  501 Dolores St., San Francisco, CA 94110   **(415) 621-4112**
  Natural foods. Grilled pineapple tofu. Indian and Japanese cuisine. Entrées include curry, miso soup, tempura. Only positive vibes, baby. Open seven days. FS,F,M,N,CH,$$

  Seventeen O Five Cafe
  1705 Haight St. (Haight at Cole)
  San Francisco, CA 94117   **(415) 387-3348**
  International. The menu here is half veg and half not. Open for all meals. For breakfast, fresh juices and frittatas are typical; for lunch, they have soups, salads, grilled veggies and tofu burgers; and for dinner, a variety of vegetarian entrées are offered. Take-out available. FS,I,V,A,J,CH,$$

- **Shangri-La**
  2026 Irving St., San Francisco, CA 94122   **(415) 731-2548**
  Strictly vegetarian and strictly Chinese—northern Chinese, that is. A Buddhist establishment. Relaxed, peaceful atmosphere. Lots of specials. Chef will make allowances for dietary restrictions. Cart of interesting ethnic appetizers. Carryout available. No MSG. FS,V,A,CC,$

  Silver Moon
  2301 Clement St., San Francisco, CA 94121   **(415) 386-7852**
  Natural foods. Known for its imitation seafood, duck and shrimp. Voted one of the top eateries in the Bay area by the *San Francisco Examiner*. A VT reader told us to be sure to try the vegetarian pressed duck. "Tastes like the real thing!" Open daily. FS,A,CC,CH,$$

CALIFORNIA

- **Taste of Honey Bakery**
  751 Diamond St., San Francisco, CA 94114   (415) 285-7979

  Mainly a juice bar, but they're now serving vegan lunches as well. No sugar or white flour used; caters to wheat-free, eggless, dairyless and oilless diets, but rich, decadent desserts available as well. Macrobiotic baked goods include tofu cheesecakes with fruit glazes, banana poppy cake and "true-blue" muffins. Frozen yogurt, smoothies, espresso, amazake and chai available. V,M,$

  Vegi Food
  1820 Clement St., San Francisco, CA 94121   (415) 387-8111

  Natural foods. Very popular with area vegetarians—and very affordable. Most popular dish is walnuts in sweet-and-sour sauce. Open daily. See Berkeley listing for more info.

SAN GABRIEL

- **Diwana**
  1381 E. Las Tunas Dr.
  San Gabriel, CA 91776   (818) 287-8743

  Traditional Indian cuisine. Max Jacobson of the *Los Angeles Times* describes Diwana's fare as "gentle cuisine of West India." Jackie Knowles, *Star News*, developed an "infatuation with Indian cuisine" after eating here. The Gujarati and Punjabi dinners are the house specialties. Buffet lunches. Carryouts are available. Closed Tuesday. FS,CAF,I, N,CC,CH,$$

SAN JOSE

Hobee's
920 Town and Country Village, Stevens Creek Blvd.
San Jose, CA 95128   (408) 244-5212

See Palo Alto listing.

SAN LEANDRO

Health Unlimited
182 Pelton Center Way
San Leandro, CA 94577   (415) 483-3630

Juice bar. Soups, sandwiches and smoothies. V,J,CC,$

KEY TO DINING GUIDE
• Vegetarian food only

FS Full service	**V** Vegan options	**CC** Major credit cards accepted
CAF Cafeteria/buffet	**M** Macrobiotic options	**CH** Children welcome
SB Salad bar	**A** Alcoholic drinks	**$** Average dinner under $5
I Informal	**N** Nonalcoholic beer/wine	**$$** Average dinner $5 to $10
F Formal	**J** Freshly squeezed juices	**$$$** Average dinner over $10

CALIFORNIA

SAN LUIS OBISPO

Hobee's
Royal Oak Motor Lodge, 212 Madonna Rd.
San Luis Obispo, CA 93403 (805) 549-9186
See Palo Alto listing. Open daily. FS,SB,I,V,N,CC,CH,$$

SAN MARCOS

Rocco's Pizza
1531 W. Mission Blvd.
San Marcos, CA 92069 (619) 744-8012
Italian. Vegetarian pizza. FS,V,N,$$

SAN RAFAEL

• Milly's
1613 Fourth St., San Rafael, CA 94901 (415) 459-1601
Natural foods. Known as one of the best. Completely eggless, and the menu lets customers know which entrées can be prepared dairy-free, oil-free or salt-free. The Warm Cabbage Salad has been a favorite since Milly's opened. Lots of pasta dishes, tofu and tempeh specials, sea veggies and a variety of beverages. Closed on major holidays. FS,I,V,M,A,N,CC,CH,$$

Pasand Madras
802 B St., San Rafael, CA 94901 (415) 456-6099
Southern Indian cuisine. Indian music on weekends. Closed Monday and Friday afternoons. FS,F,V,N,CC,CH,$$

San Rafael Health Foods
1132 4th St., San Rafael, CA 94901 (415) 457-0132
Juice bar. Extensive offering of quality vegetarian selections, featuring low-calorie and low-fat specialties. Freshly made juices and smoothies.

SANTA ANA

Good Earth
South Coast Plaza Village, 3810 S. Plaza Dr.
Santa Ana, CA 92704 (714) 557-8433
See Berkeley listing.

SANTA BARBARA

The Main Squeeze
138 E. Canon Perdido
Santa Barbara, CA 93101 (805) 966-5365

CALIFORNIA

Open five years in the middle of historic downtown Santa Barbara, The Main Squeeze caters to vegetarians. Fresh juices, soups, salads, and sandwiches round out the complete menu which includes a daily pasta special and a nightly vegetarian special—like tempeh tacos and tamale pie—and two homemade vegetarian soups. Produce is organic whenever possible. It's deli style, and you order at the counter, but there is ample table space to enjoy your meal. Sugarless desserts! Personal checks accepted. Open seven days. Live music on weekends. I,V,A,N,J,CH,$-$$

Sojourner Coffeehouse
134 E. Canon Perdido
Santa Barbara, CA 93101   (805) 965-7922

Natural foods. More than 10 years of innovative cuisine. Mexican, American, Italian dishes, soups, salads, sandwiches, coffees, hot and cold beverages. Daily dessert specials. Everything is very affordable. Carryout available. FS,V,M,N,A,J,$$

SANTA CLARA

Good Earth
2705 The Alameda, Santa Clara, CA 95050   (408) 984-0960

See Berkeley listing. Natural foods. Yogurt shakes and bakery items are noteworthy. Closed major holidays. FS,I,V,A,J,CC,CH,$$$

Pasand Madras
3701 El Camino Real, Santa Clara, CA 95051   (418) 241-5150

Southern Indian cuisine. Live northern Indian classical music Friday and Saturday nights. Open daily. Other locations in Berkeley, San Francisco and San Rafael. FS,A,CC,CH,$$

SANTA CRUZ

The Bagelry
320A Cedar St.
Santa Cruz, CA 95060   (408) 429-8049 or 425-8550

Juice bar. Fresh bagels, homemade spreads (hummus, tofu chili verde, pesto). Soups, salads and herbal teas. Liberal approach to the menu—will substitute anything. V,J,$

KEY TO DINING GUIDE
• Vegetarian food only

FS Full service	**V** Vegan options	**CC** Major credit cards accepted
CAF Cafeteria/buffet	**M** Macrobiotic options	**CH** Children welcome
SB Salad bar	**A** Alcoholic drinks	**$** Average dinner under $5
I Informal	**N** Nonalcoholic beer/wine	**$$** Average dinner $5 to $10
F Formal	**J** Freshly squeezed juices	**$$$** Average dinner over $10

CALIFORNIA

The Bagelry
1636 Seabright, Santa Cruz, CA 95062   **(408) 425-8550**
See above entry.

• Dharma's
1700 Portola Dr., Santa Cruz, CA 95062   **(408) 462-1717**
Natural foods. Used to be called McDharma's, but McDonald's didn't think it was funny. A new concept for natural food restaurants: All the old fast-food standbys are wholesome and natural. A menu sampling includes Brahma Burgers, Dharma Dogs, and I'm Not Chicken. Served with all the (natural) trimmings. Also: subs, pastas, Mexican food and whole-food desserts. Take-outs available. FS,V,M,A,N,J,

• Flavors of India
503 Water St., Santa Cruz, CA 95060   **(408) 427-0294**
Indian. Formerly Gokula's Tiffin. Can accommodate those on ayurvedic diets. Closed Sunday. FS,V,CH,$

Hobee's
The Galleria de Santa Cruz, 740 Front St.
Santa Cruz, CA 95060   **(408) 458-1212**
See Palo Alto listing.

Saturn Cafe
1230 Mission St., Santa Cruz, CA 95060   **(408) 429-8505**
"Home of the Chocolate Madness."Features ice cream from McConnell's of Santa Barbara. Open from 11:30 a.m. Monday through Friday, and from noon on weekends. I,V,A,CH,$

Seychelles
313 Cedar St., Santa Cruz, CA 95060   **(408) 425-0450**
Here's a twist: Mediterranean natural foods. Has received kudos for its cooking. Everything homemade with a nouvelle touch. Fresh breads, soups and pastas. Eat indoors or out, depending on the weather. Open daily; brunch on Sunday. Carryout available. No credit cards, but you can pay with a check if you have a credit card and a California driver's license. Open daily. FS,V,A,CC,$$$

• Staff of Life Bakery
1305 Water St., Santa Cruz, CA 95062   **(408) 423-8068**
Juice bar. Entrées, soups and a vast array of salads. Closed major holidays. Local checks accepted. SB,I,CAF,V,J,CH,$

Whole Earth
University of California, Redwood Tower Bldg.
Santa Cruz, CA 95064   **(408) 426-8255**

CALIFORNIA

Natural food deli. Fresh soups, salads and sandwiches, and vegetarian entrées. Closed on weekends and at 4 p.m. weekdays during the summer. CAF,V,A,CH,$$

Zanzibar
2332 Mission St., Santa Cruz, CA 95060   **(408) 423-9999**

International. Tantalizing tastes and romantic atmosphere at modest prices. Vegetarian cuisine from around the world. Chef will accommodate your dietary requests. Almost anything can be made vegan. Try the Phoenix Nest, a vegetable-tofu-cashew stir-fry with sweet-and-sour-glazed sweet potatoes over rice. Tofu artichoke in a cheese and wine sauce is served over saffron rice and vegetables. Open daily. FS,I,V,A,CC,CH,$$

SANTA MONICA

Bistro of Santa Monica
2301 Santa Monica Blvd.
Santa Monica, CA 90404   **(213) 453-5442**

Northern Italian cuisine with a pleasant option: You pick your pasta, then you select from the 24 pasta sauces. Closed Monday. FS,SB,I,V,N, CC,CH,$-$$

Dhaba
2104 Main St., Santa Monica, CA 90405   **(213) 399-9452**

Early World
401 Santa Monica Blvd.
Santa Monica, CA 90401   **(213) 395-7391**

All-fresh, all-natural food. Hours vary, so call first. FS,A,J,$

• Get Juiced
1423 Fifth St., Santa Monica, CA 90401   **(213) 395-8177**

Juice bar. Fruit and vegetable juices and frozen fruit creams. Also delivers gift baskets of jellies, teas, honey, muffins, cookies, nuts, and flowers throughout Los Angeles County. CC

Michael's
1147 Third St., Santa Monica, CA 90403   **(213) 451-0843**

KEY TO DINING GUIDE
• Vegetarian food only

FS Full service	**V** Vegan options	**CC** Major credit cards accepted
CAF Cafeteria/buffet	**M** Macrobiotic options	**CH** Children welcome
SB Salad bar	**A** Alcoholic drinks	**$** Average dinner under $5
I Informal	**N** Nonalcoholic beer/wine	**$$** Average dinner $5 to $10
F Formal	**J** Freshly squeezed juices	**$$$** Average dinner over $10

CALIFORNIA

Gourmet. Contemporary American and French foods. Vegetarian platter, pastas, salads. Average cost of dinner per person is about $58. Open daily. FS,N,A,J,CC

Naturaid Natural Foods
The Mall, 1220 Third St.
Santa Monica, CA 90401　　　　　　　　(213) 395-9804

Natural foods. Take out or eat in. Different veggie dishes every day. Closed Sunday. I,N,CC,CH,$$

• Oasis
1439 Santa Monica Mall, #6
Santa Monica, CA 90401　　　　　　　　(213) 393-0940

Cafe-style service with 18 fresh salads daily, plus five or six entreés. Wheatless, dairyless and sugarless desserts available. High quality, high taste, good vibes. V,M,R,J,$

One Life Natural Foods
3001 Main St., Santa Monica, CA 90405　　(213) 392-4501

Deli. Carryouts only. Open daily. M,A,N,J,CC,$

Red Sea Cuisine of Ethiopia
1551 Ocean Ave., Santa Monica, CA 90401　(213) 394-5198

Vegetarian natural foods, Ethiopian style! A vast array of vegetable dishes, many steamed and spiced with garlic, ginger, or curry. One popular dish is the lentils in sauce. Also soups and salads. Open seven days. Carryout available. FS,F,V,N,CC,CH,$$

Shambala Cafe
607 Colorado Ave., Santa Monica, CA 90401　(213) 395-2160

No eggs here. Open daily, except major holidays, for breakfast, lunch and dinner. CAF,I,M,$$

Valentino
3115 Pico Blvd., Santa Monica, CA 90405　(213) 829-4313

Nouvelle cuisine. Eggplant parmesan, pasta, eggplant timbales. Closed Sunday. CC,CH,$-$$

SANTA ROSA

• Revelation Original Sandwiches
645 Fourth St., Santa Rosa, CA 95404　　(707) 526-2225

Juice bar. Homemade soups, salads and sandwiches. Breakfast served all morning. Nightly dinner specials. Closed Sunday. I,V,J,CH,$

Ristorante Siena
1229 N. Dutton Ave., Santa Rosa, CA 95401　(707) 578-4511

Italian. Homemade pastas—many vegetarian options. Salads from organically and locally grown veggies. Open for breakfast and lunch Monday through Friday. Open for dinner Wednesday through Sunday and for brunch on Sunday. FS,V,A,N,CC,CH,$$$

SHERMAN OAKS

Foods For Health
14543 Ventura Blvd.
Sherman Oaks, CA 91413   **(818) 784-4033**

Natural foods. Closed Sunday. FS,I,V,CC,CH,$

Genmai
4454 Van Nuys Blvd., #0
Sherman Oaks, CA 91403   **(818) 986-7060**

California-style Japanese food. Open daily. FS,F,V,M,A,N,CC,CH,$$$

SIERRA MADRE

Restaurant Lozano
44 N. Baldwin, Sierra Madre, CA 91024   **(818) 355-9900**

Veg-Mex! No lard, no solid shortening, no hidden meat in the sauces and no preservatives; other than that, it's typical Mexican fare. (You can even get soy cheese if you request it.) Closed major holidays. FS,A,N,CC,CH,$$-$$$

SIMI VALLEY

Good Earth
2585 Cochran St., Simi Valley, CA 93065   **(805) 584-0484**

See Berkeley listing.

Simi Valley Adventist Hospital
2975 N. Sycamore Dr.
Simi Valley, CA 93065   **(805) 527-2462**

Natural foods. Open every day of the year. Check out this hospital food: Florentine turnovers (made with spinach and cheese), cream cheese balls and Mexican specialties. CAF,$

KEY TO DINING GUIDE
• Vegetarian food only

FS Full service	**V** Vegan options	**CC** Major credit cards accepted
CAF Cafeteria/buffet	**M** Macrobiotic options	**CH** Children welcome
SB Salad bar	**A** Alcoholic drinks	**$** Average dinner under $5
I Informal	**N** Nonalcoholic beer/wine	**$$** Average dinner $5 to $10
F Formal	**J** Freshly squeezed juices	**$$$** Average dinner over $10

CALIFORNIA

SOQUEL

The Bagelry
4763 Soquel Dr., Soquel, CA 95073   (408) 462-9888
See Santa Cruz listing.

Tortilla Flats
4724 Soquel Dr., Soquel, CA 95073   (408) 476-1754
Mexican. FS,V,N,CC,$$

SOUTH LAKE TAHOE

• Grass Roots
2040 Dunlap, South Lake Tahoe, CA 95708   (916) 541-7788
Natural food store, cafe and bakery. Just off Hwy. 50: the only road in town! Hot and cold sandwiches, fresh soups daily, salads, smoothies, juices and shakes. Known far and wide for salad sandwiches, lentil burgers and seed bread. Specials: tofu enchiladas, tamale pie, garden quesadilla. The restaurant seats only 13 at a time, so be prepared to take out. Open daily. I,V,J,$

STUDIO CITY

• Vege Gourmet
11288 S. Ventura Blvd.
Studio City, CA 91604   (818) 761-7100
Vegan dishes only. Lasagna Vegiana, eggplant casserole, tempeh chop suey. Open daily, but no breakfast on Sunday. Personal checks accepted. FS,CAF,SB,I,V,CH,$

TAHOE CITY

Hobee's
Boatworks Mall, 760 N. Lake Blvd.
Tahoe City, CA 95730   (916) 581-1166
The newest Hobee's. See Palo Alto listing.

THOUSAND OAKS

• Dharma's
2705 Thousand Oaks Blvd.
Thousand Oaks, CA 91362   (805) 373-1543
Will cater your parties at the restaurant and provide musical entertainment. Also offers retreats and yoga classes. Personal checks accepted. FS,V,J,$$

CALIFORNIA

TOPANGA CANYON

Inn of the Seventh Ray
128 Old Topanga Canyon Rd.
Topanga Canyon, CA 90290   (213) 455-1311

Acorn squash stuffed with orange, curried stuffing, steamed artichokes filled with tofu and mushrooms...Delectable! Open daily. Champagne brunch on Sunday. FS,A,N,CC,$$$

TORRANCE

Good Earth
Del Amo Fashion Center
21444 Hawthorne Blvd.
Torrance, CA 90503   (213) 370-1883

See Berkeley entry.

TUSTIN

Souplantation
13681 Newport Ave., Tustin, CA 92680   (714) 730-5443

Juice bar. Soup and salad. Homemade muffins. Fresh fruit. Closed Thanksgiving and Christmas. Locations throughout the area. CAF,A,J,CH,$$

UKIAH

Arlene's Earthly Delights
538 E. Perkins, Ukiah, CA 95482   (707) 462-4970

In the Pear Tree Shopping Center. Gourmet sandwiches, frozen yogurt and homemade soups. Arlene was too busy to talk when we called; can we assume that means a lot of people are taking up her time enjoying her cooking? Closed Sunday. I,V,CC,$

VENICE

The Comeback Inn
1633 W. Washington Blvd.
Venice, CA 90291   (213) 396-7255

KEY TO DINING GUIDE
• Vegetarian food only

FS Full service	**V** Vegan options	**CC** Major credit cards accepted
CAF Cafeteria/buffet	**M** Macrobiotic options	**CH** Children welcome
SB Salad bar	**A** Alcoholic drinks	**$** Average dinner under $5
I Informal	**N** Nonalcoholic beer/wine	**$$** Average dinner $5 to $10
F Formal	**J** Freshly squeezed juices	**$$$** Average dinner over $10

CALIFORNIA

Gourmet international natural cuisine. Live food and live music. Popular since 1973. Almost totally organic. Caters to those on special diets, including those who avoid oil, flour, salt, sugar and artificial ingredients. Music nightly and Sunday afternoons. Art exhibits. Catering service. FS,V,A,J,CC,$$

Fig Tree Cafe
429 Ocean Front Walk, Venice, CA 90291   (213) 392-4937

Dine on the beach or indoors. Scrambled tofu, mixed vegetables, cottage fries and whole-wheat scones are specialties. Open daily. FS,I,A,CC,CH,$$$

• I Love Juicy
826 Hampton Drive, Venice, CA 90291   (213) 399-1318

Natural foods. See Hollywood listing for menu information.

VENTURA

Classic Carrot
1847 E. Main, Ventura, CA 93001   (805) 643-0406

Natural foods. Homemade vegetarian soups, cold soups in summer; whole-grain desserts, like carrot cake and cookies, some fruit-sweetened. Deli salads. Year-round patio dining. Take-outs and catering available. Look for trademark carrot windsock. Open for lunch and dinner Monday through Friday. Open for lunch Saturday. Closed Sunday. FS,I,V,M,A,CH,$$

Tipps Thai Cuisine
512 E. Main St., Ventura, CA 93001   (805) 643-3040

Traditional Thai menu and a special Thai vegetarian menu. Look for tofu mock duck. No MSG or animal fat in any dishes. Reservations recommended for large groups on weekends. Closed during lunchtime Saturday and closed Sunday. FS,A,CC,$$

WESTLAKE VILLAGE

India House Restaurant
860 Hampshire Rd., Suite U
Westlake Village, CA 91361   (805) 373-6266

Lunch Tuesday through Friday. Dinner Tuesday through Sunday. Closed Mondays. FS,I,V,A,CC,CH,$$$

Rosebrock's Health Pub
968-2 Westlake Blvd.
Westlake Village, CA 91361   (805) 494-6838

CALIFORNIA

Natural foods. The tofu burgers are renowned. Patio dining. Closed Sunday. I,CH,$$

WESTWOOD

- **I Love Juicy**
  10845 Lindbrook Dr., Westwood, CA 96137
  Brand new in July. See Hollywood listing.

WESTWOOD VILLAGE

Nature's Health Cove
1010 Broxton, Westwood Village, CA 96137   (213) 208-7333
Juice bar. Soups, sandwiches, desserts and salads. N,J,CC,$$

WILLITS

- **Harvest Bounty**
  39 S. Main St., Willits, CA 95490   **(707) 459-9647**
  Juice bar. Small restaurant in natural food store. Also a pottery studio. Known for its vegetarian pizza, but there also is tamale pie, enchilada casserole, chili, mushroom stroganoff. The cooks strive for vegan dishes and are very accommodating. Some take-out. Closed weekends. V,N,CH,$

Tsunami
50 S. Main St., Willits, CA 95490   **(707) 459-4750**
Japanese—with a hefty dose of California—cuisine. Almost all of the vegetarian dishes are dairy- and egg-free. Most of the grains and produce are organic. Three kinds of vegetarian sushi every day. Counter service, or dine indoors or on the patio. Local checks accepted. Closed Sunday. Children are very welcome. FS,I,V,A,N,J,CH,$$

WOODLAND HILLS

Good Earth
23397 Mulholland Dr.
Woodland Hills, CA 91364   **(818) 888-6300**
See Berkeley listing.

KEY TO DINING GUIDE
• Vegetarian food only

FS Full service	**V** Vegan options	**CC** Major credit cards accepted
CAF Cafeteria/buffet	**M** Macrobiotic options	**CH** Children welcome
SB Salad bar	**A** Alcoholic drinks	**$** Average dinner under $5
I Informal	**N** Nonalcoholic beer/wine	**$$** Average dinner $5 to $10
F Formal	**J** Freshly squeezed juices	**$$$** Average dinner over $10

YREKA

Yrekabakery Cafe & Bagels
322 W. Miner, Yreka, CA 96097   **(916) 842-7440**

Not a vegetarian restaurant, but there are some vegetarian breakfast and lunch dishes, and all breakfasts are served with a fresh muffin or bagel, homefries and steamed veggies! There's also a homefries and steamed veggies special for breakfast that can be ordered with or without eggs and cheese. Scrambled tofu, omelets, pancakes, waffles, blintzes and french toast (made with banana nut bread) for breakfast; falafel, pita sandwiches, salads and fruit for lunch or dinner. Open for breakfast and lunch Tuesday through Sunday; open for dinner Wednesday through Saturday. Closed Mondays. V,J,$

YUBA CITY

Sunflower
726 Sutter St., Yuba City, CA 95991   **(916) 671-9511**

Juice bar. Closed weekends. FS,I,V,J,CH,$

COLORADO

ASPEN

Nature's Storehouse
620 E. Hyman, Aspen, CO 81611   **(303) 925-5132**

Eat cafeteria-style in this large, natural food cafe, on the Aspen scene for 13 years. From soup to eggroll, salad bar to desserts, this cafe probably has what you're looking for. Many macro and vegan items available. Special vegetarian entrées on most days (except Thursday) and veggie-based soup every day. Desserts are sweetened with barley malt or maple syrup, and many are wheat-free. After dinner, see what you can find to take home from the attached retail store. (Full line of natural vitamins and supplements.) Open for breakfast and lunch until 5 p.m. Closed Sunday. CAF,V,M,J,N,CC,$-$$

BOULDER

Beau Jo's
1165 13th St., Boulder, CO 80302   **(303) 449-3090**

Natural foods. Also a Denver location. FS,J,A,$$

The Harvest
1738 Pearl St., Boulder, CO 80302   **(303) 449-6223**

Natural foods. Open daily. FS,I,V,A,N,CC,CH,$$

COLORADO

- **New Age Foods**
  1122 Pearl St., Boulder, CO 80302   (303) 443-0755
  Readers report wonderful vegan entrées and salads are served here. Soups and sandwiches, too. Lunch only. Closed weekends. V,$

  Rudi's
  4720 Table Mesa Dr., Boulder, CO 80303   (303) 494-5858
  International. Several vegetarian ethnic "peasant" dishes that the menu says are "warm and heartful without too much 'la-de-da.'" Reservations recommended on weekends. FS,V,M,A,N,J,CC,$$$

COLORADO SPRINGS

The Olive Branch
333 N. Tejon St.
Colorado Springs, CO 80903   (719) 475-1199
Natural foods. The local press says it and the Olive Branch North (see below) have the best veg food in town. Homemade food, croissant sandwiches, quiches, vegetarian lasagna. Many "heart-healthy" recipes from the American Heart Association. Breakfast and lunch only. Open daily. FS,I,V,J,CC,CH,$$

The Olive Branch North
2140 Vickers Dr.
Colorado Springs, CO 80918   (719) 593-9522
See entry above. Open for dinner also.

Poor Richard's
324½ N. Tejon St.
Colorado Springs, CO 80903   (719) 632-7721
Natural foods. Homemade baked goods, vegetarian soups and entrées daily. Combination restaurant/bookstore/cinema/art gallery/espresso bar. Live music on Friday and Saturday nights. Counter service. Open daily. I,V,A,CC,CH,$$

DENVER

Beau Jo's
2700 S. Colorado, Denver, CO 80222   (303) 758-1519
Natural foods. Open daily. FS,SB,I,A,CC,CH,$$

KEY TO DINING GUIDE
• Vegetarian food only

FS Full service	**V** Vegan options	**CC** Major credit cards accepted
CAF Cafeteria/buffet	**M** Macrobiotic options	**CH** Children welcome
SB Salad bar	**A** Alcoholic drinks	**$** Average dinner under $5
I Informal	**N** Nonalcoholic beer/wine	**$$** Average dinner $5 to $10
F Formal	**J** Freshly squeezed juices	**$$$** Average dinner over $10

COLORADO

> **In the Denver area . . .**
>
> For the traveler who is not familiar with the Denver area, we suggest looking under the following listings for additional dining choices.
>
> Boulder (40 minutes)   Idaho Springs (40 minutes)
> Englewood   Littleton
> Evergreen (30 minutes)   Wheat Ridge
> Greenwood Village

Bombay Palace
910 S. Monaco, Denver, CO 80224   (303) 377-3332
Indian. Clay oven and barbecue cooking. Open daily. FS,CAF,V,A,N, CC,CH,$$

- **Genesis**
1119 S. Washington St., Denver, CO 80203   (303) 778-7822
Natural foods. FS,V,M,J,N,CC,$

Goldie's Delicatessen
511 16th St. Mall, Denver, CO 80202   (303) 623-6007
Deli-style decor with salads and a couple of vegetarian sandwiches. Closed Sunday. CH,$

Goodfriends
3100 E. Colfax Ave., Denver, CO 80206   (303) 399-1751
Natural foods. Half the menu items are vegetarian. Reservations recommended. Open daily. FS,V,M,A,N,J,CC,$$

Govinda's
1400 Cherry St., Denver, CO 80206   (303) 333-5462
Located in the Hare Krishna Temple (entrance is on 14th Street). Primarily Indian cuisine, but they also serve lasagna, quiche and enchiladas. No eggs in anything. Discounts for persons under six and over 65. Catering available, including desserts. "We do weddings!" Closed Sunday. CAF,V,CC,CH,$$

The Harvest Restaurant & Bakery
430 S. Colorado Blvd., Denver, CO 80222   (303) 399-6652
Natural foods. Open daily. FS,I,J,CC,CH,$$

COLORADO

Jerusalem Restaurant
1890 E. Evans, Denver, CO 80210 **(303) 777-8828**

Middle Eastern. No eggs or dairy products used. Stuffed grape leaves a specialty. Open daily. FS,V,CH,$$

The Macrobiotic Center
1512 Monaco Pkwy., Denver, CO 80220 **(303) 399-9511**

Natural foods. Meals at 7 p.m. Friday by reservation only, followed by discussion. Complete meals $12; children's meals half-price. Also will deliver lunches for $7. Personal checks accepted. M,$$

• Porter Memorial Hospital
2525 S. Downing, Denver, CO 80210 **(303) 778-5881**

Natural foods. Can this be a hospital? Vegan and ovo-lacto vegetarian meals in the beautiful dining room. Open daily. SB,I,CAF,V,CH,$

Rick's
80 S. Madison St., Denver, CO 80209 **(303) 399-4448**

Mexican, Italian. Special house salad and unique vegetarian entrées. Open daily for lunch and dinner; Sunday for dinner. FS,I,A,N,CC,CH,$

Samurai Nippon
2276 S. Colorado Blvd., Denver, CO 80222 **(303) 758-9981**

Natural foods. Closed Sunday. FS,V,N,CC,CH,$$

Uncle Zalmon's
1470 Sheridan Blvd., Denver, CO 80214 **(303) 893-2245**

Kosher. Well, yeah, okay, there is a sign on the front door that says, "Fresh Meat," but the meat is packaged and sold in the adjacent store; in the restaurant, only four of the nearly 60 items on the menu contain fish. Those items that sound like they contain meat actually contain meat analogs. There are sandwiches, milk shakes, knishes, soup, falafel, spaghetti, eight kinds of omelets and a salad bar. Open daily. SB,I,V

• Walnut Cafe
338 E. Colfax, Denver, CO 80203 **(303) 832-5108**

Natural foods. Breakfast and lunch. Quiche, waffles and omelets. FS,J,$

KEY TO DINING GUIDE
• Vegetarian food only

FS Full service	**V** Vegan options	**CC** Major credit cards accepted
CAF Cafeteria/buffet	**M** Macrobiotic options	**CH** Children welcome
SB Salad bar	**A** Alcoholic drinks	**$** Average dinner under $5
I Informal	**N** Nonalcoholic beer/wine	**$$** Average dinner $5 to $10
F Formal	**J** Freshly squeezed juices	**$$$** Average dinner over $10

COLORADO

Wolfe's Barbeque
333 E. Colfax Ave., Denver, CO 80203   (303) 831-1500

Vegetarian barbecue! Plus curry salad. Always one or two vegan dinner entrées. Self-service. Open Sunday through Friday for lunch and dinner. I,V,CC,CH,$

ENGLEWOOD

Twin Dragon Chinese Restaurant
3021 S. Broadway, Englewood, CO 80110   (303) 781-8068

About a dozen veggie entrées. Open daily. FS,I,A,CC,CH,$$

EVERGREEN

River Sage
Bear Creek Mall, Hwy. 74
Evergreen, CO 80439   (303) 674-2914

Natural foods. Streamside deck for outdoor dining. Indian, Mexican, Italian specialties. FS,V,M,J,N,CC,$$

FORT COLLINS

Columbine Market
1611 S. College Ave., Fort Collins, CO 80525   (303) 482-3200

Northern Colorado's largest natural food store. Deli features variety of veg salads and entrées. Open daily. $

GLENWOOD SPRINGS

Garden Cafe
1001 Grand Ave.
Glenwood Springs, CO 81628   (303) 945-0105

(Formerly Gypsy J's Cooking Naturally.) International, mostly vegetarian dishes. Specials vary. Breads are wheatless and eggless; some desserts are dairy-free. Miso soup is homemade. Eat in or out. No smoking in the restaurant. Open daily for lunch and dinner. CAF,V,M,A,N,CC,CH,$

GREENWOOD VILLAGE

The Harvest
7730 E. Belleview
Greenwood Village, CO 80111   (303) 779-4111

Natural food restaurant and bakery. Open daily. FS,V,A,J,CC,CH,$$

IDAHO SPRINGS

Beau Jo's
1517 Miner St., Idaho Springs, CO 80452 (303) 567-4376

Natural foods. Also a Denver location. FS,A,J,$$

LITTLETON

Gemini
5056 S. Wadsworth, Littleton, CO 80123 (303) 972-0210

Natural foods. Feast on vegetarian foods here, but bring along your less-daring friends, who'll find plenty of nonveg food, too. Big breakfast menu, salads, sandwiches (including The Happy Vegeburger), entrées and sweet treats. Healthful children's menu, too. Open daily. FS,I,V,M,A,N,J,CC,CH,$

WHEAT RIDGE

Gemini
Belleview-Loehmanns Plaza, 4300 Wadsworth
Wheat Ridge, CO 80033 (303) 421-4990

Natural foods. See Littleton listing.

CONNECTICUT

BRIDGEPORT

• Bloodroot
85 Ferris St., Bridgeport, CT 06605 (203) 576-9168

Natural foods. Featured in *VT* as one of the best pure vegetarian restaurants in the country. Dine in a relaxed atmosphere overlooking Long Island Sound; opt for the terrace in nice weather. Woman-owned and -managed. You can take the good taste home with Bloodroot's cookbook, *The Political Palate*. Closed Monday and Wednesday. Personal checks accepted. FS,I,V,A,N,CH,$$

KEY TO DINING GUIDE
• Vegetarian food only

FS Full service	**V** Vegan options	**CC** Major credit cards accepted
CAF Cafeteria/buffet	**M** Macrobiotic options	**CH** Children welcome
SB Salad bar	**A** Alcoholic drinks	**$** Average dinner under $5
I Informal	**N** Nonalcoholic beer/wine	**$$** Average dinner $5 to $10
F Formal	**J** Freshly squeezed juices	**$$$** Average dinner over $10

CONNECTICUT

DANBURY

Sesame Seed
68 W. Wooster St., Danbury, CT 06810   **(203) 743-9850**

Natural foods. Closed Sunday. No lunch served on Saturday. FS,N,$$

GREENWICH

• Love and Serve
35 Amogerone Expressway
Greenwich, CT 06830   **(203) 661-8893**

Natural foods. Lunch and dinner. Closed Sunday. I,V,M,CH,$$

MIDDLETOWN

• It's Only Natural
686 Main St., Middletown, CT 06457   **(203) 346-1786**

Ken Bergeron, the chef-owner, is a world-class chef who has won the silver medal at the International Culinary Competition in Frankfurt, West Germany. He's also a macrobiotic, and the menu reflects his lifestyle as well as his abilities. No eggs here, and the only dairy product we could find is the mozzarella cheese on the pizza (soy cheese can be substituted). There are the usual veggie appetizers, sandwiches, noodles and curry. Entrées include a Middle Eastern salad platter, noodles with peanut sauce and a macro platter. No meals served on Monday, but the deli's open. Brunch on Sunday, but times vary with the seasons, so call first. FS,I,V,M,N,CH,$$

La Boca
526 Main St., Middletown, CT 06457   **(203) 346-4492**

Mexican. Vegetarian platter. Open daily. FS,V,A,N,CC,CH,$$

MILFORD

El Torero
1698 Boston Post Rd., Milford, CT 06460   **(203) 878-7734**

Mexican. Primarily a Tex-Mex menu with many vegetarian options. Open daily. FS,I,N,CC,CH,$$

NEW HAVEN

Claire's Cornercopia
1000 Chapel St., New Haven, CT 06511   **(203) 562-3888**

Natural foods. Located next to the campus of Yale University. Claire's, open since 1975, is the largest veg restaurant in town. Lots of vegan dishes. Hearty soups. Check out the desserts: Claire says they're deadly (in a positive sort of way). Totally smoke-free. Handicapped access. CAF,V,M,J,N,$$

India Palace
65 Howe St., New Haven, CT 06511   **(203) 776-9010**

Indian. Many vegetarian entrées, appetizers, soups, breads and desserts. Veggie specials include homemade cottage cheese with spinach or peas, sautéed lentils, sautéed veggies, garbanzo beans with ginger and garlic, and minced vegetable balls with gravy. FS,CAF,N,CC,CH,$-$$

Mamoun's Falafel
85 Howe St., New Haven, CT 06511   **(203) 562-8444**

Middle Eastern. Open daily. FS,V,N,CH,$$

Viva Zapata
161 Park St., New Haven, CT 06511   **(203) 562-2499**

Mexican. FS,A,N,CC,$$$

WESTPORT

A Change of Seasons
256 Post Rd. E., Westport, CT 06880   **(203) 454-0737**

Natural foods. All meals can be prepared according to your individual diet. The restaurant's menu and decor change with the seasons. Want alcohol? BYOB. Lunches Monday through Saturday. Dinner and take-out buffet Wednesday through Sunday. Tuesday night macrobiotic dining club. Sunday brunch. Closed Monday evening. FS,SB,CAF,I,V,M,N,J, CC,CH,$$$

The Organic Market
285 Post Rd. E., Westport, CT 06880   **(203) 227-7728**

Natural foods deli. Self-service lunch counter. Sandwiches, muffins, cake and freshly squeezed juices. Organic produce. Open daily. I,CH,$

KEY TO DINING GUIDE
• Vegetarian food only

FS Full service	**V** Vegan options	**CC** Major credit cards accepted
CAF Cafeteria/buffet	**M** Macrobiotic options	**CH** Children welcome
SB Salad bar	**A** Alcoholic drinks	**$** Average dinner under $5
I Informal	**N** Nonalcoholic beer/wine	**$$** Average dinner $5 to $10
F Formal	**J** Freshly squeezed juices	**$$$** Average dinner over $10

DELAWARE

DOVER

El Sombrero
655 N. DuPont Hwy., Dover, DE 19901   (302) 678-9445

Mexican decor and Mexican food. All-you-can-eat lunch buffet for $3.95; dinner buffet, $6.95. Open daily. FS,A,N,CC,CH,$$

REHOBOTH BEACH

La Mexicana
112 Rehoboth Ave.
Rehoboth Beach, DE 19971   (302) 227-4140

A reader sent in the name of this one; she said it's one of her favorites in the area. (And it's a special pleasure to report because the pickings in Delaware are scarce.) Sister restaurant to El Sombrero in Dover. Open April through September only, seven days weekly. FS,V,A,N,J,CC,$$

WILMINGTON

• The Vegetarian
9 E. Eighth St., Wilmington, DE 19801   (302) 655-5523

Natural foods. Fourteen years in Wilmington, and the only all-veg restaurant in Delaware that we know of. This is primarily a lunch place, but on the first Friday of every month, dinner is served, too, accompanied by art exhibits and live music (reservations required). Everything homemade. Will accommodate vegans and macrobiotics. Closed on Saturday during the summer. SB,I,V,M,J,CH,$$-$$$

DISTRICT OF COLUMBIA

Adams Morgan Spaghetti Garden
2317 18th St. N.W., Washington DC 20009   (202) 265-6665

Real Italian food, served in the restaurant or on the rooftop outdoor cafe, open year-round, weather permitting. "A casual, family-type place, with family prices." Manicotti, fettucini Alfredo, spaghetti with mushrooms, linguini with veggies, etc. Open daily. FS,I,V,A,J,CC,CH,$$

Bombay Palace
1835 K St. N.W., Washington, DC 20006   (202) 293-3073

Indian. Locations throughout D.C. Open daily. FS,I,A,N,CC,CH,$$$

DISTRICT OF COLUMBIA

Fasika's
2447 18th Street, NW
Washington, DC 20009   **(202) 797-7673**

Inexpensive elegance distinguishes this restaurant from other Ethiopian eateries in the Adams Morgan district. Little wicker tables just fit under the large circular tray that accommodates dinner for everyone at your table; mounds of spicy lentils, split peas and stewed vegetables. Delicious pancake bread replaces the silverware, so you can scoop up your dinner by hand and sample everything. The dinner menu is cheaper before 7 p.m. Gracious service, authentic decor and the large Ethiopian clientele makes you feel like you're in downtown Addis Ababa. Open daily from 5 p.m. to 1 a.m. FS,I,V,A,CC,CH,$$

Fish, Wings & Things
2418 18th St. N.W., Washington, DC 20009   (202) 234-0322

Caribbean food a specialty. Also try Italian stew, vegetable roti and the fruit salad with yogurt dressing. All sauces are meatless. Closed Sunday. FS,CAF,I,J,CH,$$

In the Washington, D.C., area . . .

For the traveler who is not familiar with the Washington, D.C., area, we suggest looking under the following listings for additional dining choices.

In Maryland:
Baltimore (45 minutes)
Bethesda
Catonsville (45 minutes)
College Park
Riverdale
Rockville
Silver Spring
Takoma Park
Wheaton

In Virginia:
Alexandria
Arlington
McLean
Vienna

KEY TO DINING GUIDE
• Vegetarian food only

FS Full service	**V** Vegan options	**CC** Major credit cards accepted
CAF Cafeteria/buffet	**M** Macrobiotic options	**CH** Children welcome
SB Salad bar	**A** Alcoholic drinks	**$** Average dinner under $5
I Informal	**N** Nonalcoholic beer/wine	**$$** Average dinner $5 to $10
F Formal	**J** Freshly squeezed juices	**$$$** Average dinner over $10

DISTRICT OF COLUMBIA

Food For Thought
1738 Connecticut Ave. N.W.
Washington DC 20009 (202) 797-1095
Natural foods. In the DuPont Circle area. Live entertainment nightly. FS,V,A,N,CC,$$

G.G. Flips
915 21st St. N.W., Washington, DC 20006 (202) 466-5567
Indian and American. Spinach quiche a specialty. FS,I,A,CC,CH,$$

Gairsan National
1368 H St. N.E., Washington, DC 20002 (202) 396-0034
Natural foods. Carryout and health food store. All organic produce. Closed Sunday. Personal checks accepted. J,N,$$

• Indian Delight
1100 Pennsylvania Ave.
Washington DC 20004 (202) 371-2295
Fast authentic Indian food. Counter service, and you can carry out. Their special sounds interesting: Cherry potatoes in a spicy sauce (dum aloo). You can also get masala dosa, a rather dramatic potato-and-rice pancake. No eggs in anything, and the only dairy product in the place is in the yogurt shake. Entertainment nightly (seven days). Only a block away from the Washington Monument. FS,V,J,CH,$$

Islander Caribbean Restaurant
1762 Columbia Rd. N.W.
Washington, DC 20009 (202) 234-4955
"The food is gusty, spicy, rustic and good," according to the *Washington Post*. Trinidad & Tobago cuisine, in a restaurant with island motif. Mostly vegetarian, with lots of vegan (no dairy or eggs in anything). Pigeon peas and rice with cabbage in the vegetarian platter, roti (oversized burrito filled with veggies), pumpkin soup, callaloo (okra casserole) and much more. No bottled drinks, but they make their own drinks on the premises, including ginger beer made from ground ginger root. Only vegetable oils. Everything's natural and macrobiotic and most of it is brought in from the Caribbean. Closed on Monday and on all major holidays. FS,I,V,M,J,CC,CH,$$

Kalmandu
1800 Connecticut Ave. N.W.
Washington, DC 20009 (202) 483-6470
Open daily. FS,A,CC,CH,$$$

56

DISTRICT OF COLUMBIA

Kalorama
2228 18th St. N.W., Washington DC 20009   (202) 667-1022

Italian. Specializes in pastas and pizza. Whole grains served with most entrées. Vegetarian specials include broccoli-tofu stir-fry and vegetables mornay. Desserts are freshly made, with honey only. Near the Washington Hilton. FS,V,M,N,$$

• Madras Restaurant
3506 Connecticut Ave. N.W.
Washington, DC 20008   (202) 966-2541

Indian/Eastern. Oriental squash curry with rice and pakura, masala dosa—pancake made from rice and mild potato filling—with lentil soup, samosa, pakora, and deep-fried, whole-wheat bread. Yogurt shakes, mango lassi. Carryout. Open daily. I,J,CH,$

• Madurai Vegetarian Room
3318 M St. N.W. (Upstairs)
Washington, DC 20002   (202) 333-0997

Indian. Nine-Vegetable Curry and Lotus Root Curry are the specials. Mango lassi, yogurt shakes. No eggs in anything. Open daily. Sunday brunch. FS,I,V,A,J,CC,CH,$$

Meskerem Ethiopian
2434 18th St. N.W., Washington, DC 20009   (202) 462-4100

FS,V,A,CC,$$

• Paru's
2010 S St. N.W., Washington, DC 20009   (202) 483-5133

Indian. Pure vegetarian. $$

• Patrick's Good Food
1825 Columbia Rd. N.W.
Washington, DC 20009   (202) 462-5150

Patrick's is a vegetarian grocery store with a whole lot more: made-to-order fresh carrot juice combinations, sandwiches, soups (in winter) and salads. No eggs in anything. Bottled imported and domestic water. Store carries vitamins, macrobiotic supplies, organic grains and produce, etc. It's handicapped-accessible, and take-out orders are possible for everything. Closed Sunday. V,M,N,J,CC,$$

KEY TO DINING GUIDE
• Vegetarian food only

FS Full service	**V** Vegan options	**CC** Major credit cards accepted
CAF Cafeteria/buffet	**M** Macrobiotic options	**CH** Children welcome
SB Salad bar	**A** Alcoholic drinks	$ Average dinner under $5
I Informal	**N** Nonalcoholic beer/wine	$$ Average dinner $5 to $10
F Formal	**J** Freshly squeezed juices	$$$ Average dinner over $10

DISTRICT OF COLUMBIA

Red Sea
2463 18th St. N.W., Washington DC 20009   (202) 483-5000

Ethiopian. A glossary on the menu helps to familiarize customers with the foods served. Reservations recommended. Consistently voted one of the best restaurants in D.C. by the local press. Open daily. FS,I,V,A,N,CC,CH,$$

Royal Frontier
1823 L St. N.W., Washington, DC 20036   (202) 785-0785

Buffet lunch daily featuring 20 dishes. Homemade cheeses and homemade breads are specialties. No eggs in anything. Live classical Indian music at lunch and dinnertime; dancing and a DJ after 10 p.m. Open daily. FS,CAF,V,A,CC,CH,$$

• Siddhartha
1379 K St. N.W., Washington, DC 20005   (202) 682-9090

Indian. Self-service. Carryout available. Open daily. CAF,I,V,CC,CH,$$

Taj Mahal
1327 Connecticut Ave. N.W.
Washington, DC 20036   (202) 659-1544

Indian. Family restaurant. Homemade cheese cooked in special sauces. Also veggie balls, potatoes and spring peas. Buffet for lunch; regular menu for dinner. Open daily. No lunches served on Saturday and Sunday. FS,CAF,I,V,A,N,CC,CH,$$$

Thai Room
5037 Connecticut Ave. N.W.
Washington, DC 20008   (202) 244-5933

Thai. Tofu dishes, broccoli with bean sauce, sweet-and-sour vegetables and the intriguing-sounding Vegetable Deluxe with Hot Chili. Open daily. FS,M,CC,CH,$$

FLORIDA

ALTAMONTE SPRINGS

Chamberlin's
1086 Montgomery Rd.
Altamonte Springs, FL 32714   (407) 774-8866

Juice bar. Counter service only. Vegetarian chili, sandwiches. Closed Sunday. SB,I,V,CC,CH,$

FLORIDA

Vine and Harvest
Altamonte Mall, 451 E. Altamonte Ave.
Altamonte Springs, FL 32701　　　　　　(407) 331-1946

Juice bar. Light, nutritious meals, salads, meatless chili and soups, veggie sandwiches, blended juice drinks and soft frozen yogurt. J,CC,$$

AVON PARK

Walker Memorial Hospital
U.S. Hwy. 27 S., Avon Park, FL 33825　　　(813) 453-7511

Natural foods. Large salad bar. Fresh yogurt. Open daily. SB,J,$

CASSELBERRY

• Chamberlin's Natural Foods
Lake Howell Sq., Hwy. 436
Casselberry, FL 32707　　　　　　　　　(407) 678-3100

Natural foods. FS,M,N,J,$

CLEARWATER

Bunny Hop Cafe
1408 Cleveland St., Clearwater, FL 33606　　(813) 443-6703

Natural foods. Located in Nature's Food Patch natural food store. A full line of services for customers: deli, market, lectures and classes on cooking, health and related issues. If you're in a hurry, order a sandwich or smoothie. Daily specials. Mostly macrobiotic. There is pizza and turkey and tuna sandwiches are on the menu. Catering available. Closed weekends. FS,SB,I,V,M,N,J,CC,CH,$

COCONUT GROVE

• The Last Carrot
3420 Main Hwy., Coconut Grove, FL 33133　(305) 445-0805

Juice bar. Open daily. V,J,$

• The Macrobiotic Foundation of Florida, Inc.
3291 Franklin Ave.
Coconut Grove, FL 33133　　　　　　　(305) 448-6625

KEY TO DINING GUIDE
• Vegetarian food only

FS Full service	**V** Vegan options	**CC** Major credit cards accepted
CAF Cafeteria/buffet	**M** Macrobiotic options	**CH** Children welcome
SB Salad bar	**A** Alcoholic drinks	**$** Average dinner under $5
I Informal	**N** Nonalcoholic beer/wine	**$$** Average dinner $5 to $10
F Formal	**J** Freshly squeezed juices	**$$$** Average dinner over $10

FLORIDA

Macrobiotic lunch every day at noon. Dinner is at 6, usually followed by a lecture. Sunday brunch at 11 a.m. Reservations are required. It's a bed-and-breakfast, too. M,CC,CH,$$$

Touch of Nature
2829 Bird Ave., Coconut Grove, FL 33133   (305) 448-0065

All fruits, vegetables and ingredients organically grown, and only filtered water is used in cooking. Everything is freshly made, and your dietary needs will be happily catered to upon request. Open daily, including holidays. FS,M,N,CC,CH,$$

FT. LAUDERDALE

• Bread of Life
2250 Wilton Dr., Ft. Lauderdale, FL 33305   (305) 563-TOFU

Gourmet vegetarian. Freshly prepared lunches and dinners in a classic, Art Deco atmosphere. Many macrobiotic specials, homemade breads and pastries. Live jazz on the weekends. Also a natural food market stocked with many macrobiotic items. FS,M,A,J,N,CC,$-$$

Carrot Patch
1032 E. Las Olas Blvd.
Ft. Lauderdale, FL 33301   (305) 761-8263

Juice bar. Open daily. Breakfast bar has fresh fruit, whole-grain cereals, bakery items and beverages. Sandwiches and salads for lunch. Smoothies and juices. Open daily. CAF,SB,I,V,M,N,J,CC,CH,$$

Natural Foods Market
2250 Wilton Dr., Ft. Lauderdale, FL 33305   (305) 566-2799

International macrobiotic. FS,M,A,J,$$

Rice Paddy's
922 N.E. 20th Ave.
Ft. Lauderdale, FL 33304   (305) 462-5284

Natural foods deli only one mile from the beach. A refreshing chef-owned and -operated oasis in the heart of south Florida. Mostly vegan. Whole-grain vegetarian entrées, including a variety of pies, casseroles and burgers. Soups are homemade. Smoothies and desserts available, too. Chef caters to those on restricted diets. Closed Sunday and major holidays. I,V,N,$$

GAINESVILLE

Ivey's Grill
3303 W. University Ave.
Gainesville, FL 32607   (904) 371-4839

Natural foods, American style. Open for all meals, except Sunday, only breakfast and lunch are served. Omelets, French toast, scrambled tofu for breakfast. Soups, salads and veg sandwiches for lunch. Veg Mexican and pasta dishes for dinner. Homemade desserts. FS,I,V,A,CC,CH,$$

HIGH SPRINGS

The Great Outdoors Cafe
65 N. Main St., High Springs, FL 32643   (904) 454-2900

Natural foods. Gourmet food with fresh, natural ingredients. Sandwiches, salads, homemade breads and desserts. Located in an old opera house on U.S. 27 in downtown High Springs; next door to the Great Outdoors Trading Co., which specializes in classic clothing, safari clothes, tents, canoes, outdoor gear, children's wear, packs and ski wear. Open daily. Just off Interstate 75 via U.S. 441 between Lake City and Gainesville. FS,I,V,A,CC,CH,$$

HOLLYWOOD

Harvest Village
1928 Harrison St., Hollywood, FL 33020   (305) 921-5149

Juice bar in a natural foods store. Veggie burgers, spinach pies, pita sandwiches, hummus. Eat in or take out. I,V,J,CH,$

LAUDERDALE-BY-THE-SEA

• Nature's Boys Health Foods
220 Commercial Blvd.
Lauderdale-by-the-Sea, FL 33308   (305) 776-4696

Natural foods. Closed Sunday. Nori rolls, brown rice, pita salad. FS,$$

MADEIRA BEACH

Kalb's Cove
13155 Gulf Blvd., Madeira Beach, FL 33708   (813) 393-3448

Natural foods. Many veggie entrées. Pasta a specialty. Open nightly. Piano bar Wednesday through Sunday nights. FS,V,A,CC,CH,$$$

KEY TO DINING GUIDE
• Vegetarian food only

FS Full service	**V** Vegan options	**CC** Major credit cards accepted
CAF Cafeteria/buffet	**M** Macrobiotic options	**CH** Children welcome
SB Salad bar	**A** Alcoholic drinks	**$** Average dinner under $5
I Informal	**N** Nonalcoholic beer/wine	**$$** Average dinner $5 to $10
F Formal	**J** Freshly squeezed juices	**$$$** Average dinner over $10

FLORIDA

MIAMI

- **Creative Kitchens Wholesome Foods**
650 N.W. 71st St., Miami, FL 33150   (305) 756-7638
Natural foods. No eggs, little dairy used. Lunch only. Catering available. FS,M,J,$

Granny Feelgoods
190 S.E. First Ave., Miami, FL 33131   (305) 358-6233
Natural foods. For breakfast, try the soy pancakes; for lunch, the veggie burgers and sandwiches with soup and salad. Many veggie dinner entrées, but pizza is the specialty. Locally baked bread made with organic grains. Juices, smoothies and high-protein shakes. Frozen yogurt and desserts to die for. No smoking. Closed Sunday. FS,V,M,N,J,CC,CH,$$

Granny Feelgoods at Metrofare
111 N.W. First St., Miami, FL 33128   (305) 579-2104
See entry above. FS,V,M,N,J,CC,$$

Namaskar
7921 S.W. 40th St., #48, Miami, FL 33155   (305) 262-2056
Closed Sunday. FS,N,CC,CH,$$

Nora's Natural Juice Bar
5750 Bird Rd., Miami, FL 33155   (305) 666-3360
Juice bar in Beehive Natural Foods. Soups, vegetarian pizza (with soy cheese), homemade seitan. Open daily. FS,V,J,CC,CH,$

In the Miami area . . .

For the traveler who is unfamiliar with the Miami area, we suggest checking the following listings for additional dining choices.

Coconut Grove	Miami Beach
Fort Lauderdale (45 min.)	Miami Springs
Hollywood	North Miami Beach

FLORIDA

MIAMI BEACH

Granny Feelgoods at the Spa
Fountainbleu Hilton, 4441 Collins Ave.
Miami Beach, FL 33139   (305) 538-7600 ext. 39

See Miami listing. Open daily. FS,I,N,J,CH,$$

• Natural Food Express
1717 Collins Ave., Miami Beach, FL 33139   (305) 672-FOOD

Will cook and deliver vegan meals with 24 hours' notice. Deliveries made on Monday, Wednesday and Friday. Soups, grains, veggies, desserts, cakes, cookies, bean and tofu dishes. Personal checks accepted. $$$

• Our Place
830 Washington Ave.
Miami Beach, FL 33139   (305) 674-1322

Natural foods. Vegan, but you'll find honey on the tables and in some of the desserts, and the soy cheese contains calcium caseinate. No eggs in the desserts. Live entertainment on weekends. Closed Sunday. FS,V,N,J,CH,$$

Roney's Health Emporium
2385 Collins Ave., Miami Beach, FL 33139   (305) 532-0015

Juice bar. Vegetarian pizzas. Open daily. CAF,I,V,M,N,J,CC,CH,$$

NORTH MIAMI BEACH

Artichoke's
3055 N.E. 163rd St. (Sunny Isles Blvd.)
North Miami Beach, FL 33160   (305) 945-7576

It's a smallish place, but quite comfortable and accommodating, even for fairly large groups. The separate vegetarian menu is full of variety; the spring roll appetizer is incredibly delicious (especially for vegans who miss egg rolls), and even the Tokyo Tofu appetizer—simple though it is—is inspired. Veg entrées include a light tempura and the best stir-fry vegetables and pasta around. Closed Monday. FS,V,M,A,N,J,CC,CH,$$

KEY TO DINING GUIDE
• Vegetarian food only

FS Full service	**V** Vegan options	**CC** Major credit cards accepted
CAF Cafeteria/buffet	**M** Macrobiotic options	**CH** Children welcome
SB Salad bar	**A** Alcoholic drinks	**$** Average dinner under $5
I Informal	**N** Nonalcoholic beer/wine	**$$** Average dinner $5 to $10
F Formal	**J** Freshly squeezed juices	**$$$** Average dinner over $10

FLORIDA

Unicorn Village
16454 N.E. 6th Ave.
N. Miami Beach, FL 33162 (305) 944-5595

Natural foods. Soothe your jangled nerves next to the indoor waterfall as you sample one of the many vegetarian lunch or dinner specials. Restaurant includes a whole-grain bakery, an abundantly stocked deli, an organic produce center and a bulk-foods section. Exit Interstate 95 at the 826 East exit. At Northeast 6th Avenue, turn right. Go one block to Northeast 164th St. Unicorn Village is located in a small shopping center. FS,V,M,N,J,CC,CH,$$

MIAMI SPRINGS

Garden Natural Food
17 Westward Dr., Miami Springs, FL 33166 (305) 887-9238

Natural foods. Veggie specials. Decorative green plants complement the friendly service. Closed Sunday. FS,F,V,N,J,CC,CH,$$

ORLANDO

• Florida Hospital
601 E. Rollins St., Orlando, FL 32803 (407) 897-1793

Natural foods. A taco bar and a potato bar and, for breakfast, an oatmeal bar. Homemade baked goods and pastries. Open daily. The hospital is about a half-hour drive from Disney World. The cafeteria seats 250, but an expanded, 700-seat food center should be completed by mid-1990. CAF,SB,J,CH,$

Garden Patch
25 E. Church St., Orlando, FL 32801 (407) 843-7606

A lunch place, featuring sandwiches, vegetarian chili, frozen yogurt and high-protein shakes. Closed Sunday. Personal checks accepted. CAF,V,CH,$

Green Earth
2336 W. Oak Ridge Rd., Orlando, FL 32809 (305) 859-8045

Natural foods. The closest vegetarian restaurant to Disney World. Near International Drive and Convention Center. Browse through the adjoining whole-foods market. FS,V,M,N,J,CC,$

Life & Health Foods
5125 W. Colonial Dr., Orlando, FL 32808 (305) 299-2123

Juice bar. Only one vegetarian sandwich, but there are smoothies, shakes and fresh juices. Closed Sunday. I,CC,CH,$

FLORIDA

PALM BEACH

- **Sunrise Natural Foods**
233 Royal Poinciana Way
Palm Beach, FL 33480   (305) 655-3557

Juice bar. Carryout lunch only. Homemade soups, salads. Only organic vegetables used. V,M,J,CC,$

PENSACOLA

Sunshine Gardens
2904 N. 12th Ave., Pensacola, FL 32503   (904) 432-8500

The whole-foods menu features three vegetarian entrees, a vegetable soup, several veggie sandwiches and salads. Organic foods used whenever possible. Even though there are some meat dishes on the menu, people come for the vegetarian Cashew-Vegetable Stir-fry. Children's menu available. Outdoor dining in the planning stages. Closed Sundays. FS,I,V,N,CC,CH,$

ST. PETERSBURG

Kopper Kitchen
5562 Central Ave., St. Petersburg, FL 33707   (813) 345-6339

Natural foods. FS,J,$

Nature's Finest Cafe
1208 S. Pasadena Ave.
St. Petersburg, FL 33707   (813) 347-5682

Natural foods. Ninety percent of the food here is vegetarian. Up to five veg specials every day, plus menu including grilled tempeh, tofu marinade, beans and rice, and stir-fries. Primarily a lunch place, but dinner is served on Friday. Closed Sunday. FS,I,V,N,J,CC,CH,$$

SARASOTA

Wildflower
5218 Ocean Blvd., Sarasota, FL 34242   (813) 349-1758

Natural foods. A small restaurant, open since 1974, serving plenty of

---

KEY TO DINING GUIDE
- Vegetarian food only

FS Full service	**V** Vegan options	**CC** Major credit cards accepted
CAF Cafeteria/buffet	**M** Macrobiotic options	**CH** Children welcome
SB Salad bar	**A** Alcoholic drinks	**$** Average dinner under $5
I Informal	**N** Nonalcoholic beer/wine	**$$** Average dinner $5 to $10
F Formal	**J** Freshly squeezed juices	**$$$** Average dinner over $10

FLORIDA

wholesome vegetarian meals. Fast service. Closed Thanksgiving and Christmas. FS,V,M,A,N,J,CH,$$

TALLAHASSEE

Nature's Way
1932 W. Tennessee St.
Tallahassee, FL 32304 (904) 224-4525

Wooden booths with tablecloths and walls hung with the art of local students set the scene for the only mostly veg restaurant in town. Daily specials include veggies with tofu and rice, lasagna, pizza, burritos and casseroles. Twelve varieties of salad. Open daily. On weekends only breakfast is served. FS,A,J,CC,$$

TAMPA

The N.K. Cafe
4100 W. Kennedy Blvd., Tampa, FL 33609 (813) 870-1385

Natural foods. Many hot dishes, salads, sandwiches, drinks. Full vegetarian kosher menu. Anything can be packed to go. Catering available. Closed weekends. FS,I,A,N,J,CC,CH,$$

WINTER PARK

• Chamberlin's Natural Foods
Winter Park Mall, Winter Park, FL 32789 (407) 647-6661

Natural foods. FS,M,N,J,$

Power House
111 E. Lyman Ave., Winter Park, FL 32789 (407) 645-3616

Juice bar. Natural foods to go. Smoothies, sandwiches, yogurt shakes (with fantastic names like Lavender Magic, Rose Crystal), salads, herbal teas. (Soups and chili on colder days.) A few Middle Eastern dishes, too. Calorie content of most dishes listed on menu. Closed on major holidays. I,V,N,J,CH,$$

GEORGIA

ATHENS

Bluebird Cafe
199 W. Washington St., Athens, GA 30601 (404) 549-3663

Natural foods. International cuisine. Open for lunch and dinner weekdays; breakfast and lunch on weekends. FS,V,M,CH,$-$$

GEORGIA

ATLANTA

Cook's Kitchen
1395 McLendon Ave., Atlanta, GA 30307 (404) 522-8646

A new natural foods venture that caters to people on restricted diets. Deli style. International vegetarian specials; sandwiches and soups. Except for one seafood dish, it's all vegetarian. Carryout available. Open weekdays only, but the shop will cater parties on the weekends. SB,I,V,M,J,CH,$

• Eat Your Vegetables
438 Moreland Ave. N.E.
Atlanta, GA 30307 (404) 523-2671

Natural foods. Several vegetarian lunch and dinner entrées, such as tofu manicotti, vegetarian fajitas and vegetable Wellington. A macrobiotic dinner special daily. About a third of the meatless dishes contain dairy products, but they'll make them without whenever possible. Children's portions, too. Open during the week for lunch and dinner; Saturday for dinner only. Brunch on Sunday. FS,V,M,A,CC,CH,$$

Excelsior Inn
695 North Avenue N.E.
Atlanta, GA 30308 (404) 577-6455

Mostly pizza. But just about anything you want in pizza, including artichoke hearts, tofu, broccoli, and, of course, mushrooms. Vegetarian sandwiches available. FS,I,A,J,CC,CH,$$

Lullwater Tavern
1545 N. Decatur Rd., Atlanta, GA 30307 (404) 377-6598

In addition to having a few good vegetarian dishes, Lullwater reportedly has one of the best, if not the best selections of alcohol in Atlanta. Veg lasagna, baked artichoke hearts, Decatur Salad, swiss/cheddar melt sandwich and spinach salad (make sure you ask them to omit the bacon). Baked apples, fried mozzarella sticks, and french fries and onion rings (fried in vegetable oil). Open daily. FS,I,A,J,CC,CH,$$

Mad Italian
2245 Peachtree Road, Atlanta, GA 30309 (404) 352-1368

KEY TO DINING GUIDE
• Vegetarian food only

FS Full service	**V** Vegan options	**CC** Major credit cards accepted
CAF Cafeteria/buffet	**M** Macrobiotic options	**CH** Children welcome
SB Salad bar	**A** Alcoholic drinks	**$** Average dinner under $5
I Informal	**N** Nonalcoholic beer/wine	**$$** Average dinner $5 to $10
F Formal	**J** Freshly squeezed juices	**$$$** Average dinner over $10

GEORGIA

Italian food. Spaghetti, sandwiches, salad, all available in vegetarian and vegan versions. Eat in or take out. Open daily. Other locations in Chamblee and Marietta. FS,I,V,A,CC,CH,$$

Mary Mac's Tea Room
224 Ponce De Leon Ave.
Atlanta, GA 30308 (404) 875-4337

Southern country food, specializing in fresh vegetables, including potatoes, green salad, stewed corn, beets, spinach, cabbage, squash and peas. Turnip greens, green beans, Sho' 'nuff Pie, cheese souffle, cottage cheese and 16 fresh vegetables daily. The breaded vegetables are dipped in egg. Peanut oil is used for cooking and frying. Breads have lard, though. Closed weekends. Local checks accepted. FS,I,A,CH,$$

Nuts 'n' Berries
4568 Peachtree Rd., Atlanta, GA 30319 (404) 237-6829

International. Lunch only. No meals served on Sunday, but the deli's open. Everything is low in salt. FS,I,M,J,CC,CH,$

Rainbow
2118 N. Decatur Rd., Atlanta, GA 30312 (404) 633-3538

A grocery *and* a restaurant. Mostly vegetarian, specializing in soups and sandwiches, but also one or two hot entrées daily. Everything freshly made. The deli has baked goods, salads and sandwiches. Sunday brunch. A reader tells us that Rainbow is consistently excellent. It's small, though. No smoking. Wheelchair-accessible. Fast food/carryout available. FS,SB,I,M,J,CH,$

Shipfeifer
1814 Peachtree Rd. N.W.
Atlanta, GA 30309 (404) 875-1106

Mainly Greek food, with scrumptious, freshly made vegan and vegetarian specials. Veggie platters, salads and pizzas are also offered. Try their "vegetarian delight" a spanakopita platter with true filo dough, spices, spinach and feta cheese. Other items include a mushroom wrap, Mediterranean platter, falafel, hummus and other Middle Eastern/Greek delicacies. Open daily. FS,I,V,A,N,CC,CH,$

• Soul Vegetarian
551 Ashby St. S.W., Atlanta, GA 30310 (404) 752-5194

A close relation to the Soul Vegetarian eateries in Chicago and Washington, D.C. We've sampled Chicago's entrées and found them delectable. Completely vegan menu features a battered tofu sandwich, a combination veggie basket with tofu, cauliflower and mushrooms, a lentil burger and several salads. Open daily. Carryout available. FS,V,N,J,CC,CH,$$

GEORGIA

- **Veggie Land**
  211 Pharr Road N.E., Atlanta, GA 30305   (404) 231-3111
  Fast, fresh and completely vegan. Daily specials. Lunch and dinner entrées include soups, sandwiches, veggie burgers, pasta, casseroles and stir-fries. Closed Sunday. FS,I,V,M,N,CH,$-$$

CHAMBLEE

Mad Italian
2197 Savoy Dr., Chamblee, GA 30341   (404) 451-8048
See Atlanta listing.

COLUMBUS

- **Country Life**
  1217 Eberhart Ave., Columbus, GA 31906   (404) 323-9194
  Natural foods. Buffet-style dining. Closed Friday and Saturday. CAF,SB,V,CC,CH,$

MARIETTA

Mad Italian
East Lake Center, 2143-C Roswell Rd.
Marietta, GA 30062   (404) 977-5209
See Atlanta listing.

Mad Italian
Windy Hill Plaza, Marietta, GA 30080   (404) 952-1806
See Atlanta listing.

KEY TO DINING GUIDE
• Vegetarian food only

FS Full service	**V** Vegan options	**CC** Major credit cards accepted
CAF Cafeteria/buffet	**M** Macrobiotic options	**CH** Children welcome
SB Salad bar	**A** Alcoholic drinks	**$** Average dinner under $5
I Informal	**N** Nonalcoholic beer/wine	**$$** Average dinner $5 to $10
F Formal	**J** Freshly squeezed juices	**$$$** Average dinner over $10

HAWAII

HANALEI

Hanalei Health and Natural Foods
Ching Young Village, Hanalei Highway
Hanalei, Kauai HI 96714   (808) 826-6990

A deli in a natural food store. Vegetarian options include fresh soups, juices, avocado and veggie sandwich, veggie burgers, hummus, couscous salad, carrot juice and veggie burritos. "A welcome sight," according to one *VT* reader.

Pizza Hanalei
Ching Young Village, Hanalei Highway
Hanalei, Kauai HI 96714   (808) 826-9494

Lots of vegetarian pizza options, plus a Veggie Special, with mushrooms, peppers, black olives, zucchini and tomato. Whole wheat crust available. Pizzaritos feature cheeses, vegetables and spices rolled into a shell and eaten like a burrito. A *VT* reader said the chef will make a special pizza without cheese for vegans. $$-$$$

HONOLULU

The Haven
841 Bishop St., Honolulu, HI 96813   (808) 531-1851

Juice bar. Soups, salads, sandwiches, smoothies. Closed weekends. CAF,$

The Haven
700 Bishop St., Honolulu, HI 96813   (808) 533-0047

Juice bar. See entry above.

India Bazaar Madras Curry
2320 S. King St., Honolulu, HI 96826   (808) 949-4840

Vegan dishes only. Southern Indian curry a specialty. Closed Monday. I,V,N,CC,CH,$

Keo's Thai Cuisine
625 Kapahulu Ave., Honolulu, HI 96815   (808) 732-2593

Gourmet Thai. Food served in tropical garden setting—casually elegant. Everything cooked to order, so all special requests can be honored, including meatless orders. Reservations recommended. FS,V,M,A,N,CC,CH,$$$

Kokua Co-op
2357 S. Beretania, Honolulu, HI 96826   (808) 941-1922

Carryout deli. Primarily a natural foods co-op, Kokua has a deli section with a wide variety of interesting and delicious salads, salad dressings and entrées prepared by premier vegetarian chef Alan Young, former owner of the Laulima Restaurant. Open seven days a week. I,V,N,CH,$

Mekong II
1726 S. King St., Honolulu, HI 96826   (808) 941-6184

Thai vegetarian dishes are the specialties of the house, but there are meat dishes served here. Reservations recommended. FS,I,V,A,CC,$$

• The Natural Deli
2525 S. King St., Honolulu, HI 96826   (808) 949-8188

Wide variety of homestyle vegetarian low- and no-cholesterol dishes, including risotto, chili, tofu cutlets, lasagna, enchiladas, curry, Better 'n Beef Stew, salad bar, fresh whole-wheat pastries and more. No sugar, white flour, meat, fish, eggs, rennet or MSG used. Homey atmosphere. Near University of Hawaii and Waikiki. Take-out available. Open daily. FS,CAF,SB,I,V,N,CH,$

Yen King
Kahala Mall, 4211 Waialae
Honolulu, HI 96816   (808) 732-5505

Northern Chinese. Are you ready to choose from among 30 vegetarian entrées? How about mock chicken and crab? Reservations recommended. Open every day. FS,I,A,CC,CH,$$

KAILUA

• Castle Medical Center
640 Ulukahiki St., Kailua, HI 96734   (808) 263-5281

Natural foods. CAF,J,$

The Good and Natural
124 Oneawa St., Kailua, HI 96734   (808) 261-0353

(formerly Kailua Health Foods). Juice bar in a natural food store. Veggie chili, soups, sandwiches and bakery items. The only meat in the place is in the chicken soup. Closed Sunday. V,J,CC,CH,$

KEY TO DINING GUIDE
• Vegetarian food only

FS Full service	**V** Vegan options	**CC** Major credit cards accepted
CAF Cafeteria/buffet	**M** Macrobiotic options	**CH** Children welcome
SB Salad bar	**A** Alcoholic drinks	**$** Average dinner under $5
I Informal	**N** Nonalcoholic beer/wine	**$$** Average dinner $5 to $10
F Formal	**J** Freshly squeezed juices	**$$$** Average dinner over $10

HAWAII

KIHEI

Polli's On the Beach
101 N. Kihei Rd., Kihei, HI 96753   **(808) 879-5275**

Mexican food. Come here for the view: Ocean-front dining offers spectacular sunsets and whale watching. Sunsets, salsas and Polli's famous margaritas. Entertainment nightly, except Monday. Dancing on Friday and Saturday nights. Closed Thanksgiving and Christmas. FS,I,A,CC,CH,$$$

KOLOA

Koloa Ice House
5482 Koloa Road, Koloa, Kauai HI 96756   **(808) 742-6063**

Vegetarian deli items: smoothies, burritos, chili, soups and sandwiches. "Very inexpensive and excellent," according to one *VT* reader.

MAKAWAO

Polli's Mexican Cantina
1202 Makawao Ave., Makawao, HI 96798   **(808) 572-7808**

Mexican food. Best margaritas in Hawaii, so they say. Entertainment Wednesday through Saturday nights. Champagne brunch on Sunday. Closed Thanksgiving and Christmas. FS,I,A,CC,CH,$$$

MAUI

Thai Chef
Lahaina Shopping Center, Lahaina, Maui HI 96761

Thai restaurant with a vegetarian menu: spring rolls, noodle and tofu dishes.

PAIA

Dillon's
89 Hanna Hwy., Paia, Maui, HI 96779   **(808) 579-9113**

The chef will accommodate vegetarians and vegans here. The pasta is popular. Open for three meals a day, seven days a week. FS,A,CC,CH,$$$

IDAHO

BOISE

The Metro Deli
921 Jefferson St., Boise ID 83702 (208) 343-6435

Veggie burgers, whole-grain muffins, veggie lasagna, stir-fry, salads and pastas. Open daily. CAF,I,A,CC,CH,$$

COEUR D'ALENE

Coeur d'Alene Natural Foods & Restaurant
301 Lakeside Avenue
Coeur d'Alene, ID 83814 (208) 664-3452

Open only for lunch, but a widely varied menu to choose from. Vegetarian casseroles and Mexican dishes are offered. Most of the other items can be made vegan upon request, but many vegan dishes are already on the menu. Nonalcoholic beer/wine available in the store. The restaurant is closed weekends, but the store is open Saturday. FS,V,M,N,J,CC,CH,$

KETCHUM

The Kneadery
260 Leadville Ave., Ketchum, ID 83340 (208) 726-9462

Fresh, home-style food. Fancy omelets, several hot vegetable sandwiches, vegetarian soups. Big outdoor deck in summer. Breakfast and lunch only. Open daily. FS,V,A,J,CC,CH,$$

SANDPOINT

• Truby's Health Mart
113 Main St., Sandpoint, ID 83864 (208) 263-6513

Juice bar in a natural food store. Many veggie sandwiches. Soups made from scratch. Natural ice cream and shakes. For $3, get chips, a half-sandwich, soup and the salad special. Many dairyless items. I,N,J,CH,$

KEY TO DINING GUIDE
• Vegetarian food only

FS Full service
CAF Cafeteria/buffet
SB Salad bar
I Informal
F Formal

V Vegan options
M Macrobiotic options
A Alcoholic drinks
N Nonalcoholic beer/wine
J Freshly squeezed juices

CC Major credit cards accepted
CH Children welcome
$ Average dinner under $5
$$ Average dinner $5 to $10
$$$ Average dinner over $10

ILLINOIS

ARLINGTON HEIGHTS

- **Chowpatti**
  1035 S. Arlington Heights Rd.
  Arlington Heights, IL 60005   (312) 640-9554

  International gourmet. An eight-page menu of international vegetarian favorites, as well as many unique specialties. Juice bar has more than 15 combinations, squeezed to order. Large selection of imported and domestic nonalcoholic beverages, mineral waters, coffees and teas. Macrobiotic and vegan meals available, and chef will make traditional veg dishes without eggs or dairy products at your request. Just 15 minutes from O'Hare International Airport. A jewel well worth seeking out. Closed Monday. FS,I,V,M,N,CH,$$

CHAMPAIGN

Strawberry Fields
202 E. Green St., Champaign, IL 61820   (217) 359-5394

Juice bar. Baked goods, pasta salads, veg sandwiches and pizza. Open daily. A,N,J,CH,$

CHICAGO

A Natural Harvest
7122 S. Jeffery, Chicago, IL 60649   (312) 363-3939

Deli. Located in A Natural Harvest Natural Food Store, this cozy deli seats 12. Specialtes are homemade salads and unique deli items, like veggie tamales and veggie burgers. Tuna is the only nonvegetarian item. Food stamps and checks accepted. Counter service. Closed Sunday. I,V,N,CC,$

Abacus
2619 N. Clark St., Chicago, IL 60614   (312) 477-5251

Chinese. Half-price before 6:30 p.m. Authentic Mandarin and Szechwan cooking. Will accommodate special diets. Reservations encouraged. Opens at 5 p.m. daily. FS,F,V,A,CC,$$

Annadata Fast Food
2545 W. Devon Ave., Chicago, IL 60659   (312) 943-1050

Indian. India Mango Shake, and joga drink are specialties, along with vegetarian dishes from all over the subcontinent. Vegetarian buffet from noon to 3 p.m. every day. FS,V,A,J,CC,$$

ILLINOIS

Annadata Fast Food
871 N. Rush St., Chicago, IL 60611   (312) 274-4175

See entry above.

Annadata Fast Food
917 W. Belmont, Chicago, IL 60657   (312) 929-1123

See Devon Avenue listing. The vegetarian buffet on Tuesday and Thursday nights is $5.95.

Bangkok Cafe I
416 N. State St., Chicago, IL 60610   (312) 744-1115

Natural foods. Favorites are the Bamboo Stew, spring rolls and natural soups. Open for lunch and dinner Monday through Friday, but closed weekends. FS,F,V,M,N,J,CC,CH,$$

Bangkok Cafe II
9 W. Hubbard St., Chicago, IL 60610   (312) 222-1179

See entry above. Open daily. A,CC

Blue Gargoyle
5655 S. University, Chicago, IL 60637   (312) 955-4108

Natural foods. On the University of Chicago campus. Profits support Blue Gargoyle Youth Service Center. Veggie sandwiches, omelets, daily ovo-lacto special. Closed weekends. CAF,SB,I,N,CH,$

In the Chicago area . . .

For the traveler who is not familiar with the Chicago area, we suggest looking under the following listings for additional restaurant choices.

Arlington Heights   Oak Park
Evanston   Palatine
Glen Ellyn   Westmont
Joliet (35 miles)   Wheaton
Oakbrook Terrace

KEY TO DINING GUIDE
• Vegetarian food only

FS Full service
CAF Cafeteria/buffet
SB Salad bar
I Informal
F Formal

V Vegan options
M Macrobiotic options
A Alcoholic drinks
N Nonalcoholic beer/wine
J Freshly squeezed juices

CC Major credit cards accepted
CH Children welcome
$ Average dinner under $5
$$ Average dinner $5 to $10
$$$ Average dinner over $10

ILLINOIS

- **Bread Shop**
3400 N. Halsted St., Chicago, IL 60641   (312) 528-8108

Deli. Fresh soups, casseroles, veggies, sandwiches and salads daily. Vegetarian bakery. V,M,N,$

The Charlie Club
112 S. Michigan Ave., Chicago, IL 60603   (312) 726-0510

Natural foods. Eat in the Skyline Cafe overlooking Lake Michigan. Pastas, stir-fries and salads. Everything is high in fiber and low in fat and cholesterol. FS,I,A,CH,$

- **Chicago Diner**
3411 N. Halsted, Chicago, IL 60657   (312) 935-6696

Strictly vegetarian; many vegan and macrobiotic meals. Sauces and desserts are dairy-free. No smoking. Carryouts and catering available. FS,I,V,M,A,N,J,CC,CH,$$

Gaylord's of India
678 N. Clark St., Chicago, IL 60605   (312) 664-1700

Northern Indian. Buffet $6.95. FS,A,J,CC,$$-$$$

Heartland
7000 N. Glenwood, Chicago, IL 60626   (312) 465-8005

Natural foods. Good wholesome food for the mind and body. Heartland comes complete with a radical political reputation and good cornbread. Outdoor cafe in warm weather; entertainment most weekend nights after 10 p.m. Reservations recommended for parties over six. Late-night menu, too. Check out the general store for food, cosmetics, native handicrafts, books, toys and vitamins. Closed major holidays. FS,I,M,A,N,J,CC,CH,$$

- **Life Spring**
3178 N. Clark St., Chicago, IL 60657   (312) 327-1023

Juice bar in a natural food store. Juices, shakes and sandwiches. Lightning Bolt Shake, avocado-and-cheese sandwich, tempeh and tofu burgers. Open daily. I,V,J,CC,$

Mama Desta's Red Sea Restaurant
3216 N. Clark, Chicago, IL 60657   (312) 935-7561

Ethiopian cuisine with lots of vegetarian options: beans, lentils, cabbage, and spinach dishes and soups. Have your dinner by candlelight here, and listen to African classical music. Groups larger than four require reservations. Open daily. FS,I,V,A,N,J,CC,CH,$$

Mitchell's
101 W. North Ave., Chicago, IL 60610   (312) 642-5246

ILLINOIS

Large vegetarian menu and daily veg specials. Nondairy pancakes, stir-fry platters, veggie chili, lasagna, vegetarian sausage. Open daily; open all night Friday and Saturday. FS,I,CH,$$

N.E.W. Cuisine
360 W. Erie, Chicago, IL 60610   **(312) 642-8885**

Nouvelle natural foods. The anagram stands for Natural Eating Ways. Elegant cuisine with all-natural, unrefined ingredients. Closed Sunday and Mondays. FS,I,V,M,A,N,CC,$$$

- ### Natraj India
2240 W. Devon Ave., Chicago, IL 60659   **(312) 274-1300**

(Formerly Satkar.) Indian.

- ### Soul Vegetarian East
205 E. 75th St., Chicago, IL 60619   **(312) 224-0104**

Natural foods. Owned by a group of Hebrew Israelites. Food is wonderful and completely vegan. Gluten Bar-B-Que Twist on whole-wheat bun, or roast with gravy, veggie gyros. And try the peanut butter ice "cream"; it's a prized and secret recipe. Friendly service. Reservations for parties larger than eight. Open daily, but breakfast is served only Tuesday through Saturday. FS,SB,CAF,I,V,J,N,CC,CH,$$

Star of Siam
11 E. Illinois, Chicago, IL 60611   **(312) 670-0100**

Natural foods. Coconut Meal Soup, veggie egg rolls, potai noodle dishes. Open daily. FS,V,A,N,J,CC,$$

- ### Vegetaria
3182 N. Clark St., Chicago, IL 60657   **(312) 549-0808**

International. If you haven't been here for a while, check out the new decor, new recipes, new menu, salad bar, freshly ground coffee, freshly squeezed juices, and delivery and take-out services. Breakfast is served now, too. Middle Eastern, Italian and Chinese dishes are the specialties. Everything is made from fresh ingredients, and all dishes are homemade and low in salt, fat, sugar and cholesterol. Many vegan selections, and almost anything on the menu can be made without dairy products. Children's menu. Open daily. Personal checks accepted. Conference/meeting space available. FS,SB,V,M,N,CC,CH,$

KEY TO DINING GUIDE
- Vegetarian food only

FS Full service	**V** Vegan options	**CC** Major credit cards accepted
CAF Cafeteria/buffet	**M** Macrobiotic options	**CH** Children welcome
SB Salad bar	**A** Alcoholic drinks	**$** Average dinner under $5
I Informal	**N** Nonalcoholic beer/wine	**$$** Average dinner $5 to $10
F Formal	**J** Freshly squeezed juices	**$$$** Average dinner over $10

ILLINOIS

EVANSTON

- **Blind Faith**
  525 Dempster St., Evanston, IL 60201   (312) 328-6875

  Natural foods. Fresh-baked breads daily, homemade soups, chili, quiche. Peanut butter shake. Live music Tuesday and Friday nights (no cover charge). Dining room open for lunch and dinner Monday through Friday; on weekends, dinner only. Self-serve, too, is open all day Monday through Friday. Local checks accepted. Play area for kids. FS,CAF,SB,I,V,M, N,CH,$$-$$$

The Cornerstone Cafe
800 Dempster St., Evanston, IL 60202   (312) 328-6161

A reader recently called Cornerstone the most creative vegetarian and macrobiotic restaurant she'd been to. Desserts, she says, are "unbelievable" and well marked for contents. Specialties include tempura, chili, pasta stir-fry, tofu fajitas and the macrobiotic plate. You can sit down or be served at the counter. Entertainment Tuesday through Friday. Open daily. FS,I,V,M,N,CC,CH,$$

Dave's Italian Kitchen
906 Church St., Evanston, IL 60201   (312) 864-6000

Italian. Just about anything Italian with your choice of sauces. Open for dinner seven days a week. FS,I,A,CH,$$

GLEN ELLYN

- **Country Life**
  503 Duane, Glen Ellyn, IL 60137   (312) 469-3368

  See entry below. This is a brand-new restaurant. And it's also exclusively vegan. Closed weekends. SB,I,V,CC,CH,$$

OAKBROOK TERRACE

- **Country Life**
  17 W 717 Roosevelt,
  Oakbrook Terrace, IL 60521   (312) 629-2454

  Natural foods the Country Life way—completely vegan. Nice buffet, salad bar and fruit bar. Carryout available. Try the noindairy lasagna and "cream" soups—they're worldwide favorites. Natural food store, too. Health programs Monday nights. Closed weekends. CAF,SB,I,V,M, N,J,CC,CH,$$

OAK PARK

Chip & Dale's
109 N. Oak Park Ave., Oak Park, IL 60301   (312) 524-0406

Juice bar in a natural food store. Daily soup and main dish specials. Vegan entrées and treats daily. Fresh popcorn and tofu ice cream or vitari. Everything available for carryout. SB,I,V,J,$

PALATINE

The Charlie Club
Rte. 47 and Dundee Rd., Palatine, IL 60067   (312) 934-4900

See Chicago listing.

WESTMONT

- **Shree**
655 N. Cass Ave., Westmont, IL 60559   (312) 655-1021

Southern and Northern Indian. No eggs. Lunch buffet Tuesday through Friday. Open for dinner on weekends. Personal checks accepted. Closed Monday. FS,CAF,F,CC,CH,$$

WHEATON

Wheaton Natural Foods
123 N. Main St., Wheaton, IL 60187   (312) 690-8200

Juice bar. Carryout soups and sandwiches. $

INDIANA

CROWN POINT

Twin Happiness
1188 N. Main St., Crown Point, IN 46307   (219) 663-4433

Chinese. Large selection of Chinese vegetables stir-fried to order. Open daily. FS,I,CC,CH,$$

KEY TO DINING GUIDE
• Vegetarian food only

FS Full service	**V** Vegan options	**CC** Major credit cards accepted
CAF Cafeteria/buffet	**M** Macrobiotic options	**CH** Children welcome
SB Salad bar	**A** Alcoholic drinks	**$** Average dinner under $5
I Informal	**N** Nonalcoholic beer/wine	**$$** Average dinner $5 to $10
F Formal	**J** Freshly squeezed juices	**$$$** Average dinner over $10

IOWA

SOUTH BEND

Cornucopia
303 S. Michigan St., South Bend, IN 46601   (219) 288-1911

Natural foods. Reservations recommended for six or more. FS,V,N,J,CC,$$

_____ IOWA

FAIRFIELD

• A Taste of India
410 W. Lowe St., Fairfield, IA 52556   (515) 472-6530

Indian and Mexican. All-you-can-eat buffet for $5.95! Fresh soups, salads and sandwiches. Sunday brunch features scrambled tofu, veg sausage, hash browns, spinach lasagna, pancakes, waffles, croissants, donuts, fruit salads and vegetable salads. Open daily. Located four blocks southwest of Maharishi International University. CAF,N,CH,$$

Bonnie's China Deli
51 N. Second St., Fairfield, IA 52556   (515) 472-7587

Four vegetarian restaurants in the middle of the Iowa cornfields? It's because Maharishi International University is in Fairfield. Bonnie's is mostly take-out and mostly Chinese, but there are Greek and Japanese specials, too. Fresh vegetable stir-fry is a favorite. You'll find tofu in the chop suey here, and the soups are vegetarian, made with spinach and tofu. Spanakopita (spinach pie) is always a treat. Closed Sunday. FS,I,V, M,CH,$$

Smiley's Cafe
403 N. Fourth, Fairfield, IA 52556   (515) 472-6303

These people obviously enjoy what they're doing: providing fresh, organic (when possible), mostly vegan dishes, taking no shortcuts in the process. "Everyone here meditates, so the vibes in the restaurant are wonderful," says owner Jane Ryals. Smiley's specializes in wheat-, dairy- and egg-free dishes: burgers, veggie barbecue platter, homemade tofu sausage, smoothies, vegetable fritters and homemade French bread for the French toast. Friday night is Italian night. The hotcakes are special, too. Turkey hot dogs and fried clams are the only two nonvegetarian items on the menu. Open daily for breakfast and lunch. FS,I,V,CH,$

Twenty-four Carrots
508 N. 2nd., Fairfield, IA 52556   (515) 472-7343

In the Tetra Building, serving good, fast food. Not quite a deli, but be prepared to eat off paper plates. (You can sit outside on the garden terrace in good weather.) Hot and cold sandwiches on homemade five-grain bread, full breakfast menu (veg sausage), made-to-order carrot juice and smoothies. Or try the homemade tofu burger, or the veg BLT (the owner called it "very convincing"). Dinners include stroganoff, lasagna, enchiladas. Open until 5 p.m. Monday through Saturday. Closed Sunday. CAF,J,N,$$

IOWA CITY

The Brown Bottle
115 E. Washington St., Iowa City, IA 52240   (319) 351-6704

Fine Italian dining with some vegetarian entrées: lasagna, eggplant casserole, pizza. Open daily. FS,A,N,CC,$$

Great Midwestern Ice Cream Co.
126 E. Washington St., Iowa City, IA 52240   (319) 337-7243

Best ice cream in America, according to *People* magazine. The Super Premium ice cream contains no eggs. Sherbet, sorbet and frozen yogurt, too. But there're more goodies: fresh pastries, sugarless croissants, veg soups and sandwiches, hummus and tofu. Natural red-brick walls and cherrywood tables create a warm and friendly environment. Coffee-shop-style service. Open daily. I,V,CH,$

The Kitchen
9 S. Dubuque, Iowa City, IA 52240   (319) 337-5444

Fresh is the main ingredient: fresh pasta, fresh cheese cakes, fresh Italian specials. Try the spaghetti with vegetarian sauce, or the pasta primavera, the pesto sauce, or the salads. Monday is international night; on Tuesday night, regular entrées are $3.99; Wednesday is international beer and wine night; and Thursday is Cajun night. Closed Sunday. FS,I,V,A,N,CH,$$

Magnifico's Mostly Italian
1925 Broadway, Iowa City, IA 52240   (319) 337-6618

Not a vegetarian restaurant, but there are four vegetarian pasta main dishes—manicotti, ravioli and spaghetti with two different vegetable sauces—an Italian sub sandwich, five veggie salads and several Italian desserts. The dinner special is $3.69 and includes a main dish, garlic bread and tossed salad. All-you-can-eat spaghetti with garlic bread is $3.29. The pasta—and the prices—got rave reviews from two *VT* readers. Open daily. Caters to families. Personal checks accepted. CAF,A,CH,$

KEY TO DINING GUIDE
- Vegetarian food only

FS Full service	**V** Vegan options	**CC** Major credit cards accepted
CAF Cafeteria/buffet	**M** Macrobiotic options	**CH** Children welcome
SB Salad bar	**A** Alcoholic drinks	**$** Average dinner under $5
I Informal	**N** Nonalcoholic beer/wine	**$$** Average dinner $5 to $10
F Formal	**J** Freshly squeezed juices	**$$$** Average dinner over $10

KANSAS

LAWRENCE

Cornucopia
1801 Massachusetts Ave.
Lawrence, KS 66044   (913) 842-9637

International. Salad bar, spinach lasagna, stir-fried veggies, quiche, crêpes and soups. Take-out available. Open daily. FS,SB,I,A,J,CC,CH,$$

Paradise Cafe
728 Massachusetts Ave.
Lawrence, KS 66044   (913) 842-5199

Paradise in Lawrence, especially if you go for Tex-Mex specials like beans and rice on tortillas or veggie quesadillas. But there is also freshly made pasta for dinner every night and whole-wheat pancakes for breakfast. Real down home. Casual. Three meals daily. FS,A,CC,$$

OVERLAND PARK

Mother India
9036 Metcalf Ave., Overland Park, KS 66212   (913) 341-0415

Indian and kosher. Homemade cheese, homemade yogurt and fresh dishes that are contingent upon what was good at the produce market that morning. Green peas and potato dishes a specialty. Vegetarian thali. Open daily and buffet for lunch every day. FS,V,CC,CH,$$

PRAIRIE VILLAGE

Manna Nutrition Store
5309 W. 94th Terrace
Prairie Village, KS 66207   (913) 381-6604

There are seats for 10, but you order at the counter. Lots of possibilities here: veggie burgers, stuffed tomatoes, garden vegetable falafels, pita pizza, vegetarian soups, and sandwiches on whole-grain bread. With the exception of a tuna sandwich, this place is all veg. Also a retail store. Closed Sunday. FS,I,V,J,CC,CH,$

SHAWNEE MISSION

Shawnee Mission Medical Center
9100 W. 74th St.
Shawnee Mission, KS 66204   (913) 676-2496

Natural foods. Open daily. CAF,J,CH,$

KENTUCKY / LOUISIANA

KENTUCKY

LEXINGTON

Alfalfa
557 S. Limestone, Lexington, KY 40508   **(606) 253-0014**

Natural foods with a gourmet down-home flavor. The menu changes every night, but you can always expect at least three vegetarian dishes. (Look for the tofu scramble.) Also crêpes Mornay, casseroles and pasta. Wednesday night is International Night; a different cuisine is featured every week. Saturday and Sunday brunch, but closed Sunday night. Music nightly. Located across the street from main entrance to University of Kentucky. U.S. 27 South eventually becomes Limestone. FS,I,V,A,J,CH,$$

Everybody's Natural Foods
503 Euclid Ave., Lexington, KY 40502   **(606) 255-4162**

Juice bar. Open daily. FS,I,V,M,N,J,CC,CH,$

LOUISIANA

METAIRIE

Nature Lovers
3014 Cleary Ave., Metairie, LA 70002   **(504) 887-4929**

Perhaps mindful of the competition from next-door New Orleans, Nature Lovers not only offers a variety of vegetarian dishes ranging from stuffed bell peppers to lasagna, but also designs macro specials according to your desires. Homemade veggie burgers are also available, and there is carryout, too. Closed Sunday. FS,J,CC,$

KEY TO DINING GUIDE
• Vegetarian food only

FS Full service	**V** Vegan options	**CC** Major credit cards accepted
CAF Cafeteria/buffet	**M** Macrobiotic options	**CH** Children welcome
SB Salad bar	**A** Alcoholic drinks	**$** Average dinner under $5
I Informal	**N** Nonalcoholic beer/wine	**$$** Average dinner $5 to $10
F Formal	**J** Freshly squeezed juices	**$$$** Average dinner over $10

LOUISIANA

NEW ORLEANS

The Apple Seed Shoppe
346 Camp St., New Orleans, LA 70130   (504) 529-3442

A juice bar open for lunch only. Sandwiches, salads, smoothies, homemade soups. Except for three dishes, it's all vegetarian. Closed Saturday and Sunday. J,$

Back to the Garden
207 Dauphine, New Orleans, LA 70130   (504) 524-6915

Natural foods version of McDonald's: stir-fry, mushroom strudel, spinach-rice casserole, vegan soups and chili, and salads. Counter service and take-out. If the woman we spoke with is any indication, staff should be friendly and helpful. Closed Sunday. FS,I,V,M,J,CH,$

Back to the Garden
YMCA-Lee Circle, New Orleans, LA 70117   (504) 522-8792

See entry above. Closed Sunday. FS,I,N,CH,$$

Eat No Evil
405 Baronne St., New Orleans, LA 70112   (504) 524-0906

Natural foods. Salads and sandwiches. Try the avocado-cheese-and-egg sandwich, or the avocado spinach salad with carrots. Vegan soups. Counter service. Closed weekends. I,V,J,CH,$

Garden Cafe
746 Tchoupitoulas St.
New Orleans, LA 70130   (504) 561-0568

(Formerly Back to the Garden.) Daily veg lunch specials include lasagna, black beans and rice or cheese enchiladas. Two vegetarian soups every day. New items include veggie burgers, french toast, bagels, baked ambrosia and a local specialty, muffaletta. Open for three meals Monday through Saturday; open Sunday from 10 a.m. to 3 p.m. FS,I,V,A,N,J,CH,$

SHREVEPORT

Earthereal Restaurant and Bakery
3309 Line Ave., Shreveport, LA 71104   (318) 865-8947

Natural foods. A mostly vegetarian (they have chicken salad and tuna salad) health food restaurant and bakery. Sandwiches, soups, salads. Lots of fresh bread, cookies, etc. Veggie special every day, macro special on Wednesday. Closed Sunday; not open evenings. V,M,J,CC,$

MAINE

BAR HARBOR

Sunflour Bakery & Tea Room
122 Cottage St., Bar Harbor, ME 04609   **(207) 288-3696**

Inexpensive, simple and wholesome are the bywords here. Two or three vegetarian soups, salads, sandwiches on homemade, whole-grain breads. Large selection of coffees and teas. Decadent desserts. Open for breakfast and lunch Tuesday through Saturday and brunch on Sunday. In the summer, open in the evenings for tea and dessert. Closed Monday. FS,I,V,$

BELFAST

Kingsbury House
35 Northport Ave., Belfast, ME 04915   **(207) 338-2419**

Bed-and-macrobiotic-breakfast, but they'll make dinner, too, if you call ahead. M,$$$

FREEPORT

The Corsican
9 Mechanic St., Freeport, ME 04032   **(207) 865-9421**

Italian. Pesto and tomato pizza, vegetarian lasagna, avocado sandwiches. FS,J,A,N,CC,CH,$-$$

HULLS COVE

Geronimo Cafe
Breakneck Hollow Road
Hulls Cove, ME 04644   **(207) 288-5126**

Here's the ticket to a relaxing meal: Light, whole-foods vegetarian and macrobiotic suppers with no sugar and little salt or cholesterol, served in a cozy cafe that's also a bookshop, while fine music lifts your spirits and comforts your soul. Please give 24 hours' notice for the macrobiotic meals. Bring your own firewater. Browse through the antique barn after supper. Open daily. Located on Mt. Desert Island off Route 3 on the road to Bar Harbor in Hulls Cove. Turn right past the Hulls Cove General Store. FS,I,M,N,$$

KEY TO DINING GUIDE
- Vegetarian food only

FS Full service	**V** Vegan options	**CC** Major credit cards accepted
CAF Cafeteria/buffet	**M** Macrobiotic options	**CH** Children welcome
SB Salad bar	**A** Alcoholic drinks	**$** Average dinner under $5
I Informal	**N** Nonalcoholic beer/wine	**$$** Average dinner $5 to $10
F Formal	**J** Freshly squeezed juices	**$$$** Average dinner over $10

MARYLAND

RAYMOND

Northern Pines Health Resort
R.R. 1, Box 279, Raymond, ME 04071　　　**(207) 655-7624**

Natural foods. Hours vary with the seasons, so call ahead for hours and reservations. FS,CAF,V,J,CC,$$

WALDOBORO

Pine Cone Public House
220 S. Friendship Street
Waldoboro, ME 04572　　　**(207) 832-6337**

Gourmet vegetarian and seafood. French-fried artichoke hearts, salads, vegetarian Reuben, falafel plate, pasta, veggie enchilada casserole, State of Maine cheese platter. Will make anything vegetarian on request. State of Maine beer and wine, Poland Spring water. Open daily but closed Monday in the summer; open only on weekends after Labor Day. Sunday brunch. Jazz piano on weekends. Located on Route 220, one mile from U.S. Route 1. FS,I,M,A,N,CC,CH,$$

MARYLAND

BALTIMORE

• Akbar
823 N. Charles St., Baltimore, MD 21201　　　**(301) 539-0944**

Northern Indian. Baked breads. FS,A,N,CC,$$$

Bombay Grill
2 East Madison St., Baltimore, MD 21202　　　**(301) 837-2973**

Indian. The Baltimore press gave it three stars and voted it best new restaurant and best Indian restaurant in 1988. Basmati-saffron rice, stir-fried okra, stuffed green peppers, malai kofta and more. Fruit lassi (yogurt drinks). Unique veg dishes: grilled marinated vegetables, kabobs, and grilled green peppers. Twelve items on the buffet, mostly vegetarian. Breads with an assortment of veg stuffings. Open daily. FS,CAF,F,V, A,N,CC,CH,$$

• Golden Temple
2320 N. Charles, Baltimore, MD 21218　　　**(301) 235-1049**

Natural foods. No eggs used. Casseroles, soups and pizza. Hot and cold sandwiches. Specializes in healthful vegetarian cooking. Closed Sunday. CAF,SB,I,J,CC,CH,$$

MARYLAND

Harvest Moon Cafe
11 W. Preston St., Baltimore, MD 20817   (301) 685-7110

Have a delicious macrobiotic or vegan meal and then it's off to the Lyric Opera House or Meyerhoff Symphony Hall two blocks away. Try the tofu teriyaki, seitan stroganoff or the tempura. Closed Monday. No sugar or dairy products used. FS,I,V,M,N,J,CC,CH,$$

The Natural
**Cranbrook Shopping Center, 560 Cranbrook Rd.
Baltimore, MD 21030**   (301) 628-1262

Sandwich bar in a natural food store. Sandwiches and pizza. No meat, some fish. Open daily. I,V,M,N,J,CC,CH,$

Puffins
1000 Reiserstown Rd., Baltimore, MD 21208   (301) 486-8811

Natural foods. Some vegetarian dishes. Pasta, salads, homemade breads and desserts. Closed Sunday. F,N,CC,$$$

Tandoors
Harbor Place, Baltimore, MD   (301) 547-0575

See Alexandria, Va., listing. Restaurants located throughout D.C. and suburbs.

Tov's Pizza
6313 Reiserstown Rd., Baltimore, MD 21215   (301) 358-5238

Fast foods. Knishes, vegetarian egg rolls, eggplant parmesan, soups, sandwiches and pizza. $

BETHESDA

Epicure
7315 Wisconsin Ave., Bethesda, MD 20814   (301) 654-4515

Juice bar. Deli-style vegetarian sandwiches. Homemade veggie soups. Fruit salad. Breakfast and lunch. Closed weekends. SB,I,J,CH,$

Kabul West
4871 Cordell Ave., Bethesda, MD 20814   (301) 986-8566

All vegetarian dishes are dairy- and egg-free, with the exception of one yogurt dish. Four veggie dishes daily. FS,V,A,CC,CH,$$

KEY TO DINING GUIDE
• Vegetarian food only

FS Full service	**V** Vegan options	**CC** Major credit cards accepted
CAF Cafeteria/buffet	**M** Macrobiotic options	**CH** Children welcome
SB Salad bar	**A** Alcoholic drinks	**$** Average dinner under $5
I Informal	**N** Nonalcoholic beer/wine	**$$** Average dinner $5 to $10
F Formal	**J** Freshly squeezed juices	**$$$** Average dinner over $10

MARYLAND

CATONSVILLE

Bamboo Inn
1111 N. Rolling Rd., Catonsville, MD 21228 (301) 788-4777

Chinese. Thirty vegetarian entrées! Almost all can be prepared without MSG or salt. FS,V,A,N,CC,$$

COLLEGE PARK

• Berwyn Cafe
5050 Berwyn Rd., College Park, MD 20740 (301) 345-2121

Juice Bar. Open daily. Brunch on Sunday. FS,I,N,J,CH,$$

RANDALLSTOWN

The Health Department
Bradlees Plaza, 8719-A Liberty Plaza Mall
Randallstown, MD 21133 (301) 655-6618

Natural foods. Carryout available. Closed Sunday. FS,CC,$

RIVERDALE

• Leland Memorial Hospital Cafeteria
4401 East West Hwy., Riverdale, MD 20737 (301) 699-2266

Open noon to 1:30 p.m. and 5:30 p.m. to 6:30 p.m. only, but all vegetarian. CAF,SB,I,CH,$

ROCKVILLE

Hard Times Cafe
1117 Nelson St., Rockville, MD 20850 (301) 294-9720

Chili parlor. Has vegetarian chili and salads, and beer. Open daily for lunch and dinner; open Sunday for dinner. FS,I,A,N,CC,CH,$

House of Chinese Gourmet
1485 Rockville Pike, Rockville, MD 20852 (301) 984-9440

Not completely vegetarian, but three entire menu columns devoted to strictly veg foods—even appetizers. Here are some possibilities: crisp black mushroom appetizer, seaweed soup, crispy eggplant entrée and braised "chicken" (nonmeat!). Everything can be prepared without MSG. Closed weekends. FS,I,A,CC,CH,$$

Tony Lin's Kitchen
12081 Rockville Pike, Rockville, MD 20852 (301) 468-5858

Chinese. Open daily. FS,I,A,CC,CH,$$

SILVER SPRING

China Royal
8472 Piney Branch Rd.
Silver Spring, MD 20901   (301) 585-3371

Chinese. Open daily. FS,I,A,CC,CH,$$

Negril Bakery
965 Thayer Ave., Silver Spring, MD 20910   (301) 585-3000

Jamaican. Vegetarian lasagna, veggie pattie and other vegetarian sandwiches, vegetarian stew, and more. Lots of vegetables. Homemade fruit punch. Closed Sunday. FS,A,CC,CH,$$

• Siddhartha
8237 Georgia Ave., Silver Spring, MD 20910   (301) 585-0550

Indian. See Washington, D.C., entry. Open daily. CAF,SB,I,V,N,CH,$$

TAKOMA PARK

• Columbia Union College Cafeteria
7600 Flower Ave., Takoma Park, MD 20912   (301) 891-4103

Most items sold by the ounce. Open Monday through Friday for three meals a day, Saturday for lunch, and Sunday for lunch and dinner. Closed on holidays and school vacations. Located 1½ miles from 495 Beltway. Take the Langley Park exit to University Boulevard, to Carroll Avenue, to Flower Avenue. FS,CAF,SB,I,CH,$$

• Washington Adventist Hospital
7600 Carroll Ave., Takoma Park, MD 20912   (301) 891-5012

Natural foods. CAF,SB,$

TOWSON

The Health Concern
28 W. Susquehanna Ave.
Towson, MD 21204   (301) 828-4015

Juice bar in a natural food store. Sandwiches, rice and veggies, and soup. Browse the natural food, vitamin and herb departments. Juice bar closed on weekends. V,M,N,J,$

KEY TO DINING GUIDE
• Vegetarian food only

FS Full service	**V** Vegan options	**CC** Major credit cards accepted
CAF Cafeteria/buffet	**M** Macrobiotic options	**CH** Children welcome
SB Salad bar	**A** Alcoholic drinks	**$** Average dinner under $5
I Informal	**N** Nonalcoholic beer/wine	**$$** Average dinner $5 to $10
F Formal	**J** Freshly squeezed juices	**$$$** Average dinner over $10

MASSACHUSETTS

The Power House
100 Shealy Ave., Towson, MD 21204 (301) 296-0811

Juice bar. Fresh vegetable juices, yogurt shakes, soups, tofu burgers, Powerhouse sandwich. Closed Sunday. V,N,J,$

WESTMINSTER

Harvestin' Natural Foods
12 Locust Lane, Westminster, MD 21157 (301) 876-3585

Natural foods. Carryout sandwiches.

WHEATON

Nut House Pizza
11419 Georgia Ave., Wheaton, MD 20902 (301) 942-5900

Kosher pizzas and sandwiches. Subs, burgers, pizza, all with meat substitutes. Salads, juices. Closes early every Friday for the Sabbath, then reopens an hour after sunset on Saturday. Counter service and take-out. I,CC,CH,$

MASSACHUSETTS

ALLSTON

Satori Natural Foods
166 Harvard Ave., Allston, MA 02134 (617) 254-9786

Natural and top-quality ingredients, many organic. All cooking is done with filtered water in non-aluminum cookware. Sugar, chemicals and dairy products are not used. There are a few seafood dishes here, but the rest is totally veg. The menu ranges from macrobiotic to party foods. Sunday brunch features crêpes and pancakes. Informal, friendly atmosphere. FS,V,M,N,J,$$

BOSTON

Center Street Cafe
597 Center St., Boston, MA 02130 (617) 524-9217

Breakfast, lunch and dinner. Dinner menu changes every few months. Recent specials have included nachos and black beans, pizza, polenta, Thai tofu and vegetarian cassoulet. Almost every dish can be made without eggs or dairy products. The cafe is small, so be prepared to wait. Menu sounds worth it, though. Closed Tuesday night. Brunch on weekends. FS,V,M,CH,$$

MASSACHUSETTS

In the Boston area . . .

For the traveler who is not familiar with the Boston area, we suggest looking under the following listings for additional dining choices.

Allston
Brookline
Burlington (30 minutes)

Cambridge
Jamaica Plain
Stoneham (20 minutes)

- **Milk Street Cafe**
  50 Milk St., Boston, MA 02109   **(617) 542-2433**

  Kosher vegetarian. Closed weekends. Other locations in Brookline and Cambridge. CAF,J,CH,$$

  Souper Salad
  119 Newbury St., Boston, MA 02116   **(617) 247-4983**

  Natural alternatives to your all-time favorites: vegetarian burritos, quiches, sandwiches and soups. The salad bar has more than 30 items; stir-fry too. The veggie platter comes with Oriental noodles. Scrumptious desserts. Eight other locations in the Boston area. FS,V,A,J,CC,$$

  Souper Salad
  524 Kenmore Sq., Boston, MA 02215   **(617) 536-7662**

  See above entry.

  Souper Salad
  102 Water St., Boston, MA 02109   **(617) 367-2582**

  See Newbury Street listing.

  Souper Salad
  103 State St., Boston, MA 02107   **(617) 227-9151**

  See Newbury Street listing.

KEY TO DINING GUIDE
• Vegetarian food only

FS Full service	**V** Vegan options	**CC** Major credit cards accepted
CAF Cafeteria/buffet	**M** Macrobiotic options	**CH** Children welcome
SB Salad bar	**A** Alcoholic drinks	**$** Average dinner under $5
I Informal	**N** Nonalcoholic beer/wine	**$$** Average dinner $5 to $10
F Formal	**J** Freshly squeezed juices	**$$$** Average dinner over $10

MASSACHUSETTS

Souper Salad
82 Summer St., Boston, MA 02110   (617) 426-6834
See Newbury Street listing.

BRAINTREE

Souper Salad
South Shore Plaza, 250 Granite Ave.
Braintree, MA 02184   (617) 843-4658
See Boston listing.

BROOKLINE

Cafe Shalom
404 Harvard St., Brookline, MA 02146   (617) 277-0698
Kosher, with a Middle Eastern flair. Closed Friday and Saturday. FS,I,V,M,A,CC,CH,$$$

Edibles
329 Harvard St., Brookline, MA 02146   (617) 232-8835
Natural foods. Mostly vegetarian soups and sandwiches. CAF,SB,I,N,CH,$$

- **Milk Street Cafe**
Longwood Galleria, Brookline, MA 02146   (617) 739-2233
Kosher vegetarian. Closed weekends. Next to Children's Hospital. Other locations in Boston and Cambridge.

Open Sesame
48 Boylston St., Brookline, MA 02146   (617) 277-9241
Natural foods. Open daily. FS,V,M,N,J,CH,$$

BURLINGTON

Souper Salad
Burlington Mall, Burlington, MA 01803   (617) 229-2223
See Boston listing.

CAMBRIDGE

Middle East
4 Brookline St., Cambridge, MA 02139   (617) 354-8238
Middle Eastern. Plenty of vegetarian choices, homemade and delicious. Vegetarian appetizers under $3. FS,V,A,N,J,CC,$

MASSACHUSETTS

Middle East
472 Massachusetts Ave.
Cambridge, MA 02139   **(617) 492-9181**

Middle Eastern. All the usual standbys on the menu—hummus, falafel, baba ganouj—plus live international entertainment. FS,A,J,$$

• Milk Street Cafe
101 Main St., Cambridge, MA 02142   **(617) 491-8287**

Kosher vegetarian. Closed weekends. Other locations in Boston and Brookline. CAF,J,CH,$$

Souper Salad
36 Harvard Sq., Cambridge, MA 02138   **(617) 497-6689**

See Boston listing. Closed Christmas and New Year's Day. FS,SB,I,A, CC,CH, $-$$

Taha Natural Foods
162 Prospect St., Cambridge, MA 02139   **(617) 864-9368**

Middle Eastern. Reservations recommended. Vegan buffet every day for lunch and dinner. Regular menu has many vegetarian dishes, including whole-wheat pizza. Homemade desserts. Closed major holidays. FS,CAF,SB,I,V,M,N,CC,CH,$$

JAMAICA PLAIN

Five Seasons
669 A Centre St., Jamaica Plain, MA 02130   **(617) 524-9016**

Natural foods. How about grilled polenta with red peppers and cilantro sauce? Or baked Florentine lasagna? Naturally sweetened desserts? We could handle it. Not on Monday, though, when Five Seasons is closed. FS,I,M,A,CC,CH,$$

NANTUCKET

Something Natural
50 Cliff Rd., Nantucket, MA 02554   **(508) 228-0504**

Bakery and sandwich shop. A few veggie sandwiches available on wholegrain bread, and salads and beverages. Call-in orders welcome. Open daily. Seasonal hours, mid-May through mid-October. Kids can play on the boat in the yard. V,N,CH,$

KEY TO DINING GUIDE
• Vegetarian food only

FS Full service	**V** Vegan options	**CC** Major credit cards accepted
CAF Cafeteria/buffet	**M** Macrobiotic options	**CH** Children welcome
SB Salad bar	**A** Alcoholic drinks	**$** Average dinner under $5
I Informal	**N** Nonalcoholic beer/wine	**$$** Average dinner $5 to $10
F Formal	**J** Freshly squeezed juices	**$$$** Average dinner over $10

MASSACHUSETTS

NORTHAMPTON

Paul & Elizabeth's
150 Main St., Northampton, MA 01060   (413) 584-4832

Natural foods. Tempura, noodles, salads and soups. Reservations recommended. Closed Sunday. FS,I,J,A,CC,CH,$$-$$$

PITTSFIELD

• Cornucopia
424 North St., Pittsfield, MA 01201   (413) 448-8960

Cafe. Lunch only. Mostly vegan: the only dairy product is the cheese in the cheese sandwich. Macrobiotic soups, too. The specialty of the house is the Sicilian sandwich, made with nuts, olives, dill and garlic. Homemade soups, salads, vitari, bagels, carrot juice. Take lunch on the outdoor patio. Closed Sunday. I,V,M,J,CC,CH,$

SOUTH ATTLEBORO

• Fuller Memorial Hospital
231 Washington St.
South Attleboro, MA 02703   (508) 761-8500

Natural foods. Open daily during mealtimes only, but it's all vegetarian. CAF,SB,I,$

SOUTH LANCASTER

• Atlantic Union College
Main St., South Lancaster, MA 01561   (508) 368-2000

Natural foods. Reservations recommended for larger groups. No smoking. Hours vary, but usually closed weekend mornings. CAF,SB,I,J,CH,$-$$

STONEHAM

• New England Memorial Hospital
5 Woodland Rd., Stoneham, MA 02180   (617) 979-7104

Natural foods. Open daily. CAF,N,CH,$

WESTMINSTER

The Old Mill
Route 2A, Westminster, MA 01473   (508) 874-5941

Natural foods. Chef will accommodate your diet, but menu includes ovolacto and vegan dishes. Reservations recommended. FS,CAF,SB,I,V,A,N,J,CC,CH,$$$

MICHIGAN

WORCESTER

- **Annapurna**
  483 Cambridge St., Worcester, MA 01610   (508) 755-7413
  Indian. Lacto-vegetarian cuisine that "nourishes the body and mind." Special dinners and festivals to celebrate Hindu holy days. Reservations recommended at all times. Lunch Monday through Friday. Dinner daily. FS,CC,CH,$$

MICHIGAN

ANN ARBOR

- **Seva**
  314 E. Liberty St., Ann Arbor, MI 48104   (313) 662-1111
  Natural foods. Mexican and Oriental. Daily specials. Saturday and Sunday brunch. A traditional favorite in town. The warm, woody decor adds to the experience. FS,M,J,A,N,CC,$-$$

BATTLE CREEK

- **Battle Creek Adventist Hospital**
  165 N. Washington Ave.
  Battle Creek, MI 49016   (616) 964-7121 ext. 385
  Natural foods. Menu changes daily. Open weekdays during mealtimes. Closed weekends. CAF,SB,I,CH,$

BERRIEN SPRINGS

- **Andrews University Food Service**
  Campus Center, Berrien Springs, MI 49104   (616) 471-3161
  Natural foods. Open daily during mealtimes. No breakfast served on Sunday. CAF,CH,$

- **Bon Appetit**
  1501 Saint Joseph Rd.
  Berrien Springs, MI 49103   (616) 471-2445
  French vegetarian. FS,J,$

KEY TO DINING GUIDE
- Vegetarian food only

FS Full service	**V** Vegan options	**CC** Major credit cards accepted
CAF Cafeteria/buffet	**M** Macrobiotic options	**CH** Children welcome
SB Salad bar	**A** Alcoholic drinks	**$** Average dinner under $5
I Informal	**N** Nonalcoholic beer/wine	**$$** Average dinner $5 to $10
F Formal	**J** Freshly squeezed juices	**$$$** Average dinner over $10

MICHIGAN

In the Detroit area . . .

For the traveler who is not familiar with the Detroit area, we suggest looking under the following listings for additional restaurant choices.

Ann Arbor (30 miles) Royal Oak
East Lansing Toledo, Ohio (40 minutes)
Ferndale Troy

DETROIT

• The Blue Nile
508 Monroe, Detroit, MI 48226 (313) 964-6699

In Trapper's Alley, a neat place to visit even if you're not hungry. But do go hungry, just to try the cuisine: it's Ethiopian food at its best. Several vegetarian dishes, including mixed vegetables with a mild spice, collard greens with onions and peppers, and spicy lentils. And don't leave without tasting the amazing Ethiopian spiced tea. No dinner served on Monday. FS,V,A,CC,CH,$$$

Cafe Martinique
1553 Woodward Ave., Detroit, MI 48226 (313) 963-4839

Coney Island hot dogs served with chili and onions are a Detroit standard. Here you can get one to rival the best—but it's a soy hot dog and served on a whole-wheat bun. Piano music at lunchtime. Definitely worth the trip. Also try the quiche or the vegetarian lasagna. Closed weekends. FS,I,V,N,CH,$

The Corner Pocket
242 John R St., Detroit, MI 48226 (313) 965-3633

Juice bar. Maple-baked yams, fresh salads, vegetarian soups, delectable desserts. Closed Sunday. V,M,N,J,$

D.C. Watts
10223 Whittier, Detroit, MI 48224 (313) 372-7884

Several vegetarian options: spinach lasagna, pastas, stir-fries, two soups daily and vegetarian pizza. Closed Sunday and Monday. FS,V,N,CH,$$

Garden Cafe
301 Fisher Building, Detroit, MI 48203 (313) 873-7888

MICHIGAN

A unique setting for a restaurant—it's part of the Detroit Gallery of Contemporary Crafts. The Fisher Building is a Detroit landmark (the beautiful lobby is worth seeing). Open for lunch only. Vegetarian soups, quiche, lasagna, pasta, fruit salads. With the exception of two fish dishes, it's all veg. Closed Sunday and major holidays. I,$$

- **Govinda's at the Fisher Mansion**
383 Lenox St., Detroit, MI 48215   (313) 331-6740

    Krishna-style vegetarian Indian food. Restaurant is located in a famous mansion-turned-Hare Krishna-temple, complete with lotus pools and peacocks. Gorgeous inside and out. (And the food is exquisite.) Open daily for lunch and dinner. $$

    Panda's Garden
7720 W. McNichols Rd., Detroit, MI 48221   (313) 861-6966

    International and macrobiotic food. Specials include Millet Cream Du Jour, the house seven-grain burger and the house millet burger. It's one of the largest menus in Michigan. Closed Monday. FS,V,M,J,CC,CH,$$

    Traffic Jam and Snug
Canfield St. at Second Ave.
Detroit, MI 48201   (313) 831-9470

    The menu changes weekly here, but you can count on several veggie specials any time: Tex-Mex lentil burger, eggplant sandwich on pita, veggie lasagna, squash stuffed with wild rice, and linguini with cheese or pesto. Vegetarian appetizers, too. Closed Sunday. FS,I,A,N,CC,$$$

EAST LANSING

Small Planet
225 Ann St., East Lansing, MI 48823   (517) 351-6230

International. Middle Eastern, Italian, Mexican and Jamaican cuisine. FS,A,J,CC,CH,$$

FERNDALE

Om Cafe
23136 N. Woodward Ave.
Ferndale, MI 48220   (313) 548-1941

KEY TO DINING GUIDE
• Vegetarian food only

FS Full service	**V** Vegan options	**CC** Major credit cards accepted
CAF Cafeteria/buffet	**M** Macrobiotic options	**CH** Children welcome
SB Salad bar	**A** Alcoholic drinks	**$** Average dinner under $5
I Informal	**N** Nonalcoholic beer/wine	**$$** Average dinner $5 to $10
F Formal	**J** Freshly squeezed juices	**$$$** Average dinner over $10

MICHIGAN

Natural foods. Specializes in macrobiotic and vegetarian foods. Homemade desserts and breads with no sugar or dairy products. Live entertainment evenings. Closed Sunday, except for last Sunday of the month. FS,V,M,J,N,$$

FLINT

- **Merlin's Retreat**
  801 Detroit St., Flint, MI 48503 (313) 767-9050
  Natural foods. Specials every Friday. "Happy Tuna" no-tuna-fish sandwich (happy because the tuna's in the sea). No smoking. Closed Saturday through Monday. FS,I,V,M,J,CH,$

KALAMAZOO

- **Country Life**
  233 Portage St., Kalamazoo, MI 49907 (616) 343-7421
  Natural foods. Completely vegan. Specializes in sandwiches, smoothies and healthful desserts. Primarily a lunch place, but also open Wednesday for dinner. Closed Friday and Saturday. They'll be moving in 1989, so call first. CAF,SB,I,V,J,CH,$

ROCKFORD

Down to Earth
10025 Belding Rd. N.E., Rockford, MI 49341 (616) 691-7288
Natural foods. A gourmet restaurant in the country. Vegetable crêpes, soup. Six vegetarian specials daily. Reservations recommended. Open daily. Personal checks accepted. FS,I,V,CH,$$

ROYAL OAK

Cuisine Couriers
508 S. Washington, Royal Oak, MI 48068 (313) 541-2002
With the exception of a tuna sandwich, Cuisine Couriers is an all-vegetarian, whole-food, deli-style restaurant. Eat-in or carryout. There's one entrée daily plus the usual deli items, and everything but the bread is freshly made on the premises. A large variety of sandwiches, soups, chili and veggie burgers are available. Entrées include lasagna, tamale pie, baked potatoes and nachos. No sugar or white flour in anything, and nothing's fried. Closed Sundays. I,V,M,N,J,CH,$$

Inn Season
500 E. Fourth St., Royal Oak, MI 48067 (313) 547-7916
Natural foods. Dare we call it nouvelle cuisine? Photos of Chef George Vutetakis' linguine with shiro miso and fresh basil sauce certainly look

the part—and certainly look delicious. Inn Season is almost entirely veg; fish is served here, but the preparation is kept separate from the vegetarian cooking. The only eggs used are in the desserts. Two daily specials, one dairy, one vegan. Chef Vutetakis, who learned his trade in India, has 16 years of experience as a gourmet vegetarian chef. Closed Sunday. FS,V,M,N,J,CH,$$

TROY

- **Pure 'N' Simple**
  2791 Rochester Rd., Troy, MI 48084   (313) 528-0840
  Natural foods. Closed Saturday. FS,M,N,J,CC,CH,$$

MINNESOTA

BURNSVILLE

Lotus
1916 E. Highway 13, Burnsville, MN 55337   (612) 890-5573

Vietnamese. Many vegetarian dishes with tofu or "mock duck" (braised wheat gluten), including barbecue tofu. Locations also in Edina, Minneapolis and St. Paul. Closed Sunday. FS,I,V,N,CH,$

EDINA

The Good Earth
3460 W. 70th St., Edina, MN 55450   (612) 925-1001

International. Italian, Mexican, Oriental, Indian and Cajun cuisine. Open daily. FS,V,M,A,CC,CH,$$

Lotus
3907 W. 50th St., Edina, MN 55424   (612) 922-4254

See Burnsville listing.

KEY TO DINING GUIDE
• Vegetarian food only

FS Full service	**V** Vegan options	**CC** Major credit cards accepted
CAF Cafeteria/buffet	**M** Macrobiotic options	**CH** Children welcome
SB Salad bar	**A** Alcoholic drinks	**$** Average dinner under $5
I Informal	**N** Nonalcoholic beer/wine	**$$** Average dinner $5 to $10
F Formal	**J** Freshly squeezed juices	**$$$** Average dinner over $10

MINNESOTA

MINNEAPOLIS

Cafe Brenda
300 First Ave. N., Minneapolis, MN 55401   **(612) 342-9230**
International. Gourmet vegetarian options. FS,A,N,CC,$$

Caper's
2221 W. 50th St., Minneapolis, MN 55419   **(612) 927-4416**
Open daily. N,CC,CH,$$

Diamond Thai
1423 Washington Ave. S.
Minneapolis, MN 55454   **(612) 332-2920**
Thai. Vegetarian eggrolls and spring rolls. Stir-fried veggies and fried tofu in peanut sauce. Veggie noodle dishes and curry-fried rice. Open daily. FS,I,V,N,CC,CH,$-$$

Faegre's
430 First Ave. N., Minneapolis, MN 55437   **(612) 332-3515**
American. Vegetarian pasta and soups always available. Open daily. Brunch on Sunday. FS,A,N,CC,$$

The Juice Bar
2200 Dupont Ave. S.,
Minneapolis, MN 55405   **(612) 377-4630**
Juice bar. Closed Sunday. I,V,M,J,$

Lotus
3037 Hennepin Ave. S.
Minneapolis, MN 55408   **(612) 825-2263**
See Burnsville listing. Open daily.

Lotus
313 Oak St.
Minneapolis, MN 55414   **(612) 331-1781**
See Burnsville listing.

Lotus to Go
Grant Mall, 113 W. Grant St.
Minneapolis, MN 55403   **(612) 870-1218**
See Burnsville listing. Take-out.

MINNESOTA

Matin
416 First Ave. N., Minneapolis, MN 55401   (612) 340-0150

Vietnamese. Mock duck—made of soy gluten! Closed Sunday. FS,CAF,I,A,N,CC,CH,$$

• Mudpie
2549 Lyndale Ave. S.,
Minneapolis, MN 55405   (612) 872-9435

Natural foods. Lunch and dinner on weekdays. Breakfast on weekends. Reservations recommended for parties over five. FS,V,M,A,N,J,CC,CH,$$

Nature's Foods
1614 Harmon Place
Minneapolis, MN 55403   (612) 338-2363

Natural foods. FS,$

• New Riverside Cafe
329 Cedar Ave., Minneapolis, MN 55454   (612) 333-4814

Natural foods. Seasonal plate, soups, salads, sautéed dishes. Fruit-sweetened desserts. In business for more than 18 years; worker-owned and -managed. CAF,V,M,J,CH,$

Nigel's
15 S. 12th St., Minneapolis, MN 55403   (612) 338-2235

Natural foods. Lunch and dinner vegetarian specials daily. Macrobiotic options aren't on the menu but can be put together upon request. "If given enough notice, we can prepare anything." Closed Sunday. FS,I,V,M,A,N,CC,CH,$$$

Odaa
408 Cedar Ave. S., Minneapolis, MN 55454   (612) 338-4459

Ethiopian. Authentic Ethiopian cuisine and communal dining. All ingredients fresh and natural, and all dishes freshly prepared. Relaxed atmosphere. African music. Private dining available. Open daily. FS,V,A,N,CC,CH,$$

Omar's Oasis
247 Cedar Ave., Minneapolis, MN 55454   (612) 343-0252

KEY TO DINING GUIDE
• Vegetarian food only

FS Full service	**V** Vegan options	**CC** Major credit cards accepted
CAF Cafeteria/buffet	**M** Macrobiotic options	**CH** Children welcome
SB Salad bar	**A** Alcoholic drinks	**$** Average dinner under $5
I Informal	**N** Nonalcoholic beer/wine	**$$** Average dinner $5 to $10
F Formal	**J** Freshly squeezed juices	**$$$** Average dinner over $10

MISSOURI

Middle Eastern and Greek. Sample typical Middle Eastern food, such as baba ganouj, spinach pie, and hummus, or not-so-typical fare, such as mougadra—lentils on rice with deep-fried onions and homemade yogurt. Eat in the outdoor garden in summer. A reader wrote to say Omar's is a "winner" (it is—they've won several awards, including one for the best tabouli of area Middle Eastern restaurants), and that they are "happy to adapt any meal to the vegetarian palate." Entertainment on weekends, when reservations are required, too. Take-out available. FS,I,N,J,CC,CH,$$$

Seward Community Cafe
2129 E. Franklin, Minneapolis, MN 55404   (612) 332-1011

Whole and organic foods only. Secluded outdoor dining area. Specials and soups of the day made from seasonal fruits and vegetables. Open daily. FS,V,M,$

MINNETONKA

The Good Earth
1585 Plymouth, Minnetonka, MN 55343   (612) 546-6432

Natural foods. Pastas, omelets and salads. Closed major holidays. FS,V,A,J,CC,CH,$$

ST. PAUL

Lotus Victoria Crossing
867 Grand Ave., St. Paul, MN 55105   (612) 228-9156

See Burnsville listing.

MISSOURI

CLAYTON

The Lettuce Leaf
7623 Forsyth Blvd., Clayton, MO 63105   (314) 241-7773

Natural foods. Sixteen different salads, and if you don't like what you see, make a request. Locations throughout the St. Louis area and in Kansas City. Most are open daily. Menu for Little Sprouts, too. FS,CC,CH,$$

KANSAS CITY

Amber Waves Cafe
4305 Main St., Kansas City, MO 64111   (816) 931-8181

MISSOURI

It's macrobiotic, all right, but you might not know it. The hot fudge sundaes might fool you—no chocolate in these concoctions—or the dairyless ice cream. Good, healthful food made from the highest quality natural ingredients (and you can eat it all by candlelight in the evenings). Daily specials. Open Tuesday and Thursday for dinner and Saturday for lunch. Closed Monday, Wednesday and Friday. FS,I,V,M,CH,$$

The Lettuce Leaf
500 Nichols Rd., Kansas City, MO 64112   (816) 931-2000

Salads and more salads (many of them vegetarian): Italian favorites, Caesars, fresh fruit plate, pasta primavera. Also soups on most days, including a Macedonian bean and Greek lentil. Try the summer club sandwich: whole-wheat bread and cream cheese with avocado, cucumbers, sprouts and cheese. Closed Sunday. FS,A,CC,$$

Pam Pam West
401 Ward Pkwy., Kansas City, MO 64112   (816) 756-1500

Several salads and a selection of hot vegetable plates. Fruit and cheese plate, and something called the Painter's Palate, which is fresh fruit. Vegetarian sandwiches, too. Open daily for three meals. FS,A,CC,CH,$$

Ponak's Tavern
2856 Southwest Blvd.
Kansas City, MO 64108   (816) 753-0775

"Best in the West" Mexican food. Try the soft-shell tacos. Open daily. FS,A,CC,$$

The Prospect of Westport
4109 Pennsylvania St.
Kansas City, MO 64111   (816) 753-2227

Several vegetarian samplings, and everything's à la carte so there's no stopping you. Pastas, brown rice and veggies, tofu sandwich, tabouleh. Beautiful decor and when the weather's good, enjoy the poutdoor courtyard; indoors you'll sit among plants, English antiques and natural woodwork. (The sun will shine on you through the skylight if you're sitting in.) Call for days and hours. FS,A,N,J,CC,$$$

The Gold Buffet
503 E. 18th Ave.
West Kansas City, MO 64116   (816) 221-4653

KEY TO DINING GUIDE
• Vegetarian food only

FS Full service	**V** Vegan options	**CC** Major credit cards accepted
CAF Cafeteria/buffet	**M** Macrobiotic options	**CH** Children welcome
SB Salad bar	**A** Alcoholic drinks	**$** Average dinner under $5
I Informal	**N** Nonalcoholic beer/wine	**$$** Average dinner $5 to $10
F Formal	**J** Freshly squeezed juices	**$$$** Average dinner over $10

MISSOURI

Buffet-style meals with some vegetarian entrées. More than 50 types of salad available. Open daily since 1958, complete with bowling alley right next door. Open daily. CAF,A,N,CH,$

ST. LOUIS

- **Govinda's**
  3926 Lindell Blvd., St. Louis, MO 63108 (314) 535-8085

  Indian. Two bucks for all you can eat. Lacto-vegetarian and vegan meals served daily except Saturday. FS,I,CH,$

- **La Patisserie**
  6269 Delmar, St. Louis, MO 63130 (314) 725-4902

  French. Several vegetarian options for breakfast and lunch, including veggie bacon, sausage and burgers. All soups vegan. Low-cholesterol and natural French pastries. FS,I,V,N,CC,$$

  The Lettuce Leaf
  107 N. Sixth St., St. Louis, MO 63101 (314) 241-7773

  See Clayton listing.

  The Lettuce Leaf
  37 Crestwood Plaza, St. Louis, MO 63126 (314) 968-0344

  See Clayton listing.

  The Lettuce Leaf
  620 West Port Plaza, St. Louis, MO 63146 (314) 576-7677

  See Clayton listing.

  Shalimar Garden
  4569 Laclede Ave., St. Louis, MO 63108 (314) 361-6911

  Indian. Menu offers 11 different vegetarian dinners and a vegetarian buffet lunch ($4.25), all approved by the American Heart Association for low cholesterol and low calories and absence of sugar, salt and MSG. Sitar music and Indian dancers on Saturday. Open daily. Located at Euclid Avenue in the Central West End. FS,I,V,N,CC,CH,$$

  Sunshine Inn
  8½ S. Euclid, St. Louis, MO 63108 (314) 367-1413

  Natural foods. Soups, quiche, sautées, veggie burgers, soy foods, whole-grain breads. Sunday brunch. Closed Monday. Reservations recommended. FS,I,V,M,A,N,J,CC,$$

WEBSTER GROVES

Webster Grill & Cafe
8115 Big Bend Blvd.
Webster Groves, MO 63119　　　　　(314) 962-0564
Natural foods. Open daily. FS,A,CC,$$

MONTANA

MISSOULA

Lily
515 S. Higgins, Missoula, MT 59801　　　(406) 542-0002
Gourmet. Look for the bright-red awning one block south of the Higgins Avenue Bridge. Try the French-style vegetarian dishes. FS,N,CC,$$$

Mammyth Bakery Cafe
131 W. Main, Missoula, MT 59802　　　(406) 549-5542
Natural foods. Wide selection of baked goods—Italian peasant breads, croissants, whole-grain and organic breads. A gourmet pastry department was recently added, featuring French-chocolate tortes and cakes and more ethnic breads. French-chocolate truffles are also tempting to dessert lovers. (Mammyth supplies baked goods to the area's top restaurants.) Closed Sunday. CAF,SB,I,J,CC,CH,$

NEBRASKA

OMAHA

Indian Oven
1010 Howard St., Omaha, NE 68102　　　(402) 342-4856
Northern Indian cuisine. Outdoor or indoor dining in a pleasant setting. Take-out available. Closed Monday. FS,F,V,A,N,CC,CH,$$$

KEY TO DINING GUIDE
• Vegetarian food only

FS Full service	**V** Vegan options	**CC** Major credit cards accepted
CAF Cafeteria/buffet	**M** Macrobiotic options	**CH** Children welcome
SB Salad bar	**A** Alcoholic drinks	**$** Average dinner under $5
I Informal	**N** Nonalcoholic beer/wine	**$$** Average dinner $5 to $10
F Formal	**J** Freshly squeezed juices	**$$$** Average dinner over $10

NEVADA

LAS VEGAS

General Health Foods
3661 S. Maryland Pkwy.
Las Vegas, NV 89109   (702) 731-5080

Natural foods. A Las Vegas fixture for more than 17 years. Lunch only. Closed weekends. FS,J,$

• Green Goddess
953 E. Sahara, Las Vegas, NV 89104   (702) 737-0323

(Formerly Leaf and Stream). Located at the back of Rainbow's End Natural Food Store. A true oasis in the desert. Marvelous salad bar with more varieties of sprouts than we've seen in a long time. Several wheatless and dairyless entrées available. Burgers, lasagna and very simple foods, too. Fresh-baked goods daily. Extremely accommodating chef. FS,SB,V,J,$

RENO

• Blue Heron
1091 S. Virginia, Reno, NV 89502   (702) 786-4110

Natural foods. All-vegetarian breakfasts, lunches and dinners. Dinner entrées include enchiladas, baked potatoes, sautéed veggies, spaghetti, macro plate. Daily specials. No breakfast on Saturday. Closed Sunday. FS,I,V,M,N,CH,$$

NEW HAMPSHIRE

KEENE

Butternuts
7 Court St., Keene, NH 03431   (603) 352-8818

Gourmet natural. Fresh seasonal produce. Menu changes frequently. Large selection of breads and desserts. Chef will accommodate any dietary request, including low-salt and salt-free food. All-Japanese menu on Sunday nights, including vegetarian sushi. Reservations recommended. Closed Monday. FS,V,M,A,N,J,CC,CH,$$$

MEREDITH

For Every Season
66 Main St., Meredith, NH 03253   (603) 279-8875

Counter service, deli and produce market. Deluxe omelets, whole-grain pancakes, scrambled tofu and vegetables, tofu burgers, salad bar, soups and chowders, stir-fry and sandwiches. Closed Sunday. SB,I,CH,$

PLYMOUTH

Suzanne's Kitchen
36 S. Main St., Plymouth, NH 03264   (603) 536-3304

Natural foods. Live music in the evening. Whole-grain bakery on premises. Veggie burgers, vegetarian versions of Italian, Greek and Mexican dishes. Open daily. FS,V,M,A,N,J,$$

WOLFEBORO

East of Suez
R.F.D. 1, Wolfeboro, NH 03894   (603) 569-1648

Asian. Many Oriental-style vegetarian dishes. Vegetarian stir-fry, tempuras. Open for dinner only. Closed Monday. FS,I,V,N,J,CH,$$$

NEW JERSEY

CLEMENTON

Cotardo's Ristorante Italiano
Cherrywood Shopping Center, Blackwood-Clementon Road
Clementon, NJ 08021   (609) 627-2755

Italian. Macrobiotic lunches every weekday. Open daily. FS,I,M,CC,CH,$$

COLONIA

- **Siddhartha**
1133 St. Georges Ave., Colonia, NJ 07067   (201) 750-0231

Indian. Self-service. Vegan and lacto-vegetarian dishes only. Closed Tuesday. I,V,CH,$$

KEY TO DINING GUIDE
• Vegetarian food only

FS Full service	**V** Vegan options	**CC** Major credit cards accepted
CAF Cafeteria/buffet	**M** Macrobiotic options	**CH** Children welcome
SB Salad bar	**A** Alcoholic drinks	**$** Average dinner under $5
I Informal	**N** Nonalcoholic beer/wine	**$$** Average dinner $5 to $10
F Formal	**J** Freshly squeezed juices	**$$$** Average dinner over $10

NEW JERSEY

EAST RUTHERFORD

Park and Orchard
240 Hackensack St.
E. Rutherford, NJ 07073 (201) 939-9292

Gourmet. A reader poll by *New Jersey* magazine recently rated Park and Orchard one of the top 10 restaurants in the state. Open daily. FS,I,V,M,A,N,J,CC,CH,$$$

FAIR LAWN

India House
6-13 Fair Lawn Ave., Fair Lawn, NJ 07410 (201) 791-8222

Indian. Several vegetarian entrées. Open daily. FS,I,V,J,CC,CH,$$

HACKETTSTOWN

• **Hackettstown Community Hospital**
651 Willow Grove St.
Hackettstown, NJ 07840 (201) 852-5100 ext. 6980

Natural foods. Self-serve yogurt and sandwich bar. Closed holidays; no breakfast served on weekends. CAF,SB,I,J,CH,$

MONTCLAIR

Clairmont Health Food Centre
515 Bloomfield Ave., Montclair, NJ 07042 (201) 744-7122

Lunch counter in a natural food store. Hot macrobiotic and vegetarian specials daily. Hummus, tofu sandwiches, vitari. The only animal products here are the tuna and egg-salad sandwiches (tofu mayonnaise). Closed Sunday. V,M,J,CH,$

MOUNT LAUREL

Country Kitchen
Ramblewood Center, North Route 73
Mount Laurel, NJ 08054 (609) 778-1971

Macrobiotic restaurant run by a mother-daughter team in the Garden of Eden natural food store. Primarily take-out, but there are a few tables for those who prefer to eat in. Natural ingredients, low in fat and cholesterol. Desserts baked fresh daily. With the exception of the tuna sandwich, the menu is veg. Catering and cooking classes available. There are guest speakers on nutrition, health and fitness at 8 p.m. on Friday. Closed Sunday. I,V,N,J,CC,$$

NEW JERSEY

Rayetta's
Princeton Place, 3747 Church Rd.
Mount Laurel, NJ 08054   **(609) 778-4343**

Natural foods. Mostly vegan, but there are some fish dishes. Entertainment on weekends. Just minutes off the New Jersey Turnpike. Brunch on Sunday; no dinner served on Monday. FS,F,CC,CH,$$$

OCEAN CITY

The Sojourner
712 Ninth St., Ocean City, NJ 08226   **(609) 399-1554**

PRINCETON

The Whole Earth
360 Nassau St., Princeton, NJ 08540   **(609) 924-7429**

Juice bar. Carryout soups, salads and sandwiches with hot entrées during winter. Lunch only. V,M,N,J,$

RED BANK

The Garden
7 E. Front St., Red Bank, NJ 07701   **(201) 530-8681**

Natural foods. Hummus, falafel, veggie burgers, salads, baklava, rice pudding, pear crunch. You can bring your own alcohol. Closed Sunday. FS,I,CH,$$

STONE HARBOR

Green Cuisine
302 96th St., Stone Harbor, NJ 08247   **(609) 368-1616**

Located on the Jersey shore, and open only during the summer—tourist season! Many veg salads, hot and cold sandwiches. Hummus and tabouli are standards.

KEY TO DINING GUIDE
• Vegetarian food only

FS Full service	**V** Vegan options	**CC** Major credit cards accepted
CAF Cafeteria/buffet	**M** Macrobiotic options	**CH** Children welcome
SB Salad bar	**A** Alcoholic drinks	**$** Average dinner under $5
I Informal	**N** Nonalcoholic beer/wine	**$$** Average dinner $5 to $10
F Formal	**J** Freshly squeezed juices	**$$$** Average dinner over $10

NEW MEXICO

TEANECK

- **Aquarius Organic Foods**
  408 Cedar Lane, Teaneck, NJ 07666   (201) 836-0601
  Juice bar. Organic fruits and vegetables. Hot and cold sandwiches for take-out. Also tofu chili and daily soup special. V,M,N,J,CC,$

NEW MEXICO

ALBUQUERQUE

- **Adam's Table**
  3619 Copper N.E., Albuquerque, NM 87108   (505) 266-4214
  Mostly Mexican and Italian, but all vegan. Also, burgers, sandwiches, hot buffet lunch, big breakfast menu. Everything is low salt and low fat. Children's menu. Run by Seventh-day Adventists, so closed on Saturday. Personal checks accepted. FS,SB,CAF,I,V,CH,$

BK's Health Pantry
119 San Pasquale S.W.
Albuquerque, NM 87104   (505) 243-0370
Juice Bar. Homemade soups, veg chili and fresh carrot juice (pints and quarts to go) are featured. Closed Sunday. Located one block east of Rio Grande and Central. SB,I,M,N,J,CC,CH,$

The Oasis
5400 E. San Mateo
Albuquerque, NM 87109   (505) 884-2324
A Mediterranean restaurant decorated to resemble an outdoor courtyard. Quite a mixture on the menu: French, Italian, Greek, Turkish, Lebanese and Israeli. Daily entrées include falafel, veggie and cheese quiche, and yogurt salad and tabouli. For dinner, try Greek moussaka or pastitso. Open daily for lunch and dinner. Entertainment on weekends. FS,V,A, N,CC,$$

Sara's
3901 Central Ave. N.E.
Albuquerque, NM 87106   (505) 256-7272
International cuisine. Sara's offers some of the freshest food around. A light, festive atmosphere, the works of local artists highlighted on the walls, and live music on most days. Rennetless cheeses are featured. Luncheon entrées include veggie tempura, tofu and broccoli with Oriental mushrooms, and a veggie sushi roll. Dinners are similarly gourmet, and desserts are delectable. Formal and informal dining. Open Monday through Friday for lunch and dinner. Open Saturday for dinner. Closed

NEW MEXICO

Sunday. Reservations recommended for weekday lunches. FS,M,A,N, J,CC,CH,$$-$$$

SANTA FE

Cafe Pasqual's
121 Don Gaspar, Santa Fe, NM 87501   (505) 983-9340

Natural foods. Most menu items can be ordered without meat or animal products. Wholegrain cereals and pancakes for breakfast. Veggie chili, stir-fries and salads for lunch. Usually a vegetarian entrée for dinner. Macrobiotic meals can be requested. Beers are locally brewed and unpasteurized. Most produce is locally grown and organic. Open daily; no dinner on Wednesday. Brunch on Sunday. FS,SB,I,V,M,A,CC,CH,$$

• Cloud Cliff Cafe
1805 Second St., Santa Fe, NM 87501   (505) 983-6254

Vegetarian nouvelle cuisine. Beautiful Art Deco decor: antique bar, soda fountain, lights and display cases. And the food is classy, too: the chefs were trained in classic cuisine. The menu changes with the availability of locally grown produce, but you can always count on fresh salads, pizza and 20 different whole-grain breads, including French sourdough. The homemade European pastries contain no sugar, and soon there'll be locally made ice creams, also without sugar. May be serving dinner on the weekends by the time this goes to press. FS,I,V,M,A,CH,$

E.K. Mas
319 Guadalupe, Santa Fe, NM 87501   (505) 989-7121

Gourmet foods with a wholesome, natural twist. An experienced brother-and-sister team run and cook for the restaurant, and that experience shows up in the food. Be prepared for rich and creamy delights. Veg entrées include Greek salad, spanikopita, spinach rotollo with garlic cream, and hot rice noodles in Thai peanut sauce. Lovely earth-toned Southwestern decor. Closed Monday and Tuesday. FS,A,CC,$$

The Natural Cafe
1494 Cerrillos Rd., Santa Fe, NM 87501   (505) 983-1411

Traditional vegetarian fare with an international flair. Try the black bean enchilada and the Indonesian tempeh katjang with gingered peanut

---

KEY TO DINING GUIDE
• Vegetarian food only

FS Full service	**V** Vegan options	**CC** Major credit cards accepted
CAF Cafeteria/buffet	**M** Macrobiotic options	**CH** Children welcome
SB Salad bar	**A** Alcoholic drinks	**$** Average dinner under $5
I Informal	**N** Nonalcoholic beer/wine	**$$** Average dinner $5 to $10
F Formal	**J** Freshly squeezed juices	**$$$** Average dinner over $10

sauce. Szechwan vegetables, fresh pasta, homemade bread and delicious desserts. Dine on the garden patio in summer. Will accommodate vegans. Closed Monday. FS,I,V,M,A,N,CH,$$

Oliver's Whole Earth Cafe
215 Palace Ave., Santa Fe, NM 87501   **(505) 982-0280**

Best restaurant in Santa Fe for vegans, according to vegetarian activist and author Keith Akers. Mostly macrobiotic. Vegan desserts, too. Tofu quiche, broccoli-mushroom platter, corn walnut muffins. Closed Sunday. FS,V,J,$$-$$$

NEW YORK

ALBANY

• Dahlia
858 Madison Ave., Albany, NY 12208   **(518) 482-0931**

Vegetarian bistro. Kosher international. Spinach lasagna and other pasta dishes, vegetable pies, moussaka, tabouli, grain dishes and vegetarian soups. Thirty-six flavors of homemade ice cream and fruit sorbets. Reservations recommended for large parties. Take-out available. Open daily. FS,I,V,M,J,CH,$

AMHERST

The Juicery
3103 Sheridan Dr., Amherst, NY 14226   **(716) 833-2360**

In the Century Mall at Northtown Plaza. Juice bar. Veggie soups and chili, falafels, hummus, and Super Veggie pita-pocket sandwiches. Closed Sunday. Locations in Buffalo and Williamsville. CAF,I,J,CH,$

Pizza Plant
3093 Sheridan Dr., Amherst, NY 14226   **(716) 833-0882**

North of Buffalo. Eclectic pizza joint. Huge selection of pizza, sandwiches, even nachos. The owner's vegetarian, so the two area Pizza Plants have a large selection of veggie fare. Soy cheese is available for the pizzas, and most of the soups are vegetarian, including the winter special, Bread Bowl Stew—in a bowl made of bread, of course. Homemade salad dressings, and the menu reveals an offbeat sense of humor. Fifty varieties of beer. Open daily. FS,I,V,A,N,CC,CH,$$

BINGHAMTON

Whole In the Wall
43 S. Washington St.
Binghamton, NY 13903   **(607) 722-0006**

NEW YORK

Natural foods. Primarily vegetarian; stir-fried veggies, quiche, falafel, tempura. Fresh-baked breads. Pita sandwiches. Located in an old storefront rehabbed with recycled wood from local houses. FS,V,N,J,$$

BRONX

- **Nature's Exchange**
  2131 Williamsbridge Rd., Bronx, NY 10461   (212) 822-7892
  Natural foods. Open daily, but hours vary, so call first. FS,V,J,$$

BROOKLYN

- **Perelandra**
  175 Remsen St., Brooklyn, NY 11201   (718) 855-6068
  Juice bar and natural foods deli. Open daily. I,V,M,J,CH,$

BUFFALO

Amy's Place
3234 Main St., Buffalo, NY 14214   (716) 832-6666

Across from the University of Buffalo. The food is mostly vegetarian with a hint of the Middle East. Many types of sandwiches on the house's own unleavened, pita-style bread. Stuffed grape leaves, hummus, tabouli and spinach pie. Homemade dressings for the salads. Call ahead to order specially prepared dishes or if you have a large group: seating is for about 50 only. Open daily. FS,I,V,CH,$-$$

El Charro
3447 Bailey Ave. (at Winspear Avenue)
Buffalo, NY 14215   (716) 837-5300

Mexican. Closed Sunday. FS,V,A,CC,CH,$$

The Juicery
Delaware Park, Buffalo, NY 14214   (716) 873-3035

See Amherst listing.

KEY TO DINING GUIDE
• Vegetarian food only

FS Full service	**V** Vegan options	**CC** Major credit cards accepted
CAF Cafeteria/buffet	**M** Macrobiotic options	**CH** Children welcome
SB Salad bar	**A** Alcoholic drinks	**$** Average dinner under $5
I Informal	**N** Nonalcoholic beer/wine	**$$** Average dinner $5 to $10
F Formal	**J** Freshly squeezed juices	**$$$** Average dinner over $10

NEW YORK

The Juicery
Theater Place, 622 Main St.
Buffalo, NY 14202 (716) 855-1216
See Amherst listing.

Just Pasta
307 Bryant St., Buffalo, NY 14222 (716) 881-1888
Nouvelle Italian. Lots of vegetarian pastas. Pasta is made fresh daily. Catering, take-out available. Reservations recommended. Closed Sunday. FS,A,CC,$$

Rekha Indian Restaurant
271 Kenmore Ave., Buffalo, NY 14223 (716) 833-3466
Traditional Indian curries. All-you-can-eat vegetarian buffet every Tuesday night.

Sun Spirit
177 Hodge Ave., Buffalo, NY 14222 (716) 881-7108
A natural foods vegetarian deli featuring sandwiches, soups, eggrolls, hummus, casseroles, quiches, desserts, and salads. International dishes, too. All are original recipes of the chefs/owners. Take out or eat in. Homemade cookies and brownies on occasion. Seasonal menu, with more hot food in the winter. Closed Sunday. No smoking. CH,$

FRESH MEADOWS

Quantum Leap
6564 Fresh Meadow Lane
Fresh Meadows, NY 11365 (718) 461-1307
Natural foods. Established in 1973, this is one of the oldest natural food restaurants in the New York City area. International, eclectic menu. Atmosphere is casual and relaxed. No smoking. Also a Manhattan location. FS,V,M,N,J,$$

ITHACA

• Cabbagetown Cafe
404 Eddy St., Ithaca, NY 14850 (607) 273-2847
A definite pioneer in the vegetarian restaurant adventure. Daily specials, exotic salads, decadent desserts without white sugar or white flour. Internationally famous for quality food. Homemade breads and desserts. Near Cornell University, Cabbagetown has long been a favorite natural food restaurant for locals and travelers alike. Open daily. Entertainment during Sunday brunch. FS,I,V,M,A,J,CH,$-$$

NEW YORK

Moosewood Restaurant
DeWitt Mall, 215 N. Cayuga St.
Ithaca, NY 14850 (607) 273-9610

Natural foods. Collectively owned and operated. Specializes in vegetarian gourmet and international cuisine. Fresh pasta every Wednesday night and ethnic specialties every Sunday. Breads and desserts are homemade. Terrace dining in the summer. FS,V,M,A,$$

• Somadhara
DeWitt Mall, 215 N. Cayuga St.
Ithaca, NY 14850 (607) 273-8213

Deli. Mainly take-out service. Tofu salads and spreads, whole-wheat pizza, soups, knishes, samosas, eggrolls and vegetarian main-course salads. Antipasto items, dolmas, Greek olives and other savories are always in stock. Limited seating. Open daily. V,M,N,J,$

JAMAICA

• Annam Brahma
84-43 164th St., Jamaica, NY 11432 (718) 523-2600

International. Food prepared with love and care in a peaceful, soothing atmosphere. Authentic Indian dishes and American-style soups, salads and casseroles. Original artwork is displayed in the dining area, and spiritual books and tapes are available. Free meditation classes. FS,N,J,CH,$

• Smile of the Beyond
86-14 Parsons Blvd., Jamaica, NY 11432 (718) 739-7453

Natural foods. Open daily for breakfast and lunch. FS,V,M,J,$

NAPLES

Wild Winds
County Road 36, Hunt Hollow Rd.
Naples, NY 14512 (716) 374-5523

Natural foods. Unique country setting: flower, herb and theme gardens, petting zoo, hiking trails. Group tours, garden weddings. Special nature study programs for schoolchildren. Closed Monday. Personal checks accepted. FS,V,A,N,J,CH,$$

KEY TO DINING GUIDE
• Vegetarian food only

FS Full service	**V** Vegan options	**CC** Major credit cards accepted
CAF Cafeteria/buffet	**M** Macrobiotic options	**CH** Children welcome
SB Salad bar	**A** Alcoholic drinks	**$** Average dinner under $5
I Informal	**N** Nonalcoholic beer/wine	**$$** Average dinner $5 to $10
F Formal	**J** Freshly squeezed juices	**$$$** Average dinner over $10

NEW YORK

> **In the New York City area . . .**
>
> For the traveler who is not familiar with the New York City area, we suggest looking under the following listings for additional restaurant choices.
>
> The Bronx
> Brooklyn
> Fresh Meadows
> Jamaica
> Queens
>
> *On Long Island:*
> Plainview
> Sag Harbor
> Smithtown
>
> *In Westchester County:*
> White Plains

NEW YORK CITY

- **Ahimsa Cafe**
  145A First Ave., New York, NY 10003   **(212) 228-3632**
  Basic American vegetarian with several ethnic and international options. Ahimsa dishes range from sandwiches and burgers to salads made with organic ingredients whenever possible. Special entrées include curried garbanzo beans, soba noodles and a nacho deluxe. And do try the first-class desserts. Featured in *VT* as one of New York's finest. FS,V,M,$$

- **Angelica Kitchen**
  300 E. 12th St., New York, NY 10003   **(212) 228-2909**
  Natural foods. An all-around purist's dream—organic macrobiotic cuisine that strikes the right balance between absolutely delicious and wonderfully nutritious. Completely vegan and organic, and the cooks use no sugar, honey, molasses or white flour. All stainless-steel cookware. Make sure you check out the cornbread; it gets rave reviews. Selected by *VT* as one of the country's best vegetarian restaurants. Take-out available. Fresh juice bar. FS,V,M,J,$$

Beanstalk
McGraw Hill Bldg., 1221 Avenue of the Americas
New York, NY 10020   **(212) 997-1005**
Natural foods. Ample fruit salads, sandwiches, salads and hot entrées. Sunny courtyard. FS,V,J,A,CC,$$

Blazing Salads
228 W. Fourth St., New York, NY 10014   **(212) 929-3432**

NEW YORK

International. As the name tells you, salads are the specialties. There's a macrobiotic special about once a week; no particular day, though, so call first. Open daily. FS,V,M,A,N,CC,CH,$$

Boostan
85 McDougal St., New York, NY 10012   (212) 533-9561

Natural foods. Located in the heart of Greenwich Village. Greek, Italian and Creole specialties. Some dishes contain dairy but no eggs. Open daily from noon until wee hours. FS,N,J,CH,$$

Brownie Points
101 Second Ave., New York, NY 10003   (212) 505-7395

Juice bar. Sandwiches, veggie burgers, pita, quiche, salads, and, of course, brownies. Homemade varieties of frozen yogurt and ice cream. Sidewalk cafe great for people-watching. Open daily. Free delivery. I,V,M,CH,$

Buckwheat & Alfalfa
182 Eighth Ave., New York, NY 10011   (212) 463-9511

The Village Voice says it's the "best of its kind, and the only one we would recommend to friends." It's a natural food restaurant, mostly veg, although there are some fish dishes. Organic produce is used and organic wine is served whenever possible. Cafeteria service for lunch; but dinner's by candlelight. Brunch on Sunday features buckwheat pancakes and egg-white omelets. Open daily; no dinner served on Monday night. FS,CAF,A,CC,CH,$$$

- ### Country Life Buffet and Grocery
48 Trinity Place, New York, NY 10006   (212) 480-9135

Natural foods. All-vegan buffet. *VT* rated it one of New York's best vegetarian restaurants. The chefs are especially adept at Italian dishes; try the lasagna. Closed Sunday. CAF,I,V,CH,$$

- ### Country Life Vegetarian Buffet
244 E. 51st St., New York, NY 10022   (212) 980-1480

Similar to listing above, but breakfast and dinner are of the all-you-can-eat variety.

Eat at 11 St. Mark's Restaurant
11 St. Mark's Place, New York, NY 10003   (212) 477-5155

KEY TO DINING GUIDE		
• Vegetarian food only		
FS Full service	**V** Vegan options	**CC** Major credit cards accepted
CAF Cafeteria/buffet	**M** Macrobiotic options	**CH** Children welcome
SB Salad bar	**A** Alcoholic drinks	**$** Average dinner under $5
I Informal	**N** Nonalcoholic beer/wine	**$$** Average dinner $5 to $10
F Formal	**J** Freshly squeezed juices	**$$$** Average dinner over $10

Natural foods. Daily specials. The house salad dressing is great. Open daily. FS,V,M,A,J,CC,$$

Famous Dairy
222 W. 72nd St., New York, NY 10023   **(212) 595-8487**

Kosher dairy restaurant. Several vegetable dishes. Closed Friday after 2 p.m. and all day Saturday. FS,CC,CH,$$-$$$

Forty Carrots
1000 Third Ave. (at 59th Street)
New York, NY 10021   **(212) 705-2993**

You can find wholesome fast food at this juice bar in the middle of town: homemade yogurt, garden salads, veggie lasagna, baked potato with cheese and veggies. Open daily. A,N,J,CC,$$

Good Food Cafe
401 Fifth Avenue, New York, NY 10016   **(212) 686-3546**

Located in a posh natural food store across from Lord & Taylor. Closed Sunday. CAF,M,N,J,CC,CH,$$

The Great American Health Bar
35 W. 57th St., New York, NY 10019   **(212) 355-5177**

A true health food place, but fashioned after a 1940s coffee shop. Neat menu: Juices are listed under "liquid health," sandwiches and entrées under "complementing nature." Also: mixed protein-type drinks and lots of salads, veggie chili, pasta, falafel, lasagna, soups, omelets and quiche. Daily specials, take-out... and free delivery! Sit at tables or at the counter. Open daily. Locations throughout New York City, but not all are owned/managed by the same person. FS,SB,I,CH,$$

The Great American Health Bar
55 John St., New York, NY 10038   **(212) 227-6100**

See above entry.

The Great American Health Bar
821 Third Ave., New York, NY 10022   **(212) 758-0883**

See 57th Street entry.

Greener Pastures
117 E. 60th St. (between Park and Lexington Avenues)
New York, NY 10022   **(212) 832-3212**

Large menu with several selections for vegetarians, including veggie "chopped liver" and several soups. Take out a sandwich if you'd like, or go for a hot entrée: eggplant steak, vegetable cutlet, veggie "chicken" breasts (from soy) and many others, several on organic brown rice. Des-

NEW YORK

serts are baked on premises with maple syrup and blackstrap molasses and topped with sugarless whipped cream. Open daily. FS,N,J,CH,$$$

The Health Pub
371 Second Ave., New York, NY 10010   **(212) 529-9200**

Dairy-free dishes. With the exception of one salmon entrée, everything is meat-free, too. Open daily. FS,A,N,CC,CH,$$

Healthworks
153 E. 53rd St., New York, NY 10022   **(212) 838-6221**

Juice bar. Salads. Open daily. I,N,CH,$

Healthy Chelsea
248 W. 23rd St., New York, NY 10011   **(212) 691-0286**

Juice bar. Soups, sandwiches, vegetarian chili, grains. Six daily specials. Open daily. V,N,J,CC,CH,$

- ### House of Vegetarian
  68 Mott St., New York, NY 10013   **(212) 226-6572**

  Chinese vegan. Imitation fish and meat. Open daily. FS,V,CH,$$

- ### Living Springs
  116 E. 60th St. (between Park and Lexington Avenues)
  New York, NY 10022   **(212) 319-7850**

  Natural foods. Similar to the Country Life chain, and serving many of the same tried-and-deliciously-true dishes (including the famous lasagna). The all-you-can-eat buffet is $7.85 for lunch and $9.24 for dinner. Serves breakfast, lunch and dinner. Closed Friday nights and Saturday. V,CC,CH,$$

- ### Lois K. Lane's Ninth & Natural
  580 Ninth Ave., New York, NY 10036   **(212) 695-5055**

  Natural foods. Juice bar now; no longer offering hot entrées. Soups, sandwiches, smoothies and juices.

- ### Luma
  200 Ninth Ave. (at West 22nd Street)
  New York, NY 10011   **(212) 633-8033**

KEY TO DINING GUIDE
- Vegetarian food only

FS Full service	**V** Vegan options	**CC** Major credit cards accepted
CAF Cafeteria/buffet	**M** Macrobiotic options	**CH** Children welcome
SB Salad bar	**A** Alcoholic drinks	**$** Average dinner under $5
I Informal	**N** Nonalcoholic beer/wine	**$$** Average dinner $5 to $10
F Formal	**J** Freshly squeezed juices	**$$$** Average dinner over $10

NEW YORK

There are a couple of seafood dishes here, but the rest is vegan. Closed Monday. FS,V,A,N,CC,CH,$$$

- **Madras Palace**
  104 Lexington Ave., New York, NY 10016   (212) 532-3314
  A strictly kosher Indian restaurant with an elegant atmosphere that makes it perfect for business lunches or family outings. Many dishes contain dairy products and refined flours and sugars, but all the meals are delicious. Open daily. FS,V,A,CC,CH,$$$

  Marvin Gardens
  2274 Broadway, New York, NY 10024   (212) 799-0578
  Natural foods. Old-fashioned eating and drinking place with some traditional vegetarian fare: Oriental vegetables, tabouli, hummus, hot veggie plate. FS,V,A,N,CC,CH,$$

- **Nowhere**
  11 Waverly Place, New York, NY 10003   (212) 475-0255
  Owned by vegetarian pop star Howard Jones, it's the "first vegetarian rock 'n' roll bar" (the music's played on an antique Wurlitzer). Don't expect health food—but it's definitely veg. Few eggs used, and no dairy. Near New York University. Smoking allowed. Live music, too, of course. Open daily. FS,I,V,M,A,N,J,CC,$$$

- **Plum Tree**
  1501 First Ave., New York, NY 10021   (212) 734-1412
  Natural foods. Macrobiotic and vegetarian meals for lunch and dinner. Closed Monday. FS,I,M,V,N,CH,$$$

  Pumpkin Eater
  2452 Broadway, New York, NY 10024   (212) 877-0132
  Natural foods. Bills itself as a natural food restaurant with a touch of class—inviting atmosphere, after-five service and the widest variety of cuisine. Peter actually works here. Open daily. FS,A,J,CC,CH,$$

  Quantum Leap
  88 W. Third St., New York, NY 10012   (212) 677-8050
  See Fresh Meadows listing.

  Ratner's
  138 Delancey St., New York, NY 10002   (212) 677-5588
  Kosher restaurant. Open daily. FS,V,A,CH,$$

  Salad Bowl
  721 Lexington Ave., New York, NY 10022   (212) 752-7201

Salads, sandwiches, casseroles, quiches, soups and bakery. Open daily. CAF,I,V,J,CH,$

Salad Bowl
Pier 17, Third Floor, South St. Seaport, 84 South St.
New York, NY 10034   **(212) 693-9050**
See Lexington Ave. listing.

Salad Bowl
566 Seventh Ave., New York, NY 10018   **(212) 921-7060**
See Lexington Ave. listing. Closed weekends. CAF,I,V,CH,$

Salad Bowl
906 Third Ave., New York, NY 10022   **(212) 644-6767**
See Lexington Ave. listing.

• Shojin
23 Commerce St., New York, NY 10014   **(212) 989-3530**
Considered one of the finest vegetarian restaurants in New York City, its elegant style, strict standards and reasonable prices make it a "must go to." Fresh flowers, chandeliers and overall tranquil atmosphere make Shojin seem miles away from bustling Seventh Avenue. The cuisine is best described as Japanese international, but there are enough non-Oriental twists to keep things exciting—and it's completely vegan. Soups are all delicious. Try the tofu teriyaki or the sweet-and-sour tofu. Cutlet with curry, and other specials, are made with seitan. You'll have a hard time choosing. Closed Sunday. FS,I,V,M,N,$$

Souen Restaurant
2444 Broadway, New York, NY 10024   **(212) 787-1110**
Macrobiotic. Complete macrobiotic lunches and dinners daily. FS,I,M,$$

Souen Restaurant
210 Sixth Ave., New York, NY 10014   **(212) 807-7421**
See entry above.

KEY TO DINING GUIDE
• Vegetarian food only

FS Full service	**V** Vegan options	**CC** Major credit cards accepted
CAF Cafeteria/buffet	**M** Macrobiotic options	**CH** Children welcome
SB Salad bar	**A** Alcoholic drinks	**$** Average dinner under $5
I Informal	**N** Nonalcoholic beer/wine	**$$** Average dinner $5 to $10
F Formal	**J** Freshly squeezed juices	**$$$** Average dinner over $10

NEW YORK

- **Spring Street Natural**
  62 Spring St., at Lafayette St.
  New York, NY 10012   (212) 966-0290
  Natural foods. A popular vegetarian eatery for 18 years. Comfortable, spacious, airy environment. Located on a busy corner near SoHo. Serves only the freshest unprocessed foods. Unique vegetarian specialties that are both gourmet and nutritious. Open daily. FS,I,V,M,A,N,J,CC,CH,$$$

- **Vegetarian's Paradise**
  48 Bowery, New York, NY 10013   (212) 571-1535
  Chinese vegetarian. Vegan dishes exclusively. Mock chicken and beef are specialties. Closed Wednesday. FS,I,V,N,$$

  Veggies
  123 W. 39th St., New York, NY 10018   (212) 840-6560
  Natural foods. J,$

  Whole Wheat & Wild Berries
  57 W. 10th St., New York, NY 10011   (212) 677-3410
  Natural foods. Serving gourmet natural foods for 12 years. All food made from scratch. Nondairy foods always available. Open daily. FS,M,A,N,$$

  Zucchini
  1336 First Ave., New York, NY 10021   (212) 249-0559
  Natural foods. Pasta and salads. BYOB. FS,I,V,M,N,CC,CH,$$$

ONEONTA

  Autumn Cafe
  244 Main St., Oneonta, NY 13820   (607) 432-6845
  Whole-foods cooking. Closed Sunday; open Monday for lunch only. FS,V,A,N,CC,CH,$$

PLAINVIEW

  Asparagii
  379 S. Oyster Bay Rd., Plainview, NY 11803   (516) 938-4343
  Natural foods. Has pledged to accommodate veggies and vegans. Open daily. Sunday buffet. FS,V,A,CC,CH,$$$

ROCHESTER

  Jazzberry's Uptown
  50 East Ave., Rochester, NY 14604   (716) 262-3660

International. No longer exclusively a vegetarian restaurant, but eight main veg dishes are supplemented with macro, miso, stir-fry and tofu dishes. Lots of Italian, Indian, Mexican specialties. Soups and salads, too. Music or poetry readings nightly. Open every day. FS,I,V,M,A,N,J,CC,CH,$$$

SAG HARBOR

- **Provisions**
Main St., Sag Harbor, NY 11963   (516) 725-2666
Natural foods. International cuisine. FS,I,V,M,CC,CH,$$

SMITHTOWN

Jhoola, Cuisine of India
9 E. Main St., Smithtown, NY 11787   (516) 360-9861
Indian. Reservations recommended. Closed Monday. FS,V,A,CC,$$$

SYRACUSE

- **Cafe Margaux**
317 W. Fayette St., Syracuse, NY 13202   (315) 451-8172

A reader describes the cuisine here as elegant and creatively gourmet. (He also remarked on the congenial atmosphere.) There are many stir-fries on the menu, several with tofu or tempeh. And try the dairyless "cheese" sauce. Macrobiotic, wheatless foods are available, and most of the veggies are organic whenever possible. Daily dairy and nondairy specials. All eggs used are from free-range hens, and cheese is made with vegetable rennet. Chef will accommodate special diets. Toy area for children. Open daily. Cafe Margaux was moving as this went to press, so call first. FS,SB,CAF,V,M,A,N,J,CH,$$

King David's Restaurant
129 Marshall St., Syracuse, NY 13210   (315) 478-9463

Natural foods. Full vegetarian menu. Located near Syracuse Univeristy. FS,J,CC,CH,$-$$

KEY TO DINING GUIDE
• Vegetarian food only

FS Full service	**V** Vegan options	**CC** Major credit cards accepted
CAF Cafeteria/buffet	**M** Macrobiotic options	**CH** Children welcome
SB Salad bar	**A** Alcoholic drinks	**$** Average dinner under $5
I Informal	**N** Nonalcoholic beer/wine	**$$** Average dinner $5 to $10
F Formal	**J** Freshly squeezed juices	**$$$** Average dinner over $10

NEW YORK

Munjed's Mideastern Cafe
530 Westcott St., Syracuse, NY 13210   **(315) 425-0366**

Middle Eastern. Rice-lentil pilaf, stuffed grape leaves, tabouli, spinach pie, vegetarian platter—includes samples of their vegetarian foods. They "take requests" for almost anything, so just ask. Friday vegetarian specials are often vegan. Take-out available. FS,J $

WHITE PLAINS

Manna Foods
171 Mamaroneck Ave.
White Plains, NY 10601   **(914) 946-2233**

Juice bar. Vegetarian lunches. Veggie chili, hot meatball sandwiches, hoagies, pitas, stews, soups, burritos, tacos, pies and more. Prepared fresh daily. With the exception of the tuna, this place is totally vegetarian. Closed Sunday. Self-service. V,M,CC,CH,$$

Yogurt Yes
39A Mamaroneck Ave.
White Plains, NY 10601   **(914) 761-7833**

Natural foods. Closed Sunday. FS,$

WILLIAMSVILLE

The Juicery
4545 Transit Rd., Williamsville, NY 14221   **(716) 634-4020**

See Amherst listing.

Pizza Plant
8020 Transit Rd., Williamsville, NY 14221   **(716) 632-0800**

See Amherst listing.

NORTH CAROLINA

CARRBORO

Carrboro Cafe
101 E. Weaver St., Carrboro, NC 27510   **(919) 929-0010**

Near Chapel Hill. Deli in the Weaver Street Market natural food store. A thriving place that serves soups, sandwiches, and salads. The dozen or so salads offered daily include pasta, grain and bean salads, along with everyday vegetable salads. Mostly vegetarian, but some fish. V,A,N,J,$

NORTH CAROLINA

CHAPEL HILL

Pyewacket
The Courtyard, West Franklin at Roberson
Chapel Hill, NC 27514   **(919) 929-0297**

Natural foods. Recommended to us by many satisfied vegetarian diners. Live entertainment Monday, Wednesday and Friday. Closed on major holidays. FS,I,A,N,CC,CH,$$

CHARLOTTE

The Mill
1000 S. King Dr., Charlotte, NC 28207   **(704) 333-8349**

You'll find natural sandwiches and salads in this juice bar at the back of a natural food store. Daily specials. Closed Sunday. CC,$

The Mill
Quail Corners Shopping Center, 8428 Park Rd. Extension
Charlotte, NC 28210   **(704) 552-9801**

See entry above. This restaurant—also at the back of a natural food store—has the same good food as its sister on King Drive, but it's full service.

People's Natural Foods
617 S. Sharon Amity Rd.,
Charlotte, NC 28211   **(704) 364-1919**

Natural foods. Full service at night only. Dinner specials on Thursday and Friday nights, some vegetarian entrées, plus soups, salads, sandwiches, "natural" pizza, fresh juice and smoothies. Closed Sunday. FS,V,A,N,J,CC,CH,$-$$

DURHAM

Seventh Street
1104 Broad, Durham, NC 27705   **(919) 286-1019**

International lunch and dinner dishes. Closed major holidays. FS,V,A,N,CC,CH,$$

KEY TO DINING GUIDE
• Vegetarian food only

FS Full service	**V** Vegan options	**CC** Major credit cards accepted
CAF Cafeteria/buffet	**M** Macrobiotic options	**CH** Children welcome
SB Salad bar	**A** Alcoholic drinks	**$** Average dinner under $5
I Informal	**N** Nonalcoholic beer/wine	**$$** Average dinner $5 to $10
F Formal	**J** Freshly squeezed juices	**$$$** Average dinner over $10

NORTH CAROLINA

GREENSBORO

Sunset Cafe
4608 W. Market St., Greensboro, NC 27407   (919) 855-0349
International. Middle Eastern, Mediterranean and other ethnic speicals: spinach manicotti, eggplant dishes, spanakopita, Russian cheese dumplings. FS,I,V,A,N,J,CC,CH,$$

HILLSBOROUGH

The Regulator Cafe
108 S. Churton St., Hillsboro, NC 27278   (919) 732-5600
New American cuisine. A charming full-service restaurant in the Raleigh/Durham area, located in an historic district across from The Old Courthouse. Veg dishes include pita sandwiches or lasagna for lunch; lasagna, fajitas, stir-fry or pasta primavera for dinner, and salads. A seasonal menu that changes to accommodate the availability of organic produce. Homemade Carolina Cheesecake. Entertainment on weekends. No lunch served on Saturday and Sunday; no dinner Monday and Tuesday. Take-out available. Reservations requested. FS,V,A,J,CC,$$

PITTSBORO

Triangle Macrobiotic Association
50 Fearrington Post, Pittsboro, NC 27312   (919) 542-1250
The association will cook macrobiotic meals by reservation only. I,M,$$

RALEIGH

Hector's
6325 Falls Neuse Rd., Sutton Square Plaza
Raleigh, NC 27615   (919) 872-7161
A mostly Lebanese and mostly vegan restaurant run by people involved in the local vegetarian community. Vegetarians gather for meetings here, and Hector's also caters and supplies food to local natural food stores and co-ops. Specialties are hummus, falafel, pasta, salads, cheese and broccoli pies and soups. Everything's low in cholesterol and fat. Closed Sunday. I,V,A,CH,$-$$

Irregardless
901 W. Morgan St., Raleigh, NC 27603   (919) 833-9920
Natural foods. Menu changes daily—call for recorded message. Entertainment nightly. FS,I,A,CC,CH,$$

The Museum Cafe
2110 Blue Ridge Rd. (lower level)
Raleigh, NC 27607   **(919) 833-3548**

Everything is low in cholesterol, and everything is freshly made. There's a vegetarian special every day, plus veggie bean burgers and quesadillas. Open daily. FS,I,A,CC,$-$$

OHIO

AKRON

Mustard Seed Market Cafe
3885 W. Market St., Akron, OH 44313   **(216) 666-7333**

Natural foods deli and cafeteria with seating. Entertainment on weekends is planned for summer of 1989. I,V,M,N,CC,CH,$-$$$

BOARDMAN

Nature's Nook
5418 South Ave., Boardman, OH 44512   **(216) 783-1293**

Natural foods. Full-service restaurant and specialty store, with Mexican and Italian dishes. Entertainment Friday and Saturday nights. Closed Sunday and Monday. FS,N,CH,$$

CINCINNATI

Alpha
204 W. McMillan, Cincinnati, OH 45219   **(513) 281-6559**

Natural foods. Open daily. FS,SB,I,A,CC,CH,$$

Arnold's Bar & Grill
210 E. Eighth St., Cincinnati, OH 45202   **(513) 421-6234**

American. Always a vegetarian entrée on the menu. Music regularly; art displayed in dining area. Courtyard for outdoor eating in nice weather. Old establishment with lots of character. FS,V,A,CH,$$

KEY TO DINING GUIDE
• Vegetarian food only

FS Full service	**V** Vegan options	**CC** Major credit cards accepted
CAF Cafeteria/buffet	**M** Macrobiotic options	**CH** Children welcome
SB Salad bar	**A** Alcoholic drinks	**$** Average dinner under $5
I Informal	**N** Nonalcoholic beer/wine	**$$** Average dinner $5 to $10
F Formal	**J** Freshly squeezed juices	**$$$** Average dinner over $10

OHIO

Bacchus
1401 Elm St., Cincinnati, OH 45210   (513) 421-8314

International. Grilled eggplant a specialty. Usually closed Monday through Wednesday, but call: sometimes open because entertainment is planned. FS,I,V,A,CC,CH,$$$

Chin Dynasty
4609 Vine St., Cincinnati, OH 45217   (513) 641-2888

Chinese. The vegetarian menu is "excellent," according to one of *VT's* editors. FS,V,A,J,$$

The Choice Is Yours
825 Delta Ave., Cincinnati, OH 45226   (513) 871-8680

Neighborhood natural food store/restaurant, friendly and delicious, according to local press. Daily pasta special, stir-fry, three salads and soup of the day. Cheese made by local Amish. A few ultra-decadent desserts. Lunch daily; dinner Wednesday through Saturday. No smoking. FS,I,$$

Myra's Dionysus
121 Calhoun St., Cincinnati, OH 45219   (513) 961-1578

International. A deli case at the front door displays menu items. Homemade yogurt and pastas, soups, eggplant creations, hummus, tabouli and rice salads. Located on the southern edge of the University of Cincinnati campus. Open daily. FS,I,V,A,J,CC,$-$$

New World Foodshop
347 Ludlow Ave., Cincinnati, OH 45220   (513) 861-1101

Middle Eastern. All-natural macrobiotic, Middle Eastern specials. Carryout available. Closed Sunday. FS,I,J,M,$

COLUMBUS

• King Avenue Coffeehouse
247 King Ave., Columbus, OH 43201   (614) 294-8287

Good variety of sandwiches, soups, salads and daily specials. Many vegan dishes. Eggs from free-range hens. Monthly art exhibits from local and regional artists. Entertainment on Friday and Saturday nights. Closed Monday. FS,I,V,N,CC,$$

DAYTON

Courtyard
Courtyard Plaza, Dayton, OH 45402   (513) 461-3211

OHIO

The Trolley Stop
530 E. Fifth St., Dayton, OH 45402 (513) 224-1839

Natural and gourmet foods. A few vegetarian entrées, and often a vegetarian soup. It's actually in an old trolley car, and you can eat on the outdoor patio as well. They'll even provide you with magazines and newspapers to read while you dine. Open daily. Brunch on Sunday. FS,I,A,N,J,CC,CH,$

KETTERING

• Kettering Medical Center Cafeteria
3535 Southern Blvd., Kettering, OH 45429 (513) 296-7262

Open daily for three vegetarian meals. CAF,SB,CH,$

MIAMISBURG

• Sycamore Hospital
2150 Leiter Rd.
Miamisburg, OH 45342 (513) 866-2984 ext. 6063

Natural foods. Limited public seating. Three vegetarian meals daily. CAF,SB,J,CH,$

RICHMOND HEIGHTS

Akai Hana
5222 Wilson Mills Rd.
Richmond Heights, OH 44143 (216) 473-2345

Japanese. Sushi. Open daily for vegan and macrobiotic meals. Closed the first Monday of the month. FS,I,V,M,A,J,CC,CH,$$$

TOLEDO

Bassett's
3301 W. Central, Toledo, OH 43606 (419) 531-0334

Natural foods. In business over 18 years; serves vegetarian and vegan lunches. Closed Sunday. FS,SB,I,V,M,N,CC,CH,$$

KEY TO DINING GUIDE
• Vegetarian food only

FS Full service	**V** Vegan options	**CC** Major credit cards accepted
CAF Cafeteria/buffet	**M** Macrobiotic options	**CH** Children welcome
SB Salad bar	**A** Alcoholic drinks	**$** Average dinner under $5
I Informal	**N** Nonalcoholic beer/wine	**$$** Average dinner $5 to $10
F Formal	**J** Freshly squeezed juices	**$$$** Average dinner over $10

OKLAHOMA

Jalmer's
1488 Sylvania Ave., Toledo, OH 43612   **(419) 478-7918**
Juice bar. Some ovo-lacto vegetarian dishes. Closed Sunday. FS,I,J,CC,$

YELLOW SPRINGS

Wind's Cafe
230 Xenia Ave., Yellow Springs, OH 45387   **(513) 767-1144**
Natural foods. A creative menu in an artistically inspired setting. At least one vegetarian special daily; pasta, stir-fry and scrambled tofu are examples. Homemade breads and desserts. Located in an old house with a cozy fireplace. Casual. Dine on patio in good weather. Carryout available. Open daily. FS,I,A,N,CC,CH,$$$

OKLAHOMA

NORMAN

The Earth Natural Foods
309 S. Flood, Norman, OK 73069   **(405) 364-3551**
Juice bar. Sandwiches and salads to go. Fresh juices. Limited inside seating, but you can eat outdoors at the picnic table in good weather. V,M,J,CC,CH,$

Lovelight Restaurant
529 Buchanan St., Norman, OK 73069   **(405) 364-2073**
Try the lunchtime sandwich and salad "factory," where you pick the ingredients. The after-five menu offers a veggie burger, vegetable plate, pasta, beans and rice, and a special. Counter service. Open daily. I,V,A,CH,$

OKLAHOMA CITY

The Earth Natural Foods
1101 N.W. 49th St.
Oklahoma City, OK 73118   **(405) 840-0502**
Natural foods. Hot vegetarian specials daily. Soups, salads, sandwiches, baked potatoes and tacos, all served quickly. Casual setting. Open daily for lunch and dinner; Sunday for lunch only. Located two blocks from Interstate 44. FS,V,M,J,CC,CH,$

OREGON

ASHLAND

- **North Light**
  36 S. 2nd St., Ashland, OR 97520   (503) 482-9463

  Enjoy international specials on the patio of this cooperatively-run vegan restaurant (cheese or yogurt can be ordered on the side as a condiment): Oriental Sauté, Tofu Steak, Mexican Platter, sandwiches and salads. Organic, locally produced food used whenever possible; and filtered water is used in cooking. Open daily for breakfast, lunch and dinner. Children's portions available. FS,I,V,A,CC,CH,$$

CORVALLIS

- **Nearly Normals Gonzo Cuisine**
  109 N.W. 15th St., Corvallis, OR 97330   (503) 753-0791

  Natural foods. Veggie burgers, smoothies, nightly specials. Guest chefs on occasion. Beautiful outdoor summer dining. Closed Sunday. FS,I,V,M,A,N,J,CH,$-$$

EUGENE

- **The Vegetarian**
  270 W. Eighth Ave., Eugene, OR 97401   (503) 342-4335

  Full-service restaurant. Entrées, potato and salad bar, sandwiches and fresh juices. Downtown, near the Hilton Conference Center. Closed weekends. FS,CAF,SB,I,CC,CH,$

PORTLAND

- **The Daily Grind**
  4026 S.E. Hawthorne Blvd.
  Portland, OR 97214   (503) 233-5521

  Natural foods. Cafeteria line for lunch; salad bar all day. Daily: soups, chili, sandwiches, tostados, frozen yogurt. Open for lunch and dinner Monday through Thursday. Lunch only on Friday. Closed weekends. FS,CAF,I,J,CC,$

KEY TO DINING GUIDE
• Vegetarian food only

FS Full service	**V** Vegan options	**CC** Major credit cards accepted
CAF Cafeteria/buffet	**M** Macrobiotic options	**CH** Children welcome
SB Salad bar	**A** Alcoholic drinks	**$** Average dinner under $5
I Informal	**N** Nonalcoholic beer/wine	**$$** Average dinner $5 to $10
F Formal	**J** Freshly squeezed juices	**$$$** Average dinner over $10

PENNSYLVANIA

Ezekiel's Wheel
1201 N.W. 21st, Portland, OR 97209   **(503) 228-7528**

Not a vegetarian restaurant, but breakfast features pancakes, waffles, cereals and whole-grain granolas. A few veggie soups and sandwiches—including a veggie sub—are offered for lunch or dinner. Entertainment nightly. Closed Sunday. CAF,I,V,J,CH,$

• Healthway Food Center
524 S.W. 5th, Portland, OR 97204   **(503) 226-2941**

Juice bar. Located in the center of the city. Vegetarian sandwiches, soups, juices. Closed weekends. Open since 1938. I,N,CC,CH,$

• Portland Adventist Medical Center
10123 Market St., Portland, OR 97216   **(503) 257-2500**

Natural foods. Open daily, but no breakfast served on weekends. CAF, I,CH,$

SALEM

Off Center Cafe
1741 Center St. N.E., Salem, OR 97301   **(503) 363-9245**

Natural foods. FS,V,M,J,$

PENNSYLVANIA

EMMAUS

• Food Naturally
301 Main St., Emmaus, PA 18049   **(215) 967-3600**

Natural foods. Mostly macrobiotic cuisine. One-of-a-kind in the area. Also a macro and veggie natural food store: books, cookware, natural cosmetics, supplements. Closed Sunday. Macrobiotic dinner every Wednesday evening. FS,V,M,$$

GETTYSBURG

• Nature's Food
48 Baltimore St., Gettysburg, PA 17325   **(717) 334-7723**

Juice bar. Take-out available. Open for lunch only. Sandwiches, salads, smoothies; hot soups during the winter. Closed Sunday. Personal checks accepted. Handicapped-accessible. V,J,CH,$

PENNSYLVANIA

MONROEVILLE

- **Vegetarian Delight**
  4141 Old William Penn Highway
  Monroeville, PA 15146   (412) 372-7404

  Mostly vegan South and North Indian food. For $3.49, you can fill your plate and your tummy with the Vegetable Plate, featuring a chickpea, yogurt, rice and vegetable dish. Try the masala dosa; it rated a mention in the *Pittsburgh Press*. Open for dinner Wednesday through Sunday. Open for lunch on weekends. Closed Monday and Tuesday. CH,$$

NEW CUMBERLAND

- **Avatar's Golden Nectar**
  321 Bridge St., New Cumberland, PA 17070   (717) 774-7215

  Lacto-vegetarian dishes. Closed Sunday and Monday. FS,N,CH,$$

NEWFOUNDLAND

- **White Cloud**
  Rte. 447 (Panther Rd.), R.D. 1, Box 215
  Newfoundland, PA 18445   (717) 676-3162

  Natural foods. White Cloud is part of a country inn set in 50 acres of woods on top of a mountain in the Poconos. Its specialty? "Peace, quiet and good food." Also homemade quick breads, apple butter, soups. Open daily from Memorial Day through Labor Day; other times by reservation. FS,SB,I,V,M,CC,CH,$$$

PENNS CREEK

Walnut Acres
Walnut Acres Road, Penns Creek, PA 17862   (717) 837-0601

Organic salad bar features a variety of soups and whole-grain salads. (Beware—some of the soups are meat-based.) SB,I,N,CC,CH,$

KEY TO DINING GUIDE
• Vegetarian food only

FS Full service	**V** Vegan options	**CC** Major credit cards accepted
CAF Cafeteria/buffet	**M** Macrobiotic options	**CH** Children welcome
SB Salad bar	**A** Alcoholic drinks	**$** Average dinner under $5
I Informal	**N** Nonalcoholic beer/wine	**$$** Average dinner $5 to $10
F Formal	**J** Freshly squeezed juices	**$$$** Average dinner over $10

PENNSYLVANIA

PHILADELPHIA

- **Basic Four Vegetarian Snack Bar**
  446 S. 55th St., Philadelphia, PA 19143 (215) 440-0991
  Fast food for healthy eaters. Try soya "chicken" salad, veggie burgers, and all-vegetarian soups. Closed Sunday. Call for hours. V,$

  The Bourse
  21 S. Fifth St., Philadelphia, PA 19106 (215) 627-2406
  Italian. Open daily. FS,A,J,$

  Campus India
  4015 Chestnut St., Philadelphia, PA 19104 (215) 243-9718
  Indian. Open daily for lunch and dinner. FS,CC,CH,$$

  Eden
  1527 Chestnut, Philadelphia, PA 19102 (215) 972-0400
  All-natural soups, salads and whole-wheat baked goods. Special entrées include marinated tofu stir-fry and vegetable lasagna. Located in center city. Closed Sunday. CAF,V,A,N,CH,$$

  Eden
  3701 Chestnut St., Philadelphia, PA 19104 (215) 387-2471
  In West Philly. See entry above. Open daily. CAF,I,V,A,N,CC,CH,$$

- **European Dairy Market**
  2000 Sansom St., Philadelphia, PA 19103 (215) 568-1298
  Kosher vegetarian restaurant offering such traditional items as homemade cheese blintzes, borscht, potato pierogis and mushroom barley soup. Violinist every evening. Closed Friday nights and Saturday. FS,I,N,CC,CH,$$

- **Govinda's**
  529 South St., Philadelphia, PA 19147 (215) 829-0077
  This all-vegetarian restaurant serves international cuisine, especially Indian and American. The menu also includes enchiladas, lasagna, eggplant dishes and daily specials. There's informal, all-you-can-eat dining downstairs, and full-service, formal dining upstairs. Open daily. FS,SB,CAF,V,M,CH,$$

  Home Grown Foods
  Andorra Shopping Center
  Henry Avenue and Cathedral Road
  Philadelphia, PA 19128 (215) 487-1616

Natural foods. A gourmet restaurant with many vegetarian entrées and a beautiful selection of vegetarian salads. Three to four homemade veg soups daily. Nightly stir-fries. Seasonal menu includes bean enchiladas, Mediterranean pasta dishes, hummus, spanakopita and curried eggplant. On Thursday you can get a macrobiotic special dinner—soup to dessert. Sunday brunch includes scrambled tofu and a nondairy, no-egg pancake. Bring your own alchoholic drinks. FS,I,V,M,N,J,CC,CH,$$

Kawabata
2453-55 Grant Ave., Philadelphia, PA 19114   (215) 969-8225

Japanese. Open daily. Reservations recommended. FS,V,M,A,CC,$$$

Kawagiku
110 Chestnut St., Philadelphia, PA 19106   (215) 928-9564

Japanese. Many completely vegetarian offerings, including sushi and salad bar. Open daily. FS,SB,V,M,A,CC,CH,$$$

Keyflower Dining Room
20 S. 36th St., Philadelphia, PA 19104   (215) 386-2207

Located in the Divine Tracy Hotel. Inexpensive, simple, vegetarian food. Lunch and dinner entreés are regularly less than $2. Desserts are homemade. Menu changes daily. Closed weekends; call for hours. CAF,I,V,N,$

Knave of Hearts
230 South St., Philadelphia, PA 19147   (215) 922-3956

International. Thai, French and American cuisine. Eclectic menu includes baked artichoke casserole, nut loaves, lasagna, seitan with leeks and garlic. FS,A,J,CC,CH,$$$

Le Petit Cafe
8617 Germantown Ave.
Philadelphia, PA 19118   (215) 247-3215

Natural foods. The cafe is inside the Concept Natural Foods store. Daily sandwich specials. Almost all veg. Mostly take-out, but a patio for dining in nice weather. Closed Sunday. A,J,CC,$

Middle East
126 Chestnut St., Philadelphia, PA 19106   (215) 922-1003

KEY TO DINING GUIDE
• Vegetarian food only

FS Full service	**V** Vegan options	**CC** Major credit cards accepted
CAF Cafeteria/buffet	**M** Macrobiotic options	**CH** Children welcome
SB Salad bar	**A** Alcoholic drinks	**$** Average dinner under $5
I Informal	**N** Nonalcoholic beer/wine	**$$** Average dinner $5 to $10
F Formal	**J** Freshly squeezed juices	**$$$** Average dinner over $10

Middle Eastern cuisine, including many vegetarian options like salads and tabouli. Entertainment nightly. Dancing on Friday and Saturday nights. Open seven days a week. FS,I,A,CC,CH,$$$

Saladalley
1720 Sansom St., Philadelphia, PA 19103   (215) 564-0767

Natural gourmet. Besides salads, vegetarians can try the grilled eggplant sandwich or sautéed vegetables and pasta. The vegetarian soups are all made with veggie broth. Several other locations in the Philly area. (See below.) Open daily. FS,SB,I,V,A,N,J,CH,$

Saladalley/Temple University
1926 Park Mall, Philadelphia, PA 19122   (215) 787-5151

See entry above.

Saladalley
4040 Locust, Philadelphia, PA 19104   (215) 349-7644

See Sansom Street listing.

Saladalley
North East Shopping Center, 9173 Roosevelt Blvd.
Philadelphia, PA 19114   (215) 969-5969

See Sansom Street listing.

Saladalley
Bourse Bldg., 21 S. 5th St.
Philadelphia, PA 19106   (215) 627-2406

See Sansom Street listing.

South East Chinese Restaurant
1000 Arch St., Philadelphia, PA 19107   (215) 629-9095

Vegetarian entrées. Pritikin-style mock lichee duck with seitan and sea vegetables. No MSG. Open daily. FS,M,CC,CH,$$

Tang Yean
220 N. 10th St., Philadelphia, PA 19107   (215) 925-3993

Chinese. Natural foods à la Orient, in an atmosphere not unlike an intimate European cafe—no hanging lanterns or rice paper dividers here. Order from the vegetarian menu, but ask about oyster sauce, because it's used liberally in the seasonings. No MSG, all natural, fresh ingredients. Good reviews from the local press. Open daily. FS,V,M,N,CC,CH,$$

PENNSYLVANIA

- **Thai Royal Barge**
123 S. 23rd St., Philadelphia, PA 19103   (215) 567-2542
Thai vegan. FS,V,A,CC,CH,$$

Tuly's
603 S. Fourth St., Philadelphia, PA 19147   (215) 922-1003
Middle Eastern and American. Will cater to vegetarians. Home-baked pastries, lentil soup, omelets, spinach pie, salads. Open daily for dinner. FS,A,CC,$$$

PITTSBURGH

- **The Vegetarian Gourmet**
414 Semple St., Pittsburgh, PA 15213   (412) 687-2045
The Vegetarian Gourmet is owned and operated by The League of Devotees, a non-profit, interfaith spiritual community. There's no meat, fish, eggs or alcoholic beverages on the menu. For lunch, try the pita sandwiches or side orders of samosas or pakoras. For dinner, there are three different buffets, plus lasagna, eggplant parmigiana, quiche, chili, falafel, veggie burgers, steamed veggies and the veggie plate. Beverages include lassi, milkshakes and carrot juice, plus teas and sodas. And there's a dessert menu with apple crisp, fruit cakes, cheesecakes (including a non-dairy one), halva, baklava and ice creams. Open for lunch on weekdays; open for dinner Monday through Saturday. Closed Sundays. FS,CAF,SB,V,J,$$

POCONO SUMMIT

Near East
Rte. 940, Box 201
Pocono Summit, PA 18346   (717) 839-8993

Lebanese. Vegetarian soups and specials. Entertainment on Saturday nights. FS,I,A,N,J,CH,$$

KEY TO DINING GUIDE
• Vegetarian food only

FS Full service	**V** Vegan options	**CC** Major credit cards accepted
CAF Cafeteria/buffet	**M** Macrobiotic options	**CH** Children welcome
SB Salad bar	**A** Alcoholic drinks	**$** Average dinner under $5
I Informal	**N** Nonalcoholic beer/wine	**$$** Average dinner $5 to $10
F Formal	**J** Freshly squeezed juices	**$$$** Average dinner over $10

PENNSYLVANIA

QUAKERTOWN

It's Only Natural
R.D. 3, Clymer Rd., Quakertown, PA 18951   (215) 536-8005

Gourmet natural foods. Counter service and take-out. Closed Sunday and Monday. SB,I,V,M,J,CC,CH,$

READING

• Nature's Garden Natural Foods
Reading Mall, Reading, PA 19606   (215) 779-3000

Snack bar Closed Sunday. No eggs used. V,M,CC,$

SPRINGFIELD

Saladalley
Springfield Square, 1001 E. Baltimore Pike
Springfield, PA 19064   (215) 328-5880

See Philadelphia listing. No sulfites.

STROUDSBURG

• Earthlight Supplies
Quaker Plaza, Stroudsburg, PA 18360   (717) 424-6760

A natural food store with a small snack bar. Cafeteria-style service, and a glass-enclosed seating area. Soup and salads every day; usually a casserole as well. The American vegetable stew is fantastic. Open 10 a.m. to 4:30 p.m. Closed Sunday. Personal checks accepted. CAF,I,V,M,N,CH,$

SOUTH CAROLINA

CHARLESTON

Pinckney Cafe & Espresso
18 Pinckney St., Charleston, SC 29401   (803) 577-0961

An informal two-room restaurant. Order at the window and a server will bring food to your table. Try the black-bean burrito or an omelet and have a drink made with Red Zinger tea and apple juice. They make their own pimento cheese. Live music on weekends. Vegan items always on the menu, but the staff will be glad to prepare something special for you, macro, vegan or otherwise. Closed Sunday. FS,I,V,M,$$

SOUTH CAROLINA

The Primerose House
332 E. Bay St., Charleston, SC 29401 (803) 723-2954

Near the waterfront. Not a vegetarian restaurant, but a vegetarian or vegan dish can be prepared with advance notice. Emphasis on fresh, locally grown produce and local fish. Regular veg entrées (though the menu changes about every six weeks, reflecting seasonal foods) include wild mushroom crêpes, filo with vegetables and sauce, and three-layer vegetable tureen. Reservations recommended on weekends. Open daily. Brunch on Sunday. FS,I,A,CC,$$$

COLUMBIA

The Basil Pot
928 Main St., Columbia, SC 29201 (803) 799-0928

Natural foods. Creative menu with large selection of everyday items. International cuisine, organic rice, beans and produce a priority. Specialties are whole-wheat pizza and baked goods. Scheduled macrobiotic specials. Art shows in restaurant. FS,V,M,A,N,J,CC,CH,$$

Nice-N-Natural
1217 College St., Columbia, SC 29201 (803) 799-3471

Lunch only. Fresh, natural foods. Nice 'n' friendly in a house where the atmosphere is relaxed and homey. Mostly vegetarian dishes. Specialties include fruit salads, spinach salads, sandwiches. Known for its limeade, mint iced tea and frozen yogurt. Closed weekends. I,V,J,CH,$

GREENVILLE

Annie's
121 S. Main St., Greenville, SC 29601 (803) 271-4872

PENDLETON

Farmers Hall Tearoom
#1 on The Square, Pendleton, SC 29670 (803) 646-7024

Natural foods. Daily vegetarian specials. Salads, home-baked breads. Reservations recommended. FS,N,$$

KEY TO DINING GUIDE
- Vegetarian food only

FS Full service	**V** Vegan options	**CC** Major credit cards accepted
CAF Cafeteria/buffet	**M** Macrobiotic options	**CH** Children welcome
SB Salad bar	**A** Alcoholic drinks	**$** Average dinner under $5
I Informal	**N** Nonalcoholic beer/wine	**$$** Average dinner $5 to $10
F Formal	**J** Freshly squeezed juices	**$$$** Average dinner over $10

SOUTH DAKOTA

YANKTON

Body Guard
Yankton Mall, 21st and Broadway
Yankton, SD 57078 (605) 665-3482
(Formerly Fountain of Youth.) Restaurant and deli. Homemade muffins.
FS,I,J,CC,CH,$

TENNESSEE

CHATTANOOGA

- **Country Life**
3748-54 Ringgold Rd.
Chattanooga, TN 37412 (615) 622-2451
Natural foods. No dairy or eggs. FS,V,J,CC,$

COOKEVILLE

Greenside Grocery
201 S. Willow, Cookeville, TN 38501 (615) 526-4860
Juice bar. An oasis of good, natural food, almost all vegetarian. (There are chicken salad and tuna salad sandwiches on the menu.) Accommodating service. Closed Sunday. CAF,I,V,N,J,CH,$

JOHNSON CITY

Eatwell Cafe
216 E. Main St., Johnson City, TN 37601 (615) 929-8570
Natural foods. Formerly New World Foods. Lunch only: soups, salads, sandwiches, chili and smoothies. With the exception of one tuna sandwich on the menu, it's all vegetarian. Macrobiotic lunch served on Thursday. Will accommodate your special diet. Closed Sunday. FS,I,V,M,N,J,CH,$

KNOXVILLE

Chili's
7304 Kingston Pike, Knoxville, TN 37919 (615) 584-8195
Natural Mexican-style food. Vegetarian tacos, nachos. Open daily.
FS,V,A,N,CC,CH,$$

China Inn
6450 Kingston Pike, Knoxville, TN 37919   (615) 588-7815

El Palenque
6701 Kingston Pike, Knoxville, TN 37919   (615) 584-9807

Mexican. No lard used. Veg enchiladas, bean burritos, nachos, Spanish rice and beans, tacos, chalupas and tostadas. Open daily. FS,A,N, CC,CH,$-$$

Falafel Hut
601 15th St., Knoxville, TN 37916   (615) 522-4963

Middle Eastern. "The name doesn't do it justice—it's not small," said a VT reader. Most vegetarian dishes are eggless, and the chef will accommodate vegans. Specialties are hummus, tabouli, salads, vegetable stew. Vegetarian dinner specials every Thursday; sometimes other nights, too. Open daily. Thirty-six kinds of imported beer. FS,I,V,A,N,J,CC,CH,$-$$

Famous Gyros
3000 N. Mall Rd., Knoxville, TN 37924   (615) 523-4642

Fast food. The Tennessee Vegetarian Society recommends this gyros establishment because of its vegetarian pita. Salads, too. Counter service only. Open daily. CH,$

Fiesta Cantina
6600 Kingston Pike, Knoxville, TN 37919   (615) 588-9971

Mexican. Vegetarian entrées; no lard. Monday night is all-you-can-eat night. FS,CC,$

Friday's
1613 Downtown West Blvd.,
Knoxville, TN 37919   (615) 690-3273

Vegetables primavera or smoothies in a lively atmosphere. FS,A,CC,$$

Golden Buddha
4816 Kingston Pike, Knoxville, TN 37919   (615) 588-5521

Mandarin. Mixed vegetables, vegetarian eggrolls and soups. A good place to eat, according to the Tennessee Vegetarian Society. FS,$-$$

KEY TO DINING GUIDE
- Vegetarian food only

FS Full service
CAF Cafeteria/buffet
SB Salad bar
I Informal
F Formal

V Vegan options
M Macrobiotic options
A Alcoholic drinks
N Nonalcoholic beer/wine
J Freshly squeezed juices

CC Major credit cards accepted
CH Children welcome
$ Average dinner under $5
$$ Average dinner $5 to $10
$$$ Average dinner over $10

TENNESSEE

Hawkeye's Corner
1717 White Ave., Knoxville, TN 37916   (615) 524-5326
Natural foods. Dine in a refurbished plant-filled home, to live entertainment (Tuesday through Saturday nights). Top off the meal with a freshly baked dessert. Sodium-conscious cooking. Several vegan entrées. FS,V, A,CC,CH,$$

House of Chan
3701 Chapman Hwy., Knoxville, TN 37920   (615) 577-3255
Chinese. Fast-food service, but it's not fast food: Tofu Cantonese, Tofu with Szechwan Sauce, egg foo yung, chow mein. Carryouts. Open daily. I,CH,$

La Paz
8025 Kingston Pike, Knoxville, TN 37919   (615) 690-5250
Mexican. Considered among the best Mexican restaurants in the area by local vegetarians. Lively atmosphere. Closed Monday. FS,A,CC,CH,$$

Master's
5000 Kingston Pike, Knoxville, TN 37919   (615) 588-7803
Not a vegetarian restaurant, but will accommodate a veg diet. FS,A,CC, $$

Mexicali Rose
6500 Kingston Pike, Knoxville, TN 37919   (615) 588-9191
Mexican. Three vegetarian dinners nightly. Closed Sunday and Monday. FS,A,CH,$

Mom 'n' Dad's Eatin' & Drinkin'
1706 Cumberland, Knoxville, TN 37660   (615) 524-4681
Natural foods. Vegetarian buffet. FS,A,CC,$

Richard's: An American Cafe
5200 Kingston Pike, Knoxville, TN 37919   (615) 584-1323
"New food for a new age," says the menu. Innovative and eclectic macrobiotic menu, but be aware that the restaurant's specialty is wild game. The macrobiotic menu features appetizers, miso soups, salads, Raspberry Tempeh with Lotus, Seitan with Mushrooms and Leeks, Burdock-Mushroom Stew, several other unusual dishes. Carryout available. The baby grand in the dining room provides lovely entertainment in the winter months. Closed Sundays. Located in Homberg Place shopping center. FS,V,M,A,CC,CH,$$-$$$

Silver Spoon Cafe
7240 Kingston Pike, Knoxville, TN 37919   (615) 584-1066

Natural foods. Many Italian vegetarian specials. Outdoor eating area. Open daily. FS,A,CC,$$

Stephen's
7240 Kingston Pike, Knoxville, TN 37919   (615) 588-5998

Italian. Vegetarian pizza and many other Italian veg favorites. Open daily. FS,A,CC,$$

Tillie's on Homberg
5004 Homberg Dr., Knoxville, TN 37919   (615) 588-6689

Natural foods. Sandwiches, soups, pasta salads. Patio dining. FS,CC,$

Wong's Palace
4009 Chapman Hwy., Knoxville, TN 37920   (615) 573-4580

Chinese. Good veggies and tofu in a pleasant atmosphere. Will accommodate special orders. Open daily for lunch and dinner, but no lunch on Saturday. FS,A,CC

MADISON

- ## Tennessee Christian Medical Center
  500 Hospital Dr.
  Madison, TN 37115   (615) 865-2373 ext. 4518

  Open for three meals every day. CAF,SB,J,CH,$

MEMPHIS

- ## Healthy Trading Company
  1783 Union Ave., Memphis, TN 38104   (901) 278-6444

  Juice bar at the back of a natural food store. Eat inside or out. Try the hottest selling item on the menu—Drew's Delight, a huge sandwich sporting avocado, raw milk cheese, spicy mayo, tomato, sprouts and tamari-roasted sesame seeds on whole-wheat bran bread. Lunches only. You can bring your own alcoholic drinks. N,J,CC,$

KEY TO DINING GUIDE
• Vegetarian food only

FS Full service	**V** Vegan options	**CC** Major credit cards accepted
CAF Cafeteria/buffet	**M** Macrobiotic options	**CH** Children welcome
SB Salad bar	**A** Alcoholic drinks	**$** Average dinner under $5
I Informal	**N** Nonalcoholic beer/wine	**$$** Average dinner $5 to $10
F Formal	**J** Freshly squeezed juices	**$$$** Average dinner over $10

TENNESSEE

NASHVILLE

- **Country Life**
  1917-19 Division St., Nashville, TN 37203   **(615) 327-3695**
  Here's a unique idea: A vegetarian restaurant as an adjunct to a physician-staffed clinic. Buffet-style with vegetarian cooking classes in the evenings. Closed weekends. CAF,SB,I,V,CH,$$

  El Palenque
  4407 Nolensville Rd., Nashville, TN 37211   **(615) 832-9978**
  See Knoxville listing.

  Slice of Life
  1811 Division St., Nashville, TN 37203   **(615) 329-2525**
  Creative and original recipes containing no refined sugar or artificial preservatives and additives. Delicious macrobiotic fare features moros, domburi and even macro cookies. Mexican dishes are a specialty, and the breakfast menu includes a wide selection of omelets, whole-grain waffles and Danish, and soysage. Organic wines and a local "all-natural" beer are part of the beverage selection. Open daily with brunch all day Sunday. Also a whole-grain bakery. FS,I,V,M,A,N,J,CC,CH,$$

  Windows on the Cumberland
  112 2nd Avenue N., Nashville, TN 37201   **(615) 244-7944**
  Carry-out and deli. Located in a mall in a recently restored historic section of downtown Nashville, this quaint and rustic cafe overlooks the Cumberland River. Windows also sponsors entertainment and poetry readings Thursday through Sunday (small cover charge may apply). Delicious sandwiches, steamed veggies on brown rice, beans and rice, homemade soup, quiche and fruit salad. An intriguing selection of imported beers. Lunch only Monday through Thursday. Lunch and dinner Friday through Sunday. Hours vary. CAF,I,V,M,A,CH,$

TEXAS

AMARILLO

Back to Eden
2441 I-40 W., Amarillo, TX 79109   **(806) 353-7476**
Juice bar in the Eat Rite Health Food Store. Limited seating. Soups and sandwiches. Closed Sunday. SB,I,V,CC,CH,$$

TEXAS

AUSTIN

Martin Brothers Cafe
914 N. Lamar, Austin, TX 78703   **(512) 476-7601**

Mexican vegetarian, but they call it "Texican": lots of black beans in chalupas, tacos, nachos. With a few exceptions, it's almost all vegetarian. Soups, chili, sandwiches, smoothies, frozen desserts, yogurt and a deli. Homemade salad dressings, ice cream and other goodies. Located in the Whole Foods Market. Outdoor patio. V,M,J,$

Mother's Cafe & Garden
4215 Duval, Austin, TX 78727   **(512) 451-3944**

Natural foods. Features a wide variety of international selections. Soups and salads noted to be "best in town." The plant-filled garden/greenhouse provides a unique, relaxing environment. FS,V,M,A,J,CC,$$

Treaty Oak Cafe
1101 W. Fifth St., Austin, TX 78703   **(512) 482-8226**

Southwestern natural foods. Pasta and desserts are the specialties. Fresh soups, whole breads, a wide range of vegetarian entrées and unique enchiladas served in an open, plant-filled dining room. Closed Sunday evenings. FS,I,V,M,A,N,CC,$$

DALLAS

Bluebonnet Cafe
2218 Lower Greenville Ave.
Dallas, TX 75206   **(214) 828-0052**

Tex-Mex and international. Everything's fresh here. Veggie enchiladas, burgers, lasagna, submarines, plate specials. Nondairy soups and some vegan entrées. Breakfast served daily. Counter service and take-out available. SB,I,A,N,J,CC,CH,$$

Fitness Foods
Suite 112, 7879 Spring Valley
Dallas, TX 75240   **(214) 960-8658**

Cafe in a natural food store. With the exception of one tuna and one chicken sandwich, it's all vegetarian. Sandwiches, veggie burgers. "Best salad bar in town," according to a *VT* reader. One hot entrée daily. The Whole Wheat Tortilla Wrapper is a big seller. Only filtered water used in food preparation. Open every day for lunch. I,V,N,CC,CH,$-$$

KEY TO DINING GUIDE
• Vegetarian food only

FS Full service	**V** Vegan options	**CC** Major credit cards accepted
CAF Cafeteria/buffet	**M** Macrobiotic options	**CH** Children welcome
SB Salad bar	**A** Alcoholic drinks	**$** Average dinner under $5
I Informal	**N** Nonalcoholic beer/wine	**$$** Average dinner $5 to $10
F Formal	**J** Freshly squeezed juices	**$$$** Average dinner over $10

TEXAS

- **Francis Simun's**
  1507 N. Garrett Ave., Dallas, TX 75206   **(214) 824-4910**
  Natural foods. Only organic products, according to the proprietor, with an emphasis on macrobiotic foods. No dairy or eggs used here. Homemade breads, including cotton bread, and muffins, donuts and coffee cakes. Try the house tea, too. Reservations required. Fixed price for meals, but you can also eat à la carte. Closed Sunday. FS,SB,I,V,M,J,CC,CH,$

  H & M Natural Foods
  9191 Forest Lane, Dallas, TX 75243   **(214) 231-6083**
  Natural foods cafe. Sandwiches, salad bar. Try the Amazing Avocado Sandwich. Counter service and take-out. Open daily. SB,I,J,CC,$

- **Kalachandji's**
  5430 Gurley Ave., Dallas, TX 75223   **(214) 821-1048**
  Natural foods. Adjacent to the beautiful Hare Krishna Palace, the only temple in north Texas, a tourist stop. Year-round dining in the courtyard patio. The restaurant features primarily Indian cuisine, but also has specials like spinach lasagna, eggplant moussaka and batter-fried veggies. No eggs in anything, and most dishes dairyless. Reviewed in *VT* as one of the best vegetarian restaurants in the country. Children's portions available. Dinner only Tuesday through Sunday. All-you-can-eat buffet Sunday night for $5. Closed Monday. Off the beaten path, so it's better to call for directions. FS,I,V,CC,CH,$$

  Macrobiotic Restaurant of Dallas
  850 S. Greenville Ave., Dallas, TX 75081   **(214) 669-8328**
  Open daily for lunch and Thursday for dinner. Only filtered water used in the preparation of all dishes, including soups and teas. I,V,M,N,CC,CH,$$

  Plaza Health Food Store
  6924 Snider Plaza, Dallas, TX 75205   **(214) 363-2661**
  Juice bar. Sandwiches, soups and fresh juices. J,CC,$

- **Roy's Nutrition Center**
  Preston Royal Shopping Center
  Dallas, TX 75230   **(214) 987-0213**
  Natural foods. Run by Seventh-day Adventists. Lasagna and other Italian dishes. Also: sandwiches, enchiladas, avocado plate. Vitari "ice cream" made from 100 percent fruit. Smoothies, shakes. Closed Saturday. FS,V,N,CC,$

  Sundrop Nutrition
  3920 Oak Lawn, Dallas, TX 75219   **(214) 521-0550**

TEXAS

Cafe in a natural food store. Enchiladas, spinach-noodle casserole, red beans and rice. Open daily for lunch. FS,I,V,N,CC,CH,$-$$

HOUSTON

Asian Restaurant
3701 Weslayan
Houston, TX 77027   (713) 629-7805 or 850-0450

Oriental. Several varieties of Oriental cuisine, including Cantonese, Szechwan and Vietnamese. No MSG. Special vegetarian menu. Brown rice an option. FS,V,M,N,CC,CH,$$

Bombay Palace
3901 Westheimer, Houston, TX 77027   (713) 960-8472

Separate vegetarian menu features homemade cottage cheese dishes, curry, dal, masala and salads. Open daily. FS,A,CC,CH,$$$

The Hobbit Hole
1715 S. Shepherd, Houston, TX 77019   (713) 528-3418

Natural foods. That's right, someone HAS been reading Tolkien. A few vegetarian entrées, including tacos, sandwiches, salads. Fruit smoothies. Outside dining. FS,M,A,J,CC,$$

Macrobiotic Center
3815 Garrott St., Houston, TX 77006   (713) 523-0171

Macrobiotic. Primarily an educational center, but macrobiotic lunches and dinners are served five days a week. Cooks will accommodate special macrobiotic dietary needs if you call ahead. High-quality foods prepared daily. No sugar used. Closed Sunday; no dinner on Monday and no lunch on Saturday. Personal checks accepted. CAF,I,V,M,CH,$$

• Wonderful Vegetarian Restaurant
7549 Westheimer (at Hillcroft)
Houston, TX 77063   (713) 977-3137

Kosher Oriental. Literally scores of vegetarian dishes. Don't let the menu fool you—those "meat" items are imitation. And the only egg is in the

---

KEY TO DINING GUIDE
• Vegetarian food only

FS Full service	**V** Vegan options	**CC** Major credit cards accepted
CAF Cafeteria/buffet	**M** Macrobiotic options	**CH** Children welcome
SB Salad bar	**A** Alcoholic drinks	**$** Average dinner under $5
I Informal	**N** Nonalcoholic beer/wine	**$$** Average dinner $5 to $10
F Formal	**J** Freshly squeezed juices	**$$$** Average dinner over $10

TEXAS

egg foo yung. All-natural foods, no MSG and no white rice! This restaurant got rave reviews from the Austin and South Texas Vegetarian Societies and from the *Jewish Herald Voice*. Definitely worth a trip. Closed Monday. FS,CAF,V,M,N,CC,CH,$-$$

- **Ye Seekers**
  9336 Westview at Blalock
  Houston, TX 77055 (713) 461-0857

  Natural foods. The luncheon salad bar is exceptional, offering up to 10 varieties of special dishes (like mushroom-tofu salad with fennel) and a large selection of organically grown vegetables. Sandwiches and soups also available. Dinner served on Thursday. FS,N,J,CC,$$

RICHARDSON

Macrobiotic Restaurant of Dallas
850 S. Greenville Ave.
Richardson, TX 75081 (214) 669-8328

Open daily for lunch and Thursday for dinner. Only filtered water used in the preparation of all dishes, including soups and teas. I,V,M,N,CC,CH,$$

SAN ANTONIO

Gini's Home Cooking and Bakery
7214 Blanco, San Antonio, TX 78216 (512) 342-2768

Natural foods. Pritikin-style foods and "home cooking." Specialties include vegetarian lasagna and homemade Pritikin bread. Bakery items range from sugar- and oil-free goodies to chocolate cake. No smoking. Easy access from the airport and Loop 410. Open daily. FS,V,M,A,J,CC,$$

La Fiesta
1421 Pat Booker, San Antonio, TX 78148 (512) 658-5110

Mexican. Closed Monday. Personal checks accepted. FS,I,V,A,N,CC,CH,$

La Fiesta
10130 San Pedro, San Antonio, TX 78216 (512) 349-1688

See entry above. Open seven days.

Twin Sisters Bakery & Cafe
106 Sunset Ridge, San Antonio, TX 78209 (512) 822-2265

Natural foods. Closed Sunday. FS,V,A,J,$$

WAXAHACHIE

Golden's Natural Food Store
207 College, Waxahachie, TX 75165   **(214) 937-0010**

Under new management. Sandwiches, salads, homemade soups and pastas—several completely vegetarian—are the order of the day at Golden's. Fresh juices and natural sodas, smoothies and natural desserts complete the selection. Browse the natural food store after your meal. Open for lunch Monday through Saturday; dinner Thursday through Sunday. FS,I,N,J,CC,CH,$$

WESLACO

Pelly Health Farm
1616 S. Bridge Ave., Weslaco, TX 78596   **(512) 968-5343**

Natural foods. All raw foods available. All food is organically grown at its own health farm. Appointment necessary. Open noon until 4 p.m. Monday through Saturday. FS,I,J,CH,$

UTAH

MOAB

Honest Ozzie's Cafe
60 N. 100 W., Moab, UT 84532   **(801) 259-6860**

A vegetarian and seafood restaurant. Whole-foods and homemade fare. Eat outdoors in the garden or dine inside. Breakfast and dinner served daily.

PROVO

• Govinda's Buffet
260 N. University Ave., Provo, UT 84660   **(801) 375-0404**

The only completely vegetarian restaurant in the Provo and Salt Lake area. Entrées include lasagna, veggie steaks, eggplant parmesan, nut loaf and cheese enchiladas. Daily soups, even rice specials (saffron with cashews, turmeric with raisin). Home-baked breads and assorted sandwiches (try the tofu or bhima burgers). Delicious desserts, too. Closed Sunday. Catering and cooking classes available. CAF,SB,I,J,CC,CH,$$

KEY TO DINING GUIDE
• Vegetarian food only

FS Full service	**V** Vegan options	**CC** Major credit cards accepted
CAF Cafeteria/buffet	**M** Macrobiotic options	**CH** Children welcome
SB Salad bar	**A** Alcoholic drinks	**$** Average dinner under $5
I Informal	**N** Nonalcoholic beer/wine	**$$** Average dinner $5 to $10
F Formal	**J** Freshly squeezed juices	**$$$** Average dinner over $10

SALT LAKE CITY

DeLoretto's Pizzeria
2939 E. 3300 S., Salt Lake City, UT 84109   **(801) 485-4534**

The tastiest vegetarian pizza anywhere, say DeLoretto's customers. Have a pizza or try the stuffed cheese shells, vegetarian calzone and baked veggie ziti. Occasional specials include stuffed mushrooms and spinach and cheese shells. Everything freshly made. Beer is the only alcoholic beverage available, but you can bring your own. Local checks accepted. Open daily. FS,I,CH,$

DeLoretto's Pizzeria
260 E St., Salt Lake City, UT 84103   **(801) 359-8657**

See entry above.

Liaison
1352 S. 2100 E., Salt Lake City, UT 84105   **(801) 583-8144**

International. Will accommodate vegetarians, in the restaurant's typically elegant style. The restaurant is listed with the American Heart Association for serving low-fat, healthful foods. One reader said Liaison's vegetarian plate—in-season vegetables, basil vinaigrette salad and French bread—makes a visit worthwhile. Intimate dining. Closed Sunday. FS,V,M,A,N,J,CC,CH,$$$

Nature's Way Sandwich and Kite Shop
416 E. 900 S., Salt Lake City, UT 84102   **(801) 531-7572**

Fresh food with no preservatives, sugar or bleached flour. Whole-wheat bread—even on their sub sandwiches. Homegrown sprouts are on everything. Take-out available. Counter service. (And they really do sell kites!) Casual. Closed Sunday. J,CC,$

New Frontiers Market & Cafe
**1026 Second Avenue,
Salt Lake City, UT 84103**   **(801) 355-7401**

(Formerly the Second Avenue Market.) Dishes like bean and veggie pies and hummus are guaranteed to satisfy the heartiest appetite. Pasta and rice salads and scrumptious pastries round out a meal. Also: brown rice veggie burger, veggie pocket sandwich, and veggie chili or soup with cornbread. Open daily. Sunday brunch. FS,I,V,M,A,CC,CH,$$

New Frontiers Market & Cafe
2454 S. 700 E., Salt Lake City, UT 84106   **(801) 359-7913**

See listing above.

VERMONT

BRATTLEBORO

- **The Common Ground**
  25 Eliot St., Brattleboro, VT 05301   (802) 257-0855

  International natural. Eggplant parmesan. Soups and salads. Worker-owned cooperative. Large servings of "politically conscious" food. Organic whenever possible. Entertainment. Closed Tuesday. Sunday brunch. FS,SB,I,A,N,CH,$$

MONTPELIER

Horn of the Moon Cafe
8 Langdon St., Montpelier, VT 05602   (802) 223-2895

Overlooking the north branch of the Winooski River. Warm atmosphere with rotating art gallery. Artfully prepared food, too. Chef bakes bread and muffins daily. Open daily. FS,I,V,M,A,N,J,CH,$$

- **State Street Market**
  20 State St., Montpelier, VT 05602   (802) 229-9353

  Deli. Take-out from the cafe located in this natural food grocery. Juices, salads and soups. Closed Sunday. I,V,M,CH,$

VIRGINIA

ALEXANDRIA

Bamiyan
300 King St., Alexandria, VA 22314   (703) 548-9006

Afghan. Open daily. FS,I,A,CC,CH,$$

Hakim
808 King St., Alexandria, VA 22314   (703) 683-9008

Lunch Monday through Friday.

KEY TO DINING GUIDE
• Vegetarian food only

FS Full service	**V** Vegan options	**CC** Major credit cards accepted
CAF Cafeteria/buffet	**M** Macrobiotic options	**CH** Children welcome
SB Salad bar	**A** Alcoholic drinks	**$** Average dinner under $5
I Informal	**N** Nonalcoholic beer/wine	**$$** Average dinner $5 to $10
F Formal	**J** Freshly squeezed juices	**$$$** Average dinner over $10

VIRGINIA

Hard Times Cafe
1404 King St., Alexandria, VA 22314　　　(703) 683-5340

See Rockville, Maryland, listing. A jukebox filled with country and western music and vegetarian chili you could kick up your heels for. Open daily. FS,I,A,CC,CH,$$

Tandoor
719 King St., Alexandria, VA 22314　　　(703) 548-1739

The daily lunchtime all-you-can-eat buffet always features four vegetarian entrées and bread and rice, and the price is right at $7.95. (Discount for kids.) There's an extensive selection of vegetarian entrées for dinner too. Open daily. FS,I,V,A,CC,CH,$$

ARLINGTON

Bombay Curry House
2529 Wilson Blvd., Arlington, VA 22201　　　(703) 528-0849

Indian. Closed Sunday. FS,CAF,I,CC,$$

India Curry House
305 North Glebe Road
Arlington, VA 22203　　　(703) 841-0791

Indian. Five veggie entrées, including homemade cheese and spinach or peas, lentil curry, garbanzo bean curry and vegetable beriani. Carryout available. Closed Sunday. FS,A,CC,CH,$$

Kabul Caravan
1725 Wilson Blvd., Arlington, VA 22209　　　(703) 522-8394

Afghan. Open daily, but no dinner served on weekends. FS,A,CC,CH,$$

CHARLOTTESVILLE

• Garden Gourmet
811 W. Main St., Charlottesville, VA 22901　　　(804) 295-9991

International vegetarian, featuring Italian, Mexican, Greek, Oriental, Indian and Mediterranean specials. Homemade pastas and breads. Sandwiches, subs, whole-grain pizza, salad, deluxe coffees. No eggs in anything. Entertainment on weekends. Closed Sunday. V,M,N,J,CH,$$

FREDERICKSBURG

Sammy T's
801 Caroline St., Fredericksburg, VA 22401　　　(703) 371-2008

VIRGINIA

Natural foods. Vegetarian lasagna, sandwiches. Most dishes can be modified for specific diets. Enter on the Hanover Street side for the nonsmoking room. FS,V,A,N,CC,$

MCLEAN

- **Sprouts**
  6216 Old Dominion Dr., McLean, VA 22101   (703) 241-7177
  Carry-out from a natural food store. Items prepared fresh daily and displayed in deli case. Special sandwiches upon request. Most natural food stores in the Washington, D.C., area carry Sprouts' sandwiches. Closed Sunday. V,N,J,CC,$

RICHMOND

- **Grace Place**
  826 W. Grace St., Richmond, VA 23220   (804) 353-3680
  Natural foods. Dinner specials nightly. Homemade bread, desserts, soups daily. Closed Sunday and Monday. FS,I,V,M,A,N,J,CH,$

VIENNA

Naturally Yours
330 Maple Ave. W., Vienna, VA 22180   (703) 938-4485
Juice bar. Tofu burgers, fruit salad, avocado and mushroom spreads, cream cheese coolers. Closed Sunday. SB,I,V,N,J,CC,CH,$$

VIRGINIA BEACH

Tyhe Fresh Market & Deli
#309 Hilltop Square, 550 First Colonial Rd.
Virginia Beach, VA 23451   (804) 425-5383
Natural foods. International cuisine. Veg chili, soups, sandwiches. And for dessert, the specialty: freshly baked fruit pies. Closed Sunday. FS,I,N,J,CC,CH,$$

KEY TO DINING GUIDE
• Vegetarian food only

FS Full service	**V** Vegan options	**CC** Major credit cards accepted
CAF Cafeteria/buffet	**M** Macrobiotic options	**CH** Children welcome
SB Salad bar	**A** Alcoholic drinks	**$** Average dinner under $5
I Informal	**N** Nonalcoholic beer/wine	**$$** Average dinner $5 to $10
F Formal	**J** Freshly squeezed juices	**$$$** Average dinner over $10

WASHINGTON

BAINBRIDGE ISLAND

Natural Gourmet
345 Winslow Way
Bainbridge Island, WA 98110   (206) 842-2759
Natural foods. Soups, sandwiches, salads. Take-out available. Open daily.
FS,N,CC,$

BELLEVUE

Thai Chef
1645 140th Ave. N.E., Bellevue, WA 98005   (206) 562-7955
Thai. Separate vegetarian menu that includes tofu dishes, soups, appetizers and curry. Try the tofu spinach with peanut sauce or broccoli sautéed with cashews. A,CC

Twelve Baskets
201 106th Ave. N.E., Bellevue, WA 98004   (206) 455-3684
Natural foods. Named for the 12 baskets of food left after Jesus fed the multitudes. Pasta, veggie burgers, stir-fry, salads, soups, zucchini casserole, vegetarian chili and homemade whole-grain breads. Live Christian entertainment on Saturday nights; no cover charge. Reservations recommended. FS,I,A,N,J,CC,CH,$$

COLLEGE PLACE

• Walla Walla College Cafeteria
32 S.E. Ash, College Place, WA 99324   (509) 527-2732
International vegetarian cuisine for daily breakfast, lunch and dinner. The "Treat-Yourself-Right" bar open during lunch offers foods without oil, sugar, white flour, eggs or dairy products. Open daily, including during school vacations. CAF,FS,SB,I,V,CH,$

EDMONDS

Soup's On
201 Fifth Ave. S., Edmonds, WA 98020   (206) 775-1677
Natural foods. A lunch place with salads, veggie soup, a vegetable and fruit plate, and a couple of vegetarian sandwiches. You can customize your food by ordering the sandwich filling or salad toppings of your choice. Open daily. FS,I,V,N,CH,$

WASHINGTON

ELLENSBURG

Valley Cafe
105 W. Third, Ellensburg, WA 98926   **(509) 925-3050**

Natural foods. Some vegetarian entrées made with fresh foods. FS,A,J, CC,CH,$$

EVERETT

The Sisters
2804 Grand Ave., Everett, WA 98201   **(206) 252-0480**

Natural foods. Closed weekends. CAF,I,A,CC,CH,$

FEDERAL WAY

Marlene's Market & Deli
31839 Gateway Center Blvd. S.
Federal Way, WA 98003   **(206) 839-0933**

Deli. Entrées, salads and baked goodies. Everything fresh daily. Closed Sunday. CAF,J,CC,CH,$

KIRKLAND

Pleasant Peasant
132 Central Way, Kirkland, WA 98033   **(206) 827-5313**

Natural foods. Vegetarian soups and salads made fresh daily. There are a couple of vegetarian sandwiches and occasionally a veggie quiche or lasagna. Yogurt shakes. Closed Sunday. CAF,I,V,A,CC,CH,$-$$

LAKE CITY

Taj Mahal
12345 Lake City Way, Lake City, WA 98125   **(206) 367-4694**

(Formerly Geogy's.) "Real Indian food." The chef has 16 years of experience, here and in India. Open daily. Reservations recommended. FS,A,CC,CH,$$

KEY TO DINING GUIDE
• Vegetarian food only

FS Full service	**V** Vegan options	**CC** Major credit cards accepted
CAF Cafeteria/buffet	**M** Macrobiotic options	**CH** Children welcome
SB Salad bar	**A** Alcoholic drinks	**$** Average dinner under $5
I Informal	**N** Nonalcoholic beer/wine	**$$** Average dinner $5 to $10
F Formal	**J** Freshly squeezed juices	**$$$** Average dinner over $10

WASHINGTON

MERCER ISLAND

- **Alpine Health Foods**
  7611 S.E. 27th, Mercer Island, WA 98040   (206) 232-7900
  Juice bar. Lunch only. Soups, chowders, sandwiches, taco salad. N,J,$

OLYMPIA

- **New Moon Cafe**
  111 Legion Way, Olympia, WA 98501   (206) 943-8692
  Breakfast and lunch served Monday through Saturday; dinner only on Friday and Saturday nights. Eggplant lasagna, spanakopita, tamale pie, tofu stroganoff, curried rice and vegetables—almost any dish can be made without dairy or eggs. All baked goods are homemade and are dairy- and egg-free. Entertainment for dinner. Closed Sunday. FS,I,V,M,CH,$$

Urban Onion
Olympian by the Park, Olympia, WA 98501   (206) 943-9242
Natural foods. Owners are doubling the size of the restaurant. Located near Legion Way and Washington Street in the old hotel building. Closed Sunday. FS,V,J,CC,CH,$$

SEATTLE

Bagel Express
205 First Ave. S., Seattle, WA 98104   (206) 682-7202
Deli. Bagels and fresh juice and fruit for breakfast; a few veggie sandwiches and soups for lunch. Homemade lemonade and hot spiced cider in season. $

Bahn Thai
409 Roy, Seattle, WA 98109   (206) 283-0444
Thai. Near Seattle Center. Noodles, soups and rice dishes. Separate vegetarian menu with a dozen entrées. Open daily. FS,V,A,CC,CH,$$

Bangkok Hut I
170 S. Washington St., Seattle, WA 98104   (206) 624-7565
Northern Thai cuisine. Special vegetarian dinner menu. Choose hot-and-spicy or mild. Also in Belltown area. Open daily.

Bangkok Hut II
2126 Third Ave., Seattle, WA 98121   (206) 623-4425
Thai. See entry above.

Cafe Counter Intelligence
94 Pike, Suite 32, Seattle, WA 98101   (206) 622-6979

All natural and wholesome ingredients are behind the variety of foods served here. Everything freshly made and attractively served. Hearty soups throughout the year. Soups, salads, fruit and cheese plates, desserts and espresso. Closed Sunday. Hours vary seasonally; you may want to call ahead. FS,F,V,M,A,J,$

Cafe Loc
407 Broad St., Seattle, WA 98109   **(206) 441-6883**

Vietnamese. Tofu and fresh veggies always available. Reservations recommended. Closed Sunday. Also in the Seattle Center. FS,I,V,A,CH,$

Cafe Loc
Center House, Seattle Center
Seattle, WA 98109   **(206) 728-9292**

See entry above.

Cafe Mars
2416 Western Ave., Seattle, WA 98121   **(206) 441-1677**

Veggie sandwiches. Try the Silochard: braised cabbage, onions, spinach and mustard on French bread. Open daily. FS,I,CH,$$

Danny's Wonderfreeze
97B Pike St., Seattle, WA 98122   **(206) 382-0932**

Treats. In the Pike Street Market. Besides frozen dairy treats, Danny's serves Worthington vegetarian hot dogs. Nice treats to eat while walking around the market. Open daily.

Elliott Bay Cafe
101 S. Main, Seattle, WA 98104   **(206) 624-6600**

Natural foods. At least one vegetarian soup daily. Also, veggie chili, quiches, lasagna, salads, hummus sandwich, Middle Eastern plate. Open daily. CAF,I,A,CC,CH,$$

• The Globe Cafe
1531 14th Ave., Seattle, WA 98122   **(206) 324-8815**

Almost everything is vegan, and almost everything is organic. Dinner always a surprise: There's no menu, but two specials every night. Maybe

---

KEY TO DINING GUIDE
• Vegetarian food only

FS Full service	**V** Vegan options	**CC** Major credit cards accepted
CAF Cafeteria/buffet	**M** Macrobiotic options	**CH** Children welcome
SB Salad bar	**A** Alcoholic drinks	**$** Average dinner under $5
I Informal	**N** Nonalcoholic beer/wine	**$$** Average dinner $5 to $10
F Formal	**J** Freshly squeezed juices	**$$$** Average dinner over $10

curried vegetables with peanut sauce, or pasta or stuffed grape leaves. Lunches are soups, salads, steamed veggies and bakery items. Many baked goods are wheat- and sugar-free. Some, however, are "relatively decadent," says the owner. Counter service during the week; full service and brunches on the weekends. Closed Monday and Tuesday. I,V,CH,$

The Grand Palace
417 Second Ave., Seattle, WA 98104   **(206) 624-3825**

Natural foods. Curried vegetables and tofu. Noodles and vegetable soup. Open weekdays for lunch. FS,V,N,CC,$$

Gravity Bar
86 Pine, Seattle, WA 98101   **(206) 443-9694**

Juice bar. Exotic juice and snacks. The fastest slow food in town, so they say. Salads, miso soup, brown rice and steamed vegetables and soups. If you have a craving for fresh wheatgrass, this is the place to go. The owners describe the decor as a cross between the Flintstones and the Jetsons. Hmmmmm... Open until 5 p.m. during the week and until noon on Sunday. Two locations in Seattle. I,V,M,J,CH,$$

Gravity Bar
415 Broadway E., Seattle, WA 98102   **(206) 325-7186**

See entry above. Open daily for breakfast, lunch and dinner.

The Haven
1522 Third Ave., Seattle, WA 98101   **(206) 622-2030**

Juice bar. Veggie sandwiches, salads and soups. Also a vegetarian chili. Caters to the breakfast and lunch crowds. Daily breakfast specials. Open very early in the a.m. for the convenience of early-morning types. Closed weekends. CAF,V,$

Hi-Spot Cafe
1410 34th Ave., Seattle, WA 98122   **(206) 325-7905**

A tavern with great veggie food for breakfast and lunch. Homemade veggie soups every day. Sandwiches, too. Outdoor patio for summer dining. Open daily. I,N,CC,CH,$$

• Honey Bear Bakery
2106 N. 55th, Seattle, WA 98103   **(206) 545-7296**

Natural foods. Not really a restaurant, but the bakery chefs prepare two veggie soups, black-bean chili and two veggie salads daily. All whole grains and natural sweeteners in the fresh bakery items. Open every day. Entertainment most nights. I,CH,$

India House
4737 Roosevelt Way N.E.
Seattle, WA 98105   **(206) 632-5072**

Indian. Extensive selection of northern Indian vegetarian cuisine cooked in authentic tandoori. Closed Monday. FS,I,V,A,CC,CH,$$$

Julia's 14 Carrot Cafe
2305 Eastlake Ave. E., Seattle, WA 98102   (206) 342-1442

Natural foods. Breakfast, lunch and dinner daily. Vegetarian nut burgers and baked goods. In-house bakery. Also in Wallingford area. No smoking. FS,A,N,J,CC,CH,$$

Julia's in Wallingford
4401 Wallingford Ave. N.
Seattle, WA 98103   (206) 633-1175

See entry above. The bakery features whole-grain breads, carrot cake and cookies. Open daily. No dinner served on Sunday. Closed major holidays. FS,I,V,A,J,N,CC,CH,$$

The Kaleenka
1933 First Ave., Seattle, WA 98101   (206) 728-1278

Ukrainian. Cabbage or cheese piroshki, vegetarian borscht. Mushroom-stuffed potato cakes on Friday. Desserts sound wonderful. Personal checks accepted. Closed Sunday. FS,CAF,I,V,A,J,CH

Kokeb
926 12th Ave., Seattle, WA 98122   (206) 322-0485

Ethiopian. Open daily. Entertainment and dancing. FS,V,A,N,J,CC,CH,$$

Lao Charearn
121 Prefontaine S., Seattle, WA 98104   (206) 223-9456

Go for Laotian cuisine here. Try the stir-fried tofu, Pad Thai and spring rolls. Closed Monday. FS,A,$

Lemon Grass
7200 E. Greenlake Drive N.
Seattle, WA 98103   (206) 525-6510

Natural foods. A few vegetarian and vegan dishes. Open daily. FS,I,V,A,CC,$$$

KEY TO DINING GUIDE
• Vegetarian food only

FS Full service	**V** Vegan options	**CC** Major credit cards accepted
CAF Cafeteria/buffet	**M** Macrobiotic options	**CH** Children welcome
SB Salad bar	**A** Alcoholic drinks	**$** Average dinner under $5
I Informal	**N** Nonalcoholic beer/wine	**$$** Average dinner $5 to $10
F Formal	**J** Freshly squeezed juices	**$$$** Average dinner over $10

WASHINGTON

• Morningtown
4110 Roosevelt Way N.E.
Seattle, WA 98105   **(206) 632-6317**

Sit at a table or enjoy full service in the patio of this natural foods international restaurant. Except for cheese on the pizza, all the food is vegan. No salt or sugar either. Pizza, tostados, burritos, falafel, vegan pastries. Daily brunch features scrambled tofu and blue-corn pancakes. Carryout available. FS,V,M,J,$

Neighborhood Kitchen
524 15th Ave. E., Seattle, WA 98112   **(206) 323-1888**

(Formerly Cause Celebre, but under new ownership.) Natural foods. Cafeteria-style breakfast, but full-service lunch and dinner. Sandwiches and salads for lunch. International dinner entrées: Mexican, Oriental, Middle Eastern, European and American. Homemade ice cream! Open daily. Entertainment Friday and Saturday nights. FS,CAF,V,A,N,CH,$

New Orleans
114 First Ave. S., Seattle, WA 98104   **(206) 622-2563**

Creole, Cajun. A bit of old New Orleans in Seattle: Live jazz, swing and blues every night and a piano player at lunch. Nationally known acts every month or so. All this and veggie food! Vegetarian gumbo, eggplant, red beans and rice. Open daily. FS,I,V,A,N,CH,CC,$-$$

Rachel's
5004 University Way N.E.
Seattle, WA 98105   **(206) 524-TOFU**

Completely macrobiotic. Some fish dinners are available, but otherwise, there's no meat, animal fat, eggs, poultry, dairy products, refined sugars, honey, artificial drinks or processed foods here. A full menu wasn't available at press time, but veggie burgers, soups, beans, chili and cornbread, salads, pita pizzas, hummus, desserts and noodle dishes are the usual at Rachel's. Open for breakfast, lunch and dinner. FS,I,V,M,A,N,CC,CH,$$

Rama House Thai Restaurant
2228 Second Ave., Seattle, WA 98121   **(206) 728-0900**

Thai. Open daily. FS,I,V,A,CC,CH,$$

Rasa Malaysia
7802 E. Greenlake Dr., Seattle, WA 98103   **(206) 526-5864**

Indian. All-vegan, noodle/rice and vegetarian selections for lunch and dinner daily. Six locations in Seattle. FS,CAF,I,V,CH,$

Rasa Malaysia
Columbia Center, Fifth and Columbia
Seattle, WA 98104   **(206) 682-6688**

See entry above.

Rasa Malaysia
Broadway Market, Seattle, WA 98102   **(206) 328-8882**

See entry above.

Rasa Malaysia
60th and Phinney, Seattle, WA 98103   **(206) 781-8888**

See entry above.

Rasa Malaysia
4341 University Way N.E.
Seattle, WA 98105   **(206) 545-7878**

See entry above.

Rasa Malaysia
1514 Pike Place, Seattle, WA 98101   **(206) 624-8388**

See entry above.

Ristorante Pony
621½ Queen Anne N., Seattle, WA 98109   **(206) 283-8658**

Mediterranean. Lots of salads (including Arab salad), rice and vegetables, soups and pasta dishes. Sunday brunch. Closed Monday. FS,V,A,J,CC,$$

Roosevelt Cafe
4759 Roosevelt Way N.E., Seattle, WA 98105 (206) 632-7977

Natural foods. Not entirely vegetarian, but absolutely no hidden animal products (in soups, for instance). Several vegetarian entrées, salads and fruit plates, and extraordinary desserts. Closed Monday. FS,A,J,CC,CH,$$

Sahara
4752 University Way N.E.
Seattle, WA 98105   **(206) 527-5216**

Mediterranean, Lebanese. Falafel, vegetarian grape leaves, vegetarian appetizers. Open daily. FS,I,V,A,N,CC,CH,$$

• Silence-Heart-Nest
5247 University Way N.E.
Seattle, WA 98105   **(206) 524-4008**

KEY TO DINING GUIDE
• Vegetarian food only

FS Full service	**V** Vegan options	**CC** Major credit cards accepted
CAF Cafeteria/buffet	**M** Macrobiotic options	**CH** Children welcome
SB Salad bar	**A** Alcoholic drinks	**$** Average dinner under $5
I Informal	**N** Nonalcoholic beer/wine	**$$** Average dinner $5 to $10
F Formal	**J** Freshly squeezed juices	**$$$** Average dinner over $10

Eastern Indian and international. "Not a place of worship, but for those of us whose religion begins with the tastebuds, it's close." Closed Sunday. Personal checks accepted. FS,V,J,CH,$$

Silver Dragon
421 Seventh Ave. S., Seattle, WA 98104   (206) 621-9354

Sound View Cafe
1501 Pike Place, Seattle, WA 98101   (206) 623-5700

Natural foods. Fresh market produce from Seattle's Pike Place market. Several specialty salads daily, plus two (and sometimes three) vegetarian soups. Desserts are mostly whole grain. It's not called Sound View for no reason: The view of Elliott Bay is breathtaking. Personal checks accepted. Open daily. CAF,V,A,J,CH,$

• The Sunlight Cafe
6403 Roosevelt Way, Seattle, WA 98115   (206) 522-9060

Natural foods. A definite presence in the vegetarian establishment of Seattle. Delicious vegan meals. Salads, soups and super waffles. One VT reader calls it "terrific." FS,I,V,A,J,CH,$$

Tanooki Cafe
6311 Roosevelt Way N.E.
Seattle, WA 98115   (206) 526-2935

Oriental natural foods. Vegetarian yakisoba, tofu dishes, humbow and kabob dishes. No MSG. Closed Sunday. FS,I,V,A,CC,CH,$$

Thai Palace
2224 Eighth Ave., Seattle, WA 98121   (206) 343-7846

Thai. Separate vegetarian menu that includes tofu dishes, soups, appetizers and entrées like Paht Thai and vegetarian curry. FS,A,N,J,CC,$$

Viet-My Restaurant
129 Prefontaine Place S.
Seattle, WA 98104   (206) 382-9923

Vietnamese. Vegetarian selections, some with tofu. FS,$

Vietnam's Pearl
914 E. Pike, Seattle, WA 98122   (206) 322-4080

Vietnamese. Tofu, seitan dishes. Vegetarian curries. Closed Sunday. FS,A,CC,$

Wanza
6409 Roosevelt Way N.E.
Seattle, WA 98115   (206) 525-3950

Ethiopian. No lunch on Sunday and closed Monday. FS,I,V,A,CC,CH,$$

STANWOOD

Cookie Mill
9808 State Rd., #532, Stanwood, WA 98292   (206) 629-2362

Readers wrote to tell us the Cookie Mill is a true haven for local vegetarians. Not strictly vegetarian, the Cookie Mill does have vegetarian soups (vegetable and minestrone), a couple of good veggie salads, and a veg sandwich: cream cheese, cukes, tomato, shredded carrots and lettuce. Cheerful, clean and friendly. By the way, lots of homemade cookies and muffins, too. Counter service only. Closed Sunday. V,CH,$

VASHON ISLAND

Sound Food
Rte. 2, Box 298, Vashon Island, WA 98070   (206) 463-3565

Natural foods. Country cuisine with fresh, unprocessed food; fine California and European wines; homemade breads and desserts. Country brunch on Saturday and Sunday. Only seven miles from either Tacoma or Seattle ferry. FS,V,A,N,CC,$$

WEST VIRGINIA

MORGANTOWN

• Mountain People's Co-op
1400 University Ave.
Morgantown, WV 26505   (304) 291-6131

A food co-op that's burgeoning. In the past few months, it's added a mostly vegan and mostly organic deli and a bakery, and there should be a salad bar by the time this goes to press. Pick out fruits and vegetables from the store and make your own juice to eat-in or carryout at the self-serve juice bar. Open daily. I,V,N,J,CH,$

KEY TO DINING GUIDE
• Vegetarian food only

FS Full service	**V** Vegan options	**CC** Major credit cards accepted
CAF Cafeteria/buffet	**M** Macrobiotic options	**CH** Children welcome
SB Salad bar	**A** Alcoholic drinks	**$** Average dinner under $5
I Informal	**N** Nonalcoholic beer/wine	**$$** Average dinner $5 to $10
F Formal	**J** Freshly squeezed juices	**$$$** Average dinner over $10

WISCONSIN

MOUNDSVILLE

- **Imperial Elephant**
Hare Krishna Ridge, R.D. 1
Moundsville, WV 26041   (304) 843-1600 ext. 255

It's called "Designer Cuisine," and it contains no meat, fish or eggs. It's Indian-style American food: broccoli, cauliflower or potatoes sautéed in butter with roasted pecans, sour cream and homemade fried cheese; basmati rice with peas and cheese; veggie prawns and cocktail sauce. Located in "America's Taj Mahal," the gorgeously appointed Krishna palace. Open daily June through October from noon until dark. FS,I,CH,$$

WISCONSIN

MADISON

Antonio's
1109 S. Park St., Madison, WI 53715   (608) 251-1412

Closed Sunday. FS,V,A,N,CC,CH,$$

- **Country Life**
2465 Perry St., Madison, WI 53713   (608) 257-3286

Natural foods. Featured in *VT*'s March 1987 issue as one of the country's finest vegetarian restaurants. Country Life's motto is "Uplifting humanity through service and love." And they do their best. Sit by the stone fireplace if you can, and enjoy the country decor. Completely vegan (some honey). Homey menu includes nut roasts, and the desserts (especially the tofu cheesecake) are wonderful. You can take it all home, too—by buying Country Life's cookbook! Reservations recommended for groups of eight or more. Carryout available. Closed Friday and Saturday; schedule of days and hours are a bit unusual, so call ahead. FS,V,N,J,CC,CH,$$

Husnu's
547 State St., Madison, WI 53703   (608) 256-0900

This may be unique: a Turkish/Italian vegetarian restaurant. Vegetarian couscous, eggplant in yogurt sauce, cold soups. Also pastas, fruit salads and a vegetarian lasagna with broccoli. Personal checks accepted. Open daily. FS,V,A,N,J,CC,CH,$$

Mt. Everest
1851 Monroe St., Madison, WI 53711   (608) 255-1704

Indian. The first Indian restaurant in the city. Closed Sunday. Personal checks accepted. FS,SB,I,N,J,CC,CH,$$

WISCONSIN

Ovens of Brittany
305 State St., Madison, WI 53703   **(608) 257-7000**

California gourmet. A limited selection of fresh vegetarian items available. Madison's first wholesome, all-natural, French gourmet bakery; available for take-out. Four locations in Madison. FS,A,N,CC,$$

Ovens of Brittany
1831 Monroe St., Madison, WI 53711   **(608) 251-2119**

See entry above.

Ovens of Brittany
3244 University, Madison, WI 53705   **(608) 233-7701**

See entry above.

Ovens of Brittany
1718 Fordem Ave., Madison, WI 53704   **(608) 241-7779**

See entry above.

The Second Story
508 State St., Madison, WI 53703   **(608) 256-2434**

Natural foods. Several vegetarian gourmet salads and entrées: Spinach Feta Strudel, Mushrooms St. George, cheese ravioli, sautéed eggplant with yogurt and tomato-mint sauce. Open daily. FS,A,N,CC,CH,$$$

Sunprint Cafe
638 State St., Madison, WI 53703   **(608) 255-1555**

Natural foods. European-style cafe and coffee house for breakfast, lunch and dinner. Mostly veg; some chicken and fish served. Homemade soups, salads, sandwiches, gourmet desserts. It's an art gallery, too. Open daily. FS,I,J,CC,CH,$$

Supreme Pizza
912 E. Johnson, Madison, WI 53703   **(608) 255-2500**

A neighborhood-type pizzeria with toppings galore: artichoke hearts, sauerkraut, avocado, pesto, tofu...and more. Or try the "soysage" special. Also: sandwiches, soups, salads, spaghetti. And the specialty is spinach lasagna. Carryout and delivery available. Open daily. Local checks accepted. FS,$

KEY TO DINING GUIDE
• Vegetarian food only

FS Full service	**V** Vegan options	**CC** Major credit cards accepted
CAF Cafeteria/buffet	**M** Macrobiotic options	**CH** Children welcome
SB Salad bar	**A** Alcoholic drinks	**$** Average dinner under $5
I Informal	**N** Nonalcoholic beer/wine	**$$** Average dinner $5 to $10
F Formal	**J** Freshly squeezed juices	**$$$** Average dinner over $10

MILWAUKEE

Abu's
1978 N. Farwell Ave., Milwaukee, WI 53202   (414) 277-0485
Middle Eastern. Mint tea, Arabic and Turkish coffees. Several vegan dishes available. Open daily. Reservations suggested for large parties. FS,V,$$

Beans & Barley
1901 E. North, Milwaukee, WI 53202   (414) 278-0234
Natural Foods. Mexican. Also: veggie burgers, salads, sandwiches, soups, stir-fry. FS,V,M,A,N,J,CC,$$

West Bank Cafe
732 E. Burleigh St., Milwaukee, WI 53212   (414) 562-5555
Natural foods. Vietnamese, Chinese and European specialties. Open daily. Brunch on weekends. FS,A,N,J,CC,$$

WYOMING

CASPER

Wyoming Natural Foods
242 S. Wolcott, Casper, WY 82601   (307) 234-4196
Simple, wholesome meals include many sandwiches and soups, as well as fresh juices. Juice-bar format. Closed weekends. CC,$

PUERTO RICO

HUMACAO

- **Nutrilife**
  Calle Miguel Casillas #9
  Humacao, PR 00661   **(809) 852-5068**

  Lacto-vegetarian dishes: soups, sandwiches and burgers with a Puerto Rican flavor. Closed Sunday. FS,I,N,J,CH,$

RINCON

Rosa's Patio Restaurant
Maria's Beach, off Rte. 115
Rincon, PR 00743   **(809) 823-4500**

Chinese. Enjoy your dinner from the patio as you watch one of Puerto Rico's glorious sunsets. There may not be a vegetarian selection on the ever-changing menu but the chef will gladly accommodate you if you call ahead. Delicious stir-fries are made from quality, fresh ingredients. Seating is limited so make reservations if coming with four or more. Full bar and game room available. Dinner Monday through Saturday, lunch daily and brunch on Sunday. FS,I,A,CH,$$

KEY TO DINING GUIDE
• Vegetarian food only

FS Full service	**V** Vegan options	**CC** Major credit cards accepted
CAF Cafeteria/buffet	**M** Macrobiotic options	**CH** Children welcome
SB Salad bar	**A** Alcoholic drinks	**$** Average dinner under $5
I Informal	**N** Nonalcoholic beer/wine	**$$** Average dinner $5 to $10
F Formal	**J** Freshly squeezed juices	**$$$** Average dinner over $10

GUIDE TO NATURAL FOOD RESTAURANTS

IN CANADA

BRITISH COLUMBIA

VANCOUVER

Ashiana Restaurant & Sweet Shop
5076 Victoria Drive, Vancouver, BC   (604) 321-5620

Indian.

• Buddhist Vegetarian Restaurant
363 E. Hastings St., Vancouver, BC   (604) 687-5231

Rated three stars from a *VT* reader.

Grand View Restaurant
60 W. Broadway, Vancouver, BC   (604) 879-8885

Szechuan.

Greens & Gourmet Restaurant
2681 W. Broadway, Vancouver, BC   604) 737-7373

Varied menu. Full service and buffet-style.

Naam
2724 W. Fourth Ave.
Vancouver, BC V6K 1R1   (604) 738-7151

Natural foods. Vancouver's oldest natural foods restaurant. Features an extensive menu: scrambled eggs, scrambled tofu, or granola for breakfast; macrobiotic specials for dinner; veggie burgers, Mexican and Middle East specials all day. Even tofu hot dogs for the kids. Three meals daily. Musicians serenade you at lunch and dinner. Eat by the open-air fireplace or on the lovely garden patio, depending on the weather. Open 24 hours, seven days a week. Reservations recommended on the weekends. FS,SB,I,V,M,A,N,J,CC,CH,$$

• Woodlands
2582 W. Broadway (upstairs)
Vancouver, BC V6K 2G1   (604) 733-5411

You might find some Hollywood celebs here—they've been known to come up for the great Woodlands food. International entrées include tofu lasagna, Japanese sea vegetable dishes, East Indian and French cuisine. Extensive salad bar. Breakfasts are a treat, too: sesame waffles, fruit pancakes and fruit salads, muffins and scones...and all made without eggs. Choose the specials from an à la carte menu, and dine in a serene environment. Open daily for three meals. FS,CAF,SB,I,A,N,J,CC,CH,$$

- **Woodlands**
  93 Lonsdale Ave.
  North Vancouver, BC V7M 2E5   (604) 985-9328

  See above entry for description. Very much the same, but not full service. Buffet and salad bar. Also a retail outlet. CAF,V,N,CC,CH,$

NOVA SCOTIA

HALIFAX

- **Satisfaction Feast**
  1581 Grafton St., Halifax, Nova Scotia   (902) 422-3540

  Have breakfast, lunch or dinner in a serene atmosphere, under skylights, surrounded by fresh flowers and soothed by Indian music. The restaurant is run by disciples of Sri Chinmoy. There are two daily specials, two soups and two currys. Known for the West Africa Nut Stew and the Mushroom-Spinach Torte. All dishes can be made without dairy products. All the breads are made on the premises. Smoking not permitted. Open daily, but only dinner served on Sundays. FS,I,V,N,CC,CH,$$

ONTARIO

DOWNSVIEW

- **The Ainger**
  Calumet College, 4700 Keele St.
  Downsview, ON M3J 1P3   (416) 736-5449

  Natural foods. Daily vegetarian soup and entrée. Watch for anchovies in vegetable paté. A must for vegetarians on York University campus. Closed on the weekend. CAF,CH,$

KEY TO DINING GUIDE
• Vegetarian food only

FS Full service	**V** Vegan options	**CC** Major credit cards accepted
CAF Cafeteria/buffet	**M** Macrobiotic options	**CH** Children welcome
SB Salad bar	**A** Alcoholic drinks	**$** Average dinner under $5
I Informal	**N** Nonalcoholic beer/wine	**$$** Average dinner $5 to $10
F Formal	**J** Freshly squeezed juices	**$$$** Average dinner over $10

ONTARIO

ELORA

Desert Rose Cafe
42 Mill St. W., Elora, ON N0B 1S0   (519) 846-0433

Cafe, bed and breakfast and a take-out place. With the exceptions of a tuna salad and a salmon salad sandwich, all menu items are vegetarian. Soups, salads, quiche, bean burgers, falafel, burritos and a daily special. Desserts, too. Open daily. Longer hours in summer. Series of musical performances every couple of months. Elora is about 15 minutes north of Guelph. FS,I,A,CC,CH,$$$

GUELPH

Bookshelf Cafe
41 Quebec St., Guelph, ON N1H 2T1   (519) 821-3333

It's truly a bookstore, plus a cinema with a rooftop bar and a terrace. And there's plenty to eat, like hummus pita, vegetarian lasagna and a daily quiche. Also veg pizza and salads. Dinner and lunch specials sometimes include a vegetarian entrée. FS,V,A,CC,CH,$$-$$$

KINGSTON

- **Le Kasfmir**
479 Princess St., Kingston, ON K7L 1C3   (613) 548-7053

See entry under Toronto location:

- **Sunflower Natural Foods**
20 Montreal St., Kingston, ON K7L 3G6   (613) 542-4566

Not just a restaurant: Also contains gallery space for local artists and a theater for musicians and actors. Two or three luncheon and dinner specials daily, including quiche, pasta, a spicy dish (curry or Mexican). Or try the Sunflower Sandwich: open-face on whole wheat with mayo, scallions, tomatoes, cheese and sprouts. The specialty desserts should be worth a try, too: carrot cake, shortcake, sour-cream chocolate cake. Closed Monday. No smoking. FS,I,V,M,A,N,J,CC,CH,$$

OTTAWA

Cafe Crépe de France
76 Murray St., Ottawa, ON K1N 5M6   (613) 235-2858

French. Vegetarian crépes galore. Also omelets, ratatouille. No lunch served on Monday. FS,I,V,A,N,CC,CH,$$

Domus Cafe
269 Dalhousie St., Ottawa, ON K1N 7E3   (613) 235-4586

Considered one of the best restaurants in town. Sells its own cookbook in the store. Soups and salads are specialties. Open daily. FS,I,CC,$$$

Hacienda Dos Gringos
594 Rideau, Ottawa, ON K1S 1W8 (613) 230-1185

Open daily. I,V,A,CC,CH,$$

Khyber Pass
271 Dalhousie St., Ottawa, ON K1N 7E5 (613) 235-0881

Afghani. Open daily. FS,I,V,A,J,CC,CH,$$$

Mexicali Rosa's
895 Bank St., Ottawa, ON (613) 236-9499

Open daily. FS,I,V,A,CC,CH,$$

Rosie Lee Cafe
167 Laurier Ave. E., Ottawa, ON K1N 6N8 (613) 234-7299

Organic ingredients used whenever possible. Located near University of Ottawa. Generally open daily, but call if you plan to be there on a weekend. FS,I,A,N,$$

Silk Roads
300 Sparks St., Ottawa, ON (613) 236-4352

Afghani. Authentic Afghan cuisine. All dishes homemade. Soups, desserts. Open daily. FS,A,J,CC $-$$

SCARBOROUGH

- ### Buddhist Vegetarian Restaurant
  3290 Midland Ave., Unit 9
  Scarborough, ON M1V 4W8 (416) 292-7095

  Cantonese. Located in the Scarborough Village Mall. A reader recommended this one. . .with empathy for all the times we're told something is vegetarian, and it's not. At this restaurant, it's guaranteed. (The soup stocks, for example, are made from mushrooms.) Closed Wednesday. FS,I,V,CC,CH,$$

KEY TO DINING GUIDE
• Vegetarian food only

FS Full service	**V** Vegan options	**CC** Major credit cards accepted
CAF Cafeteria/buffet	**M** Macrobiotic options	**CH** Children welcome
SB Salad bar	**A** Alcoholic drinks	**$** Average dinner under $5
I Informal	**N** Nonalcoholic beer/wine	**$$** Average dinner $5 to $10
F Formal	**J** Freshly squeezed juices	**$$$** Average dinner over $10

ONTARIO

STRATFORD

The Loading Dock Cafe
245 Downie St., Stratford, ON N5A 1X5   (519) 273-3107

Self-service salads, pita sandwiches, homemade soups. Closed on the weekend. I,CC,CH,$$

THORNHILL

Checkerberries
2300 John St., Thornhill, ON   (416) 881-7240

Continental cuisine that's all homemade. A neighborhood restaurant with about a half-dozen vegetarian entrées, although the chef will prepare other dishes without meat. Daily pasta and stir-fried specials. Closed Sunday. Located on northern edge of Toronto. FS,A,CC,CH,$$-$$$

TORONTO

• Annapurna
1085 Bathurst St., Toronto, ON M5R 3G8   (416) 537-8513

Primarily South Indian dishes complemented by European-style vegetarian food. Sri Chinmoy books and tapes are available at the restaurant. No smoking. Closed Sunday. On your birthday, they'll bake you a birthday cake and cater your party, too. FS,I,V,M,J,CH,$$

• The Chaat Hut
1438 A Gerrard St. E., Toronto, ON   (416) 466-2264

East Indian. Fast-food restaurant specializing in East Indian savories, including veggie samosas, and natural ice creams in a wide selection of unusual flavors: mango, rose, saffron, cardamom and others. Open daily. V,N,CH,$

• Earth Tones
357 Queen St. W., Toronto, ON M5V 2A4   (416) 977-8044

Natural foods. Celebrating its fifth year. All natural foods and freshly made. Unusual salads. Daily specials include quiche, spanakopita, chili and tacos, plus baked goods made on premises with whole grains and honey as sweetener. Gourmet coffees. Catering available. Closed Sunday. CAF,I,V,M,A,N,CC,CH,$$

EastWest
807 Bloor St. W., Toronto, ON M6G 1L8   (416) 530-1571

Natural foods. Formerly Real Foods Cafe, but has new name and new management. Restaurant also is a natural foods store, Toronto's macrobiotic center, and a bookstore specializing in macrobiotics with many hard-to-find titles. Restaurant serves home-cooked macrobiotic and vegan meals twice daily, using organic ingredients whenever possible. Pasta and (homemade) seitan are specialties. Convenient to several subway stops. Closed Monday. FS,V,M,N,CC,CH,$$

The Groaning Board
131 Jarvis St., Toronto, ON M5C 2H6   **(416) 363-0265**

Salad bar has 75 items—no wonder it groans. Located at Richmond Street, one block south of Queen. FS,CAF,SB,I,M,N,J,CC,CH,$$$

• Hare Krishna Dining Room
243 Avenue Rd., Toronto, ON   **(416) 922-5415**

Indian natural. Formerly Gopi's. CAF,J,$$

Indian Rice Factory
414 Dupont St., Toronto, ON   **(416) 961-3472**

Indian. Good selections of fresh veggies daily. All-vegetable oil. Chef is conscientious about never mixing meat products with veggie meals. Open daily. Reservations preferred. FS,J,CC,$$

Jake's
406 Dupont St., Toronto, ON M5R 1V9   **(416) 961-8341**

Closed Monday. FS,I,V,A,CC,$$$

Jerusalem
955 Eglinton Ave. W.
Toronto, ON M6E 2E4   **(416) 783-6494 and (416) 783-3931**

Middle Eastern. Hummus, tahini, fried eggplant and tomatoes, falafel, homemade soups. Take-out, too. Open daily. FS,I,V,A,N,CC,CH,$$$

• Kensington Kitchen Cafe
124 Harbord St., Toronto, ON   **(416) 961-3404**

Primarily a vegan restaurant: No eggs are used, but there are dairy products in some of the sauces. Vegetarian specials daily, including pasta, couscous, falafel, chili, eggplant provencal, pizza, curried okra. Open daily. FS,I,V,A,CC,CH,$$$

La Ina
116 Avenue Rd., Toronto, ON   **(416) 960-8579**

Spanish. Endive salads, orange salads, rice and bean dishes. Closed Monday. FS,I,A,CC,CH,$$$

KEY TO DINING GUIDE
• Vegetarian food only

FS Full service	**V** Vegan options	**CC** Major credit cards accepted
CAF Cafeteria/buffet	**M** Macrobiotic options	**CH** Children welcome
SB Salad bar	**A** Alcoholic drinks	**$** Average dinner under $5
I Informal	**N** Nonalcoholic beer/wine	**$$** Average dinner $5 to $10
F Formal	**J** Freshly squeezed juices	**$$$** Average dinner over $10

ONTARIO

La Maison
1404 Yonge St., Toronto, ON M4T 1Y5   (416) 960-3396

Vegetarian lasagna, eggplant curry, quiche, salads and sandwiches for lunch and dinner daily; brunch on Sunday. FS,A,CC,CH,$$$

• Le Kasfmir
605 Bloor St. W., Toronto, ON M6G 1K6   (416) 533-5955

Indian. Vegetarian buffets during the week. Fifteen vegetarian dishes on the regular menu. Open daily. FS,A,CC,$$$

Le Papillon
106 Front St. E., Toronto, ON M5E 1E1   (416) 363-0838

French. Closed Monday. FS,V,A,CC,CH,$$$

Motimahal
1422 Gerrard St. E., Toronto, ON M4L 1Z6   (416) 461-3111

Indian. Lots of vegetable curries. Closed Tuesday. CAF,I,CC,CH,$$$

Piece of Cake Cafe
7 Balmuto St., Toronto, ON   (416) 923-9494

Home cooking. Open daily. FS,A,$$

Queen Mother Cafe
208 Queen St. W., Toronto, ON   (416) 598-4719

Natural foods. Beautiful garden patio for outdoor summer dining. Closed Sunday. FS,V,A,CC,CH,$$

Raja Sahib
254 Adelaide St. W., Toronto, ON M5X 1X6   (416) 593-4756

Indian. Open daily. FS,I,A,CC,CH,$$

• The Renaissance Cafe
509 Bloor St. W., Toronto, ON   (416) 968-6639

International vegetarian gourmet. Dal and curry are the specialties of the house, and the lasagna and fresh stir-fries are good, too. The chef will accommodate any diet; many of the items are wheat, dairy- and egg-free. Children love the colorful, unusual artworks. Terrace open during summer months. Open daily. FS,SB,V,M,A,N,J,CC,CH,$$

The Rivoli
332 Queen St. W., Toronto, ON   (416) 597-0794

Laotian. Sit on the sidewalk patio during the summer and early fall. Closed Sunday. FS,V,M,A,J,CC,$$

ONTARIO

Sher-E-Punjab
351 Danforth Ave., Toronto, ON   **(416) 465-2125**

East Indian. Reservations recommended. Open daily. FS,I,A,N,CC,CH,$$$

Sonny Langer's Dairy Vegetarian Restaurant
180 Steeles Ave. W., Toronto, ON L4J 2L1   (416) 881-4356

With the exception of a few fish dishes, the menu is vegetarian. The ingredients are fresh, the food is homemade, and the sandwiches are triple-decker! For dinner, there's the quiche of the day (for real men...and women), lasagna, mushroom crêpes, veggie chili, eggplant parmesan and manicotti crêpes. Open daily. FS,I,A,CC,CH,$$

- ## Soy City Foods
  2847 Dundas St. W., Toronto, ON M6P 1Y6   (416) 762-1257

  Juice bar. All vegan. A soyfoods information center that also makes soyfoods for its diners and for other local mestaurants. Menu includes take-out sandwiches and natural juices, sodas and soymilks. Closed Sunday and Monday. I,V,CH,$

- ## Top Vegetarian House
  393 F Dundas St. W., Toronto, ON M5T 1G6   (416) 971-8632

  Chinese vegetarian cuisine. Vegan dishes only. Open daily. FS,V,N,CH,$$

United Bakers Dairy Restaurant/Uptown
506 Lawrence Ave. W., Toronto, ON M6A 1A1(416) 789-0519

Polish, Jewish. Over 70 years in business. Wonderful vegetarian soups, cheese blintzes, potato and cheese kreplach (pierogi), cabbage rolls with mushrooms, stuffed peppers. Open daily. FS,I,N,CC,CH,$$

- ## The Vegetarian
  4 Dundonald St., Toronto, ON M4Y 1K2   (416) 961-9522

  Natural foods. One block north of Wellesley Street and just east of Yonge. Closed on major holidays. See description for second location, The West End Vegetarian, below. CAF,I,V,J,CC,CH,$$

- ## The West End Vegetarian
  2849 Dundas St. W., Toronto, ON   (416) 762-1204

  Natural Foods. Now cafeteria-style with the same great food—just faster

	KEY TO DINING GUIDE	
	• Vegetarian food only	
FS Full service	**V** Vegan options	**CC** Major credit cards accepted
CAF Cafeteria/buffet	**M** Macrobiotic options	**CH** Children welcome
SB Salad bar	**A** Alcoholic drinks	**$** Average dinner under $5
I Informal	**N** Nonalcoholic beer/wine	**$$** Average dinner $5 to $10
F Formal	**J** Freshly squeezed juices	**$$$** Average dinner over $10

service. Features new soy products not available in any other Toronto location. Soyettes and soy falafel are made by the restaurant's affiliate, Soy City Foods. No smoking and no caffeine drinks. A minimum of dairy products and frying. Accommodates allergic customers by offering alternatives to dairy and wheat. Uses only stainless steel cookware, and makes all desserts from scratch on the premises. CAF,J,CC,$$

Yofi's Restaurant & Cafe
19 Baldwin St., Toronto, ON   **(416) 977-1145**

International, featuring salads, pita sandwiches, falafels, homemade soups and daily specials. Vegetarian lasagna, falafel, burritos and cabbage rolls are the specialties. Delicious desserts, too. Best yogurt in town. Fresh-frozen fruit yogurt and fresh carrot juice, too. Closed Sunday. FS,N,J,CC,CH,$$

Yonge Garden
5186 Yonge St., Toronto, ON   **(416) 225-2383**

Chinese. FS,A,$

WILLOWDALE

- ### North York Branson Hospital Cafe
  555 Finch Ave. W., Willowdale, ON   **(416) 633-9420**

  Seventh-day Adventist-affiliated hospital; cafeteria open to the public. CAF,J,$

QUEBEC

MONTREAL

- ### The Herb Garden (Les Jardins du Soleil)
  201 St. Viateur W., Montreal, PQ H2T 2L6   **(514) 279-3828**

  Juice bar. Also an organic produce market. Open daily. SB,N,J,CC,CH,$$

- ### Le Commensal
  2115 St. Denis, Montreal, PQ H2X 3K8   **(514) 845-0248**

  International. More than just a restaurant, Le Commensal also is a conference center on healthful living, alternative lifestyles, women's and environmental issues, astrology, natural foods, nutrition. At 7 p.m. Mondays through Thursdays, just take your plate downstairs to the "communication center" and fill up on wholesome vegetarian food and talk. Homemade desserts and bread. There are three other locations; this one is full service, with salad bar, live food bar, and carryout available. Open daily. FS,V,CC,CH,$$

QUEBEC

- **Le Commensal**
  680 Sainte-Catherine ouest, Montreal, PQ   (514) 871-1480
  See above listing.

- **Le Commensal**
  400 Sherbrooke est, Montreal, PQ   (514) 849-9388
  See above listing. This is the take-out restaurant of the chain.

- **Le Commensal**
  5043 St. Denis, Montreal, PQ   (614) 843-7441
  This is the chain's bakery and pastry shop.

- **Restaurant Au Jardin**
  330 Marie Anne, Montreal, PQ H2W 1B1   (514) 849-8867
  International. Opened in 1976 and billed as the first vegetarian restaurant in Montreal. Daily lunch and dinner specials are either vegan, macrobiotic or lacto-vegetarian. Several varieties of coffee available. Located near the Mont-Royal metro stop. No dinner served on the weekend. FS,N,J,CH,$

QUEBEC

Cafe Le Hobbit
700 Rue St. Jean, Quebec, PQ G1R 1P9   (418) 647-2677
Cafe on one side, formal dining on the other. Open daily. FS,I,V,A,N,CC,CH,$$-$$$

SOUTH DURHAM

- **The Vegetarian Village**
  P.O. Box 136, South Durham, PQ J0H 2C0   (514) 843-9331
  Located on a lot of land with a small lake on the grounds. Dine inside or outside. Offers yoga, exercise programs and cooking classes. Restaurant isn't open on a regular basis, so call ahead. South Durham is between Montreal and Sherbrooke City.

KEY TO DINING GUIDE
• Vegetarian food only

FS Full service	**V** Vegan options	**CC** Major credit cards accepted
CAF Cafeteria/buffet	**M** Macrobiotic options	**CH** Children welcome
SB Salad bar	**A** Alcoholic drinks	**$** Average dinner under $5
I Informal	**N** Nonalcoholic beer/wine	**$$** Average dinner $5 to $10
F Formal	**J** Freshly squeezed juices	**$$$** Average dinner over $10

APPENDIX

MEXICO

ACAPULCO

100% Natural
Av. Sunyaxchen 6, Cancun, Mexico   436-17

This is a chain with one restaurant in Cancun and seven in Acapulco. This isn't a vegetarian restaurant, but there are a few vegetarian and vegan dishes available here, as well as a large assortment of fresh fruit and vegetable drinks. Vegetarian dishes include quesadillas, pasta, some sandwiches and soup. FS,A,J

100% Natural
Costera M. Aleman 2280, Acapulco, Mexico   439-28

See above listing. Check the phone directory for more. There are eight of these restaurants in Cancun and Acapulco. Some have a bar. FS,J

Satvico's
Diego 8. de Mendoza, No. 55
Centro Acapulco, Guerrero, Mexico   317-20

There are 265 (count 'em) items on the menu—all vegetarian. If you can't find anything to eat here, you aren't hungry. Salads, veggie sandwiches, soups, main dishes and desserts. Many dishes with imitation meats. Everything's homemade. Closed Sunday. FS,A,J,CH,$

KEY TO DINING GUIDE
• Vegetarian food only

FS Full service	**V** Vegan options	**CC** Major credit cards accepted
CAF Cafeteria/buffet	**M** Macrobiotic options	**CH** Children welcome
SB Salad bar	**A** Alcoholic drinks	**$** Average dinner under $5
I Informal	**N** Nonalcoholic beer/wine	**$$** Average dinner $5 to $10
F Formal	**J** Freshly squeezed juices	**$$$** Average dinner over $10

Discover Vegetarian Times Magazine

Special Introductory Offer

If you enjoy vegetarian food, you'll love *Vegetarian Times* magazine. Each issue contains recipes, health advice, consumer information, news and much more. And, when it comes to vegetarian restaurants, we wrote the book on it! Get 6 issues for just $12.47.

It's like getting a free issue.

☐ YES, send me the next 6 issues of *Vegetarian* Times for just $12.47.
☐ Bill Me   ☐ Payment Enclosed   ☐ Mastercard ☐ Visa

Card No. _____ Signature _____ Exp. Date _____
Name _____
Address _____
City _____ State _____ Zip _____

TD89

Mail to:
VEGETARIAN TIMES, P.O. Box 446, Mt. Morris, IL 61054-9894

Order these fine books from Book Publishing Company:

Cooperative Method of Natural Birth
   Control $5.95
Dreamfeather 9.95
Fertility Question 5.95
George Bernard Shaw Vegetarian Cookbook .. 8.95
Guide to Natural Food Restaurants 9.95
How Can One Sell the Air? 4.95
Judy Brown's Guide
   to Natural Foods Cooking 9.95
Kids Can Cook 8.95
Murrieta Hot Springs Vegetarian Cookbook .. 9.95
New Farm Vegetarian Cookbook 7.95
No Immediate Danger 11.95
Shepherd's Purse:
   Organic Pest Control Handbook 5.95
Song of Seven Herbs 9.95
Spirit of the White Bison 5.95
Starting Over:
   Learning to Cook with Natural Foods 9.95
Tempeh Cookbook 9.95
Ten Talents 16.95
this season's people 5.95
Tofu Cookery 11.95
Tofu Quick & Easy 5.95
Vegetarian Cooking for Diabetics 9.95

Please send $1 per book for postage and handling.

Mail your order to:
Book Publishing Company
PO Box 99
Summertown, TN 38483